Beyond Truman

Beyond Truman

Robert H. Ferrell and Crafting the Past

Douglas A. Dixon

LEXINGTON BOOKS
Lanham • Boulder • New York • London

Published by Lexington Books
An imprint of The Rowman & Littlefield Publishing Group, Inc.
4501 Forbes Boulevard, Suite 200, Lanham, Maryland 20706
www.rowman.com

6 Tinworth Street, London SE11 5AL, United Kingdom

Copyright © 2020 Douglas A. Dixon

All rights reserved. No part of this book may be reproduced in any form or by any electronic or mechanical means, including information storage and retrieval systems, without written permission from the publisher, except by a reviewer who may quote passages in a review.

British Library Cataloguing in Publication Information Available

Library of Congress Cataloging-in-Publication Data Is Available

Library of Congress Control Number: 2020935397

ISBN 978-1-7936-2781-0 (cloth)
ISBN 978-1-7936-2783-4 (pbk)
ISBN 978-1-7936-2782-7 (electronic)

For My Wife
Who always supports my historical journeys
and
To the memory of Robert H. Ferrell, lifelong mentor

[In] the atmosphere of the Cold War . . . Communist advocacy of the interests of the masses, belief in the "laws" of history and progress, and enthronement of ideology and belief at the center of the historical process and historical interpretation were thought of by liberals and conservatives as principles to be combated in the interests of the freedom of the individual. Soviet historians, it was believed, had betrayed the ideals of factual accuracy, neutrality, and detachment in the same way as Nazi historians had. History had become a means of indoctrination, pressed into service of the state, and of the spread of Communism. Western history, on the contrary, was now held to represent the virtues of accuracy, objectivity, and truthfulness.

—Richard J. Evans, *In Defense of History* (New York: W. W. Norton & Company, 1999), p. 30

Contents

Preface	xi
Acknowledgments	xv
Introduction	xvii
PART I: THREE VIGNETTES	**1**
1 Midwest to Yale and World War	3
2 Two Lovers	23
PART II: BEGINNINGS AND SCHOLAR-ACTIVIST	**47**
3 Ferrell in the Making	49
4 Dear Senator Taft: "Heads Ought to Roll"	71
PART III: DISTINCTIONS	**97**
5 Traditionalists, Debunkers, and Revisionism	99
6 Then and Now	127
Appendix	141
Bibliography	147
Index	153
About the Author	163

Preface

Robert H. Ferrell (1921–2018) earned the title "Distinguished Professor of History" at Indiana University in 1974. Some might honor him with a more colloquial moniker such as the Midwest's best Ivy League storyteller. But in an era when the media emphasizes dramatic and overstated claims suggesting that someone is the best at anything will likely evoke skepticism, so it deserves explanation. Ferrell could claim to be the best Midwestern historian on any number of counts. He wrote or edited sixty books, many after his retirement; the writing continued into his eighties.[1] The first volume, *Peace in Their Time*, came in 1952 and won top prizes at Yale and the American Historical Association. The most recent book, published in 2011, very likely showed a marked progression in subject focus in the eyes of postmodern critics—African American troops in the Great War, *Unjustly Dishonored*. Ferrell's correspondence, however, reveals that his concern for others' mistreatment did not come late in life.[2] He also guided a record number of dissertations to completion as published books, perhaps seventeen at one count, and shepherded males and female students alike, despite a more Victorian-era view of women's roles. On the basis of scholarship alone few Middle West historians of any stripe can best Ferrell.

The qualifier best could also attach to Ferrell's omnipresence among colleagues, whether editing their work, founding or serving historical organizations, contributing as a highly sought-out publishing consultant, authoring a top-selling *American Diplomacy* textbook, and as importantly, serving as a friend and mentor to many in the field. The adjective best also may allude to a certain moral insight and behavior. Ferrell was an Eagle Scout, with a true compass that pointed the right way, in the Lincolnian sense, as God gives us the ability to see it. His moral rectitude flared in his role as historian as well as democratic citizen. U.S. presidents, senators, and military brass got the

Ferrell treatment as did well-known fellow authors, academic or otherwise; David McCullough or Merle Miller are good examples of the latter. Ferrell called for President Clinton's resignation after the pitiful dalliance with the well-known intern, and he had plenty of thoughts on Woodrow Wilson, Franklin Roosevelt, Dwight Eisenhower, and Richard Nixon. This best historian also found critical words for other notable figures, Collin Powell or Margaret Truman.

From another vantage point, former Ferrell students attributed their professor's exceptionalism to the helpful, if paternalistic, attitude he displayed as one found his or her way into that sparse Ballantine Hall office on the seventh floor. Surrounded by books and dressed in a clean, iron-pressed pin-striped dress shirt, Ferrell always had the appearance of professionalism and that of a busy scholar, more often than not facing a manual typewriter, yet he always found time for students. A former student of his, presently serving as an executive associate dean at Indiana University's School of Global and International Studies, shared an apt illustration: One day I relayed the difficulties of student monies arriving after the semester started, which each year put me in a probationary status with finances. Professor Ferrell picked up the phone, called the Bursar's Office, and solved the problem on the spot, then turned to me and said, now let's focus on your interest in history. The present author can attest to the enormous energies Ferrell expended across three independent-study history courses and the marked-up papers to prove the point. These experiences are hardly uncommon. Into the present decade, the Indiana University Alumni Association continues to find him a "favorite professor" in polls conducted and anecdotes shared.[3]

In addition to his respected professional status, or better said, infusing it, Ferrell represents the Midwest in birth, career attachment, and in many ways, outlook. Born in a Cleveland, Ohio, hospital May 8, 1921, he and a younger brother, June, and parents Ernest Sr. and Edna, faced the volatility rooted in the economic swings of his age, living at times near urban environs, then on a family farm (a savior from bank collapse), near Custar, Ohio. As with perhaps the majority of heartland faithful Americans, the budding Bob Ferrell attended a Methodist church in his early years. Teachers of the Good Book, family and friends, inculcated a lifelong, evangelical orthodoxy that continued with extended family, including endless correspondence with Aunt Ocie. Ocie, a sister of Ferrell's mother, alongside Uncle Mark, spread the Gospel as missionaries in China, and the message was rarely lost on Ferrell in the letters passed to him. Ernest Sr. and Edna made the evangelical tie indelible by assigning the middle name Hugh to their son, the namesake of a missionary in China, Hugh Hubbard, a cousin. One might say, Ferrell's genealogical roots grew from white, Anglo Saxon, Protestant soil (the derided WASP to many postmodernists), and, by extension, he consciously or otherwise internalized

Midwest breadbasket conservatism, that of close family ties with fealty to faith and farming. Ferrell grew out of the family shell to become more iconoclastic in outlook and values than his progenitors.

The zig-zag in other-than-Midwestern birthright came twice for the future historian, and these were significant changes of scenery. Ferrell packed his bags for the Second World War after three years at Bowling Green State University (1939–1942), a school just a few miles from his home at the time. The war years would expand the horizons of Ferrell, which led to momentous decisions afterward, namely the focus on history and away from music education. The second Midwest variance came with acceptance to Yale, the Ivy League school in New Haven, Connecticut, and history graduate studies (1947–1951). Much will be said about this fortunate connection, and it certainly colored his world, to his benefit. New Haven trumped a Bowling Green pedigree, and Ferrell capitalized on the former. After graduation, the Yale alum with distinction unhappily held a one-year appointment to an Air Force intelligence job in Washington, D.C. The Pentagon work reintroduced the war veteran to the Washington-based bureaucracy he came to abhor as part of his service. By the fall of 1952, Ferrell found his way back to the Midwest—this at Michigan State College (later university) by means of Yale mentor Samuel Flagg Bemis's former school chum. The move permitted the final leap to Indiana's flagship state university the following year, another Yale network advantage. This is where Bob Ferrell found fertile ground, in one of those "I" states that Midwestern outsiders can never keep straight (not Illinois or Iowa), but in some ways very similar to them along with Ferrell's native Ohio, thus, the title the Midwest's best Ivy League storyteller.

NOTES

1. Robert H. Ferrell, "*Contemporary Authors Online,*" Gale, 2018. *Biography In Context*, http://link.galegroup.com/apps/doc/H1000031397/BIC?u=loc_main&sid =BIC&xid=2d7b177a. Accessed October 2, 2018. Ferrell's *Unjustly Dishonored*, published in 2011, is not included in the citations.

2. Letter to Murf, Marion, Karl and Stephen, February 25, 1952, Box 84; letter to Bob and Kit, July 12, 1953, Box 44; letter to Chris and Bob, September 15, 1953, Box 44; All correspondence referenced is housed at the Lilly Library, Indiana University, Bloomington, Indiana, unless otherwise noted. Letters cited are from Robert H. Ferrell unless otherwise identified.

3. "Favorite Profs," *Indiana University Alumni Magazine* (Fall 2013), 11.

Acknowledgments

Showing appreciation is an opportunity to reflect on friends and colleagues whose efforts have made this work possible. As the Preface underscored, the late Robert Ferrell contributed the most. Carolyn (Ferrell) Burgess, Mr. Ferrell's daughter, along with her husband Lorin, indulged my exploration and opened their home and life to me as I sought background information and photographs on her father and family. Historians Michael Brooks and Gregory Pfitzer read the entire manuscript, provided insightful suggestions, and supported the project; efforts like these remind us of what true mentorship continues to be, without expectation of reward. Their positive feedback, along with James Gifford at Fairleigh Dickinson University Press, got the manuscript through the editorial doors of several publishers. Other historians, academics, and constructive critics improved the end-product by their engagement with various chapters, most notably, historians David Brown (Elizabethtown College) and Eric Sandweiss (Indiana University) and social science education professor Ronald VanSickle (University of Georgia). Professor Randy Mills (Oakland City University) shared sage publishing advice. Nick Cullather (Indiana University), a former student at IU, reflected on stories of Ferrell's inspiration and later-day professional frustration. Amy Spungen (Editing and Writing Service), smoothed the initial draft of chapter 2 and celebrated the drama I sought to convey in storytelling. San Antonio's Jim Lowry, Jr. provided significant legal advice while I worked my way through publishing contracts.

Other Ferrell family members, friends, and beneficiaries of his efforts deserve recognition for sharing their insights about his personality, ideology, hard-driven nature, kindness, angst, relationships, and much more: Dr. Robert Bryant, Charles Blankenship, A. Lovell Elliot, Dennis Ferrell, Terry Feehan, and David Frasier, to name several writ large in my notes.

Institutions and their representatives were also integral to the completion of the project. Generous guidance from Sarah and Jody Mitchell at the Lilly Library at Indiana University helped me navigate Ferrell's Papers and the reading room challenges and capture camera-ready images. Erika Dowell and Joel Silver, associate director and director of the Lilly Library, respectively, made the archives readily accessible and user-friendly for researchers. Other institutional representatives of great value to the project included Verna and John Rose and Jim Conrad, at the Waterville Historical Society; Lisa Alsee, at the Lakewood Public Library; Martha Gubernath, at the Lakewood United Methodist Church; Nanci Young, at Smith College Archives; Tiffany Tully, at Anthony Wayne High School and Beth Walker and Jenean Carlson, at Lakewood High School and City School District Office; Connor Wagner, a former Scout at Boy Scout Council #440 in Cleveland. Of import too were the efforts of Eric Kuntzman, editor, and his assistant, Alexandra Rallo, at Lexington Books, for shepherding this project to completion.

Unfortunately, not all who merit attention for their efforts on the book's behalf may be identified, so let me thank them even as they remain anonymous. This, along with the other shortcomings in the book, are mine alone.

Introduction

So why a book titled *Beyond Truman: Robert H. Ferrell and Crafting the Past*? It is almost unimaginable for any devotee of twentieth-century presidential biography to be unaware of Robert Ferrell. Well known for painting intimate details of political elites, famous and infamous, the Hoosier author steadied his microscope on President Truman more than most. Other presidents had to endure the stethoscope, one might say, of Ferrell's search for medical malpractice. Diplomats and soldiers also did not elude the historian's investigative eye. Yet, looking at the content of books alone misses the larger story, the intrigue, or better said, the man, the motivations, even the mischief of Ferrell and his times.

This Buckeye-turned-Hoosier found his way of thinking about and doing history at odds with a growing chorus of colleagues during his career. A self-described "traditionalist" or empiricist, he criticized the efforts of many postmodernists, the New Left, and social and cultural historians because they were upending the basis of what he, and many others, believed was legitimate, worthwhile, ethical history. Concentrating on the subfields of American diplomacy, the presidency and war, itself, was a sign that his training owed much to the nineteenth-century Leopold von Ranke school, which emphasized that statecraft was the legitimate area of historical inquiry and that state documents were the proper sources to excavate. Elite, Eurocentric, and top-down foci were also part of this mix.

Various strands of postmodernism challenged the Indiana University historian's approach to the past. Ironically, Ferrell's experiences soldiering in the Second World War, application to Yale, or courtship of lifetime mates, explored in the following chapters, serve as exemplars of the potency of postmodernist claims. Serving in the Army Air Force in the unique way that Staff Sergeant Ferrell did provides alternatives to mainstream narratives of the war; finding his way into an Ivy League graduate history program defies one's attempt at a unified, singular, coherent explanation; defining Ferrell's persona leading to marriage points to multiple realities of truth. So, though Ferrell defended the empirical tradition against these challenges, some evidentiary trails of his life reinforce his opponents' beliefs—illusive truthful essences of the past, multiple realities, male-dominated history, the merits of bottom-up history, and so on. Broadly speaking, postmodernism rattled Ferrell's orientation toward historical topics, sources, perspectives, claims to a singular, truthful historical reality, and disciplinary boundaries; yet his lived experiences might be considered at odds with traditional historical and social values. These debates continue to be worthy of our attention.

The stories shared here also reveal something of the character, one might say bias, that inevitably lay behind the public face of historians like Ferrell. Truth seekers claim that the experiences, background, values, or demographic traits that historians bring to the task influence the topics explored, sources used, the topical framework or arguments proffered, in the end, the illusion some project of objectivity. Ferrell's characteristics and background match those traits, in many ways, of President Harry Truman (as examined in chapter 4). Thus, it is not too difficult to imagine that this, in part, may explain why the president's most prolific biographer was apologist for the struggles of, as well as advocate for ranking highly, the thirty-third chief executive. Readers can see how well the Indiana storyteller adhered to several conventional criteria of historical objectivity defined by the profession in other instances too.

One can find plenty of enjoyment solely in reading the intrigue that infused Ferrell's world. Overall, this book illuminates in a personal way the ongoing struggles that producing history can present to the storyteller. The lessons of historian Ferrell continue to inform current practices, even today.

Part I
THREE VIGNETTES

Chapter 1

Midwest to Yale and World War

Truth does not always run down the middle.

—Robert H. Ferrell (Letter to
Margery M. McKinney, July 23, 1973)

In the last half of the twentieth century and beyond, Indiana University's Robert Ferrell was caught up in the battle raging among historians characterized as the "quasi-scholarship of revisionists."[1] Critics accused revisionists of impugning the intentions of the United States. Revisionists were tattooed "ideological," and ironically, denied awards due to their political beliefs.[2] Ferrell branded them the "Cannon to the Left," and if not anti-capitalists then at least budding socialists.[3] Arthur Schlesinger Jr. labeled them the self-appointed "moral censors of the history profession."[4] Protagonists of this "new school of revisionism," as Ferrell described it, found their way into several discussions of the past such as events leading the United States into the Great War or those preceding the attack on Pearl Harbor, or the origins of the Cold War and characterizations of presidents Franklin Roosevelt and Harry Truman.[5] In a poignant example, the new collegial breed offered a radical storyline for Pearl Harbor that questioned President Roosevelt's judgment if not intentions.[6] Editors at *The Historian* and *The Review of Politics* and leaders of the American Historical Association aired the fight in journals and newsletters.

Not surprisingly, the rebel storytellers were questioning generally accepted understandings of the past at a time when United States was caught in the tumultuous era of civil rights protests, Vietnam, and President Nixon's implosion. But fertile ground for the new revisionism had been laid in the postmodernist push in other professions such as art, literature, and sociology, well before the 1960s.⁷ While different in most respects, the chaos of postmodernism and revisionism in this context had some overlap. Revisionists, in the middle of Cold War angst, mixed Marxist ideology with history making according to Ferrell traditionalists; facts were chosen to lead to preordained conclusions (anticapitalist/imperialism), and at times made up altogether.⁸ Cold War revisionists as they came to be categorized, viewed in the context of conventional standards of history practice and theory, were considered unprofessional scoundrels.

Although too multiheaded to address fully here, postmodernism as described by historian Callum Brown contrasted sharply with how traditionalists practiced and thought about history. The following explanation underscores a basis for the difference.

> The event is something that happened in the past, the fact is a human construction (or representation or statement) of it. The event occurred; the fact is a record and expression of it. The event is neutral. But the fact is built upon documents or records of the event, making it laden with problems of accuracy, bias, editing, significance, and the sheer restrictions of human description. This is the shift from that which can be ascertained to have happened to that which is being packaged by an historian in statements.⁹

An example Brown described of postmodernists' critique focused on the commonly understood narrative of the French Revolution, an interpretation of its beginning at the storming of the Bastille on July 14, 1789. The fact that the Bastille was overrun is placed with numerous other facts to create a narrative of significance, one celebrated today. Yet, the historian bunches the Bastille episode with an assortment of other events and facts out of an infinite possibility to create the narrative of the revolution's starting point. As the storyteller characterizes the facts from the chaos of the past, orders and interprets them, neutrality is lost to imposition, so the theory goes. The grander the scale of interpretation, the further the facts from the events, the more problematic as the basis for objective claims to what happened. Different event selections result in different potential narrative statements and interpretations and approaches to truth.¹⁰ A recent discussion among French Revolution experts contrasts the Bastille beginning with a long-term view resting on the decline of the French nobility.¹¹ There is much to postmodernism that is disputed by historians that stem from the evaluation of events, to selection of facts, to narrative interpretation, to whether in fact, one can recapture a/the past. Ferrell and colleagues rejected a specific group of Cold War revisionists based on more than interpretation. They argued that these revisionists also resorted to unethical historical practices to arrive at their interpretations. Aside from Cold War antagonists, Ferrell was experiencing postmodernist influences from scholars at Indiana in other disciplines too.¹²

Ferrell labeled one group of these followers "crackpot" sociologists.[13] In college classes, history students, following the postmodernist philosophy, were dismissing facts and singularly true narratives as only one person's reality; to some professors, so students shared, "nothing was certain or even true in this world."[14] Ferrell's response to the new revisionists suggested he questioned stories of the past that did not have a unified coherence, a truthful essence, a right and wrong. Notre Dame colleague Stephen Kertesz, among others (Robert Maddox or Oscar Handlin), agreed with the thrust of Cold War antirevision criticism.[15] Ferrell and Kertesz reasoned that these young college students and their green-eared professors had not experienced the world sufficiently to understand it, especially during the decades immediately following the Second World War, as they had.[16]

With the postmodernist controversy as canvas, there is some irony embedded in three episodes that characterize Ferrell himself, as reflected in the artifacts in his collection at the Lilly Library at Indiana University. These personal episodes are framed using the following questions. How did this future Hoosier historian find his way into the PhD History Program at Yale University? How did his soldiering experience fit with the larger understanding of the Second World War? How might we characterize Ferrell's matrimonial courtship? Seemingly disparate events, they present a puzzle to those who would draw a straight-line narrative of reality, one with the certainty of truth or appeal to moral judgment. While of no wider historical significance beyond themselves, as Ferrell no doubt would agree, the three stories stand as postmodern allegories, as antithesis, to the Ferrell way of knowing what happened.

In pursuing these questions of the past, Ferrell himself had some advice: Search the archives.[17] Some historians have labeled such artifacts "surrogates of the past," a phrase used to describe remnants that have a history of their own.[18] It is argued that this history is separate from what happened. How Ferrell, in fact, got into Yale, for example, may be impossible to know, but the documents that rest at various repositories have their own tale, in collaboration with the sense making of whomever chooses to interpret them, and those who made them available or did not. Ferrell himself had some choice as to what he would save (or create) or not for posterity and for reasons known to him alone. Processes of evaluating evidence, that is experiencing evidence and applying inductive reasoning, are shared by both postmodernists and "scientists of the past" or empiricists.[19] But the two types of historical approaches differ on the meaning they impute to artifacts, and indeed, whether one can recover "the" or any past, whether bias toward it can be minimized, or whether a coherent, singular, truthful narrative is possible. Differences are also rooted in the end goals for historical study. In the episodes presented here, the prevalence of evidence and a sense of narrative and biography drove the process initially.

Another Ferrell recommendation guided the search: Find the incongruencies, follow the evidence to address them, and create an accurate and faithful narrative that solves the puzzle.[20] As one reads the narrative elaborated below, it is hard to overlook evidence first encountered; that is, course grades, exam feedback, military correspondence, parental reflections, Ferrell's conjecture, and so forth. The initial artifacts reviewed raised questions about how Ferrell found his way into a prestigious graduate history program at Yale. The head scratching subsided as an alternative narrative appeared. The alternative gained more steam, if more complexity, as young Bob's extracurricular activities came to the fore. Another missing piece was a complete college transcript, this by way of Bowling Green State University. What resulted from this search for historical answers achieved some coherence and unity, but truth is hard to come by. The same may be said of Ferrell's courtship and military service stories. The topic of Ferrell's path to Yale comes first.

MIDWEST TO YALE

Ferrell's rise to well-respected historian by way of Yale's graduate school is a useful prelude to the puzzling narratives of his war service and matrimonial courtship. Each vignette highlights postmodernism's tussle with the Hoosier historian's singular, unified, truthful history approach.[21] Considering Ferrell's path to Yale, there is reason that he was reluctant to share his early life experiences with the present author since they encompass both highs and lows and personal vulnerability. He may have found it undesirable to share his lack of interest in history in the first several years as a student at Bowling Green State University (BGSU) beginning in the late 1930s.[22] In an interview years later, the emeritus professor Ferrell noted that BGSU professors awarded him a grade of D and C in his initial world civilization courses. This was the first sign that Ferrell may not have been invited through the front door at Yale's graduate history program. Another artifact, a World Civilization Exam bluebook marked C-, described another deficiency—not writing to the question.[23] Several BGSU transcripts for the semesters from 1939 to 1940, aside from music, show Ferrell to be a good student overall, though hardly top notch.[24]

Bowling Green State University, itself, was a surprising launching point given Ferrell's critique of it through the years. In two missives to BGSU presidents, the Indiana University historian said as much years after graduating. In a letter to President Ralph McDonald, the former alum pointed to the "inadequacy of [BGSU] undergraduate training," "poor teaching," and faculty who were "asleep intellectually." BGSU, as with many other schools, had gained university status even though its faculty produced a "scarcity of scholarship since 1910." The reality in Ferrell's eyes: "the graduate school" was a "solemn farce."[25] The Indiana professor's opinions stood unchanged a decade later, as President Sumner Canary received Ferrell's critique on a wide array of issues including the lack of quality history faculty and the scholars needed to recruit PhD students and establish a program.[26] Such shortcomings may explain why his favorite history professor at BGSU, Walter Sanderlin, left after the initial year, transferring to Jefferson and Washington University in Pennsylvania in the fall of 1946. Even if one discounts the inveterate critic's remarks, a BS degree in Music Education with a minor in English and German would hardly have included the prerequisites for a middle class Midwesterner to hope for admission to a history program at an Ivy League school.[27] Additional archival evidence, for instance, Ferrell's remark to an acquaintance, Mark Gallagher, raised more questions than it answered: "I went back to Bowling Green for two years and change[d] courses from music education to history."[28] There was also an abbreviated vita attached to a letter Ferrell sent to Philip E. Mosley as part of an application to do research for the Council on Foreign Relations in New York. In it, the future Yale graduate student noted that he earned a BA in Music with minors in history and political science.[29]

The puzzle of how the future historian came to Yale is muddled more by his inconsistent thoughts shared at the early and late stages of his military service. Staff Sergeant Ferrell's interest in the discipline of history came partly during his travels overseas in Uncle Sam's fight against totalitarianism.[30] Repeatedly cycling out to the pyramids in Egypt, near the army base, certainly had a pronounced effect; long after, Ferrell continued to recall it as pivotal.[31] History as a vocation began creeping into the horizon, if only mutedly, a year into the war and only partly because music held out such lousy prospects as a career.[32] A letter responding to his dad's query stimulated the following response:[33] "[T]he prospect of going out and teaching public school music [psm] is not especially interesting to me. The more I think about it the less I like it. There are so many young girl [teachers] who can go out [and] teach psm much better than I can. It is essentially a job of singing, which is not for me." Ferrell found the inherent limitations of schools to develop acceptable orchestra and band programs impractical. He lacked the skills to play professionally. The Army soldier shared that "I became dissatisfied with [music education] by degrees" and "the Army" had given him "plenty of time to think. This history business at present seems the best to me," but it would fall short of "working for [ones]self." Soldier Ferrell went on to judge the advantages and disadvantages of teaching regardless of discipline—"English, language or history." Sociology and economics were also on his radar. Striving for a master's or PhD degree was imperative to obtain a teaching job due to the glut of teachers and might work to his advantage at the college level, he believed. "Stability and safety" were the highest priorities, the result likely of living through the Great Depression, his dad's loss of a banking job, and move away from friends and boyhood home.[34]

Another letter in response to Ferrell's dad, Ernest Sr., came late in the war. Despite the early pronouncements, young Bob was ambivalent about his future or at least what he felt comfortable sharing with his parents.[35] In letters back and forth, his dad repeatedly shared what he thought best for his son, and young Bob's replies reflected this: "As you said Dad, it is important to get into something where there will be dough. That is one of the big assets of the medical business, besides the fact that you work for yourself. In the army, I've had some experience working for other people, and naturally one would get along best working for himself. . . . The trouble is, though, that I'm not sure yet just what I want to do." Ferrell thought that taking a leisurely course load, perusing the BGSU catalogue, and sorting out his options were important. The only certainty was to avoid a career in music education.

A wonderful BGSU mentor and professor of history, Sanderlin, facilitated the progression toward history after the former Staff Sergeant Ferrell was released from service and found his way back home in 1945.[36] Youthful, handsome, and student-friendly, Sanderlin's effect made sense since he joined the faculty at BGSU in 1945 and taught the sorts of courses that would have attracted the by-then widely traveled Ferrell—"Oriental Civilizations" or "Africa and the Near East";[37] Sanderlin would publish his first book in 1946, and this gave him the expertise and scholarly approach that no doubt inspired his protégé. According to various campus newspaper reports in the *Bee Gee News*, Sanderlin was a constant social presence around campus too, whether at dances, debates, or volleyball matches. Ferrell played organ at campus concerts, and the two likely grew close both academically and through informal events. The returning student finished his Music Education degree by the spring semester. Robert Ferrell's note to Robert Gallagher suggested Ferrell's preparation continued beyond music education, and perhaps the full academic record would shed more light, if obtainable.[38]

Two sources pointed to potential saving graces for Ferrell's acceptance to Yale, though hardly watertight justifications, given other evidence. Following graduation from Bowling Green State, the war veteran sat for the Graduate Record Exam (GRE) at his alma mater.[39] Overall scores were not stellar. In the hard sciences—mathematics, physics, chemistry—the scores came in below average. His verbal skills and literature background did little more to recommend him. Yet importantly to the Yale History Department, Ferrell found himself toward the top few percentiles in history and social studies. Ernest Sr. later pontificated that this must have been the reason his son found his way to Yale, noting, "with the discharge of so many soldiers in 1945–1946 seeking higher degrees, colleges were filled, but he took an examination and on the basis of this test was, much to his surprise, admitted to Yale."[40] Ferrell himself explained, perhaps in gest, that his acceptance was merely on the basis that the department "needed someone West of the Hudson . . . and I was the person."[41] There was no mention of other factors by Ernest Sr. or his son, for or against, that colored the pathway, as the record eventually displayed.

The evidence reviewed to this point hardly made the case for how this young Midwest-rooted former enlisted soldier came to Yale, or rather, was invited. At least several extant BGSU grade cards demonstrate a less-than-exceptional student, Bs primarily with the exception of As in music. An exam blue book comment was decidedly below average. His music degree did not include evidence that history was a pursuit. Above average marks at a lesser school, Bowling Green State, would not be an Ivy League launching pad. While the GRE scores also did not mark him as exceptional, except of course for those top scores in the target area, they would not predict competitive status. There were, nevertheless, signs that Ferrell had attended to history courses beyond those that received poor marks. No records of these were available at this point, but it was an opening to pursue. Military correspondence suggested history was only one of several possible career avenues and one he did not consistently rate highly. Years later, Ferrell shared that cycling trips to Egyptian pyramids during service drew him to history, but the war letters on career choice do not make the case.

Several points may have counted in applicant Ferrell's favor at Yale, aside from the GRE scores. Young Bob had two Yale-connected family members, both highly respected surgeons in New Haven, who no doubt may have leveraged their weight in his favor. Certainly Uncle Burt paved the way for Ernest Jr. (June), Bob's younger brother, to intern then gain residency at Grace Hospital, later a Yale Medical teaching facility.[42] The elder son also came to Yale and New Haven at his Uncle Burt's invitation as the Indiana historian later recounted.[43] Young Bob also enjoyed other pursuits in high school and college that may have supported his application. He participated in numerous extracurricular activities, achieving the rank of Eagle Scout, excelling at music (and teaching others those skills), swimming competitively, and performing journalist duties. It is possible too that an essay that gained national recognition from *The American Magazine*'s Youth Forum contest added the extra feather needed to tilt the scale with Yale admissions committee members.[44] The award fell somewhere outside the top group, gaining Ferrell five dollars, whereas the top winners earned $1,000 (grand prize), $500 (second place), $100 (third place), $50 (15 winners), and $10 (50 winners). Hundreds of winners received $5. Nevertheless, the award was significant if one considers the 317,161 article entries across the country.[45] Young Bob's 2,000 or so words addressed a topic that might have gained the attention of patriots on Yale's faculty in the early post–world war period—"What I owe America and What America Owes Me." Hilda Scott, a fellow competitor from Hickman Springs High in Columbia, Missouri, won the Grand Prize, perhaps producing some irritation given Ferrell's views toward women.[46]

Again, considering the times, not so long beyond the victorious troops returning from Europe, Ferrell's war service certainly may have contributed to gaining admission. Contrarily, neither a war hero nor combatant, he might have encountered an uphill climb against many returning combat soldiers competing for a spot as Ernest Sr. relayed. Indeed, the veteran staff sergeant admitted how safe he was during his assignment while "at war" in correspondence.[47] Yet, Ferrell had gone from private to staff sergeant in less than a year outside of the rigors of warfare. As a competent organist and pianist, he played for military-run religious services and at informal celebrations. Officially a chaplain's clerk, he ingratiated himself with superiors by performing a variety of official and unofficial duties, and in appreciation, these earned him opportunities to travel extensively on generous weekends during the war, gaining a breath of international experience that fit well with scholarly interests of Samuel Flagg Bemis, his eventual mentor at Yale. End-of-war recognition came in the form of a "Bronze Star Medal for non-combatants" that he could list on the Yale application.[48]

Higher education historians have described the context and criteria of college admissions during the late 1940s. Elite schools such as Yale were relying less on subject matter mastery (as demonstrated in high school coursework) and more on intelligence testing.[49] Granted this was for undergraduate admissions, but researchers at the time noted that "statistical studies showed that general verbal and mathematical ability predicted college grades better than did achievement tests in particular subject matter."[50] In this context, Ferrell's mediocre mathematics and verbal GRE scores would not have proven useful. Post–Second-World-War students also demonstrated a higher level of competence thus raising the level of competition against returning veterans. Even more, some in the academic community at Ivy League schools were complaining that their admissions committees were placing too much emphasis on academic criteria and too little on the attributes that contributed to a well-rounded student; not until the late 1950s, however, would other factors such as geographic balance or extracurricular activities be advantageous. This, again, discounts what might be thought as part of Ferrell's admission advantages.[51] Another factor, legacy admissions, trended upward through the first half of the twentieth century at elite institutions for a variety of reasons (e.g., excluding minorities, say Catholics or Jews, or bolstering needed alumni contributions, especially sagging since the Great Depression; Ferrell's use of the GI Bill may have added to his attractiveness in this latter point).[52] David O. Levine, an historian, found that these schools even invited alumni to participate in admission decisions, serving "to give legacy applicants an added advantage . . . ensuring the admission of their own children and those of others with whom they closely identified."[53]

One can speculate on the path that cleared Robert Ferrell's way to Yale, including at least two narratives, WASP-advantaged, alumni-connected insider (e.g., Uncle Burt Rentsch) or multitalented, late-to-history, war veteran bloomer.[54] It is important not to discount other factors that may have played into either hypothesis directly: the background (and possible empathy) of Ferrell's second-year mentor, Bemis, who came from a rural farming community in western Massachusetts similar to this applicant or Ivy League officials pushing to broaden the representation of Midwesterners.[55] Bob had an endearing personality too, which no doubt contributed to graduate school recommendations or any interviews with Yale officials that may have taken place. A telling document, Ferrell's second degree (completed in a year) at Bowling Green State University, listed all "A's" in history and political science, and this during his return from service. These marks no doubt reaffirmed his purposefulness, if not level of academic rigor or equivalent excellence to east coast elite schools. Once accepted in New Haven, those less-than-exceptional GRE scores, aside from history and social studies, may have given the admissions committee pause as Yale graduate student Ferrell struggled in his first year there.[56] Moreover, he and fellow student Lawrence Kaplan failed the initial attempt to pass the required German examination, "a pre-requisite . . . to formal admission to the doctoral program."[57] Of course, the much later celebrated Truman and diplomatic history storyteller went on to gain top honors from both Yale and the American Historical Association for his first book, proving that he belonged.

The postscript to Ferrell earning his PhD is less unwieldy. The path to initial professorship is hardly disputable. Bemis's ties to F. Lee Benns (friends at Clark University) smoothed the way to IU's History Department along with Ferrell's characteristics: male, white, protestant (Methodist), Ivy League–trained, and well-connected. The newly published Yale thesis-to-book *Peace in Their Time* no doubt provided a boost, though it did not prove advantageous a year earlier in a competition for a Michigan State College professorship. Gaining the tenure-track post at IU was just the beginning of Ferrell's path to prominence. There is more to contemplate before casting judgments on him as an exemplar of postmodernist angst. Ferrell's war story is another vignette worth considering.

FERRELL AT WAR?

When you read about rear echelon troops, just imagine that I am behind them. I've never seen a German plane in action and never heard a bomb of any kind.

—Robert Ferrell
(Letter to Mom and Dad, December 25, 1944)

There are multiple narratives that would put Ferrell, in the end, at Yale and by his second year under the guidance of one of the nation's most highly respected American foreign relations historians. It was Bemis who knew Benns at Indiana University and others so useful to Ferrell's early career trajectory. Contingency has its place: What if the faculty member had been someone else? Or if there had been no meeting with William Castle, a U.S. State Department connection to former Secretary of State Kellogg or no Castle diary, events critical to the success of RHF's prize winning first book published by Yale in 1952. Just as with the narrative of Ferrell's rise through Yale to prominent historian, his Second World War participation sheds light on the multiple perspectives on that war, how soldiers experienced it, its meaning, its purposes, its chroniclers, its subject matter, from the top-down, middle out, and Ferrell up, and even more, as written by unrecognized historians. For young Bob, it began with enlistment, still an option before the draft-only Army closed that door to others.[58] Soldier Ferrell bemoaned that enlistees such as himself were shut out of officer candidate school (OCS) competition simply by bad luck of not finishing college, a seemingly minimalist requirement. Enlistment itself evaporated as an option for others precluding their noncombat choices. Even those "lucky enough" to obtain a coveted OCS spot had few options outside combat. Ferrell, later realizing this, stopped pushing to be an officer.

Certainly, postmodernism would have no reason to deny soldier Ferrell as an appropriate historical focus, given the historical gap his case is worthy of filling, even as it lacks the intrigue of Rick Blaine in *Casablanca*. Although a WASP, his story is not top-down and even more it is not the mainstream battle narrative. Private Ferrell wrote his itinerary in a little red book to organize the chronology of this civilian-turned-soldier's early war sojourn to Cairo. Egypt was the first lengthy posting, this at Headquarters, 9th Air Force Service Command (AFSC), by the end of 1942.[59] But before arriving and after all the intermediate steps, from beginning of service at Patterson Field to assignment with the 9th AFSC in early September, and after the usual marching, inculcation of military bearing, rifle range practice, and so forth, recruit Ferrell joined a few others at a six-week air "flight operations" clerk school.[60] By October, he was on his way to embarkment from Staten Island's docks aboard the USS West Point, Compartment

B-13.⁶¹ And this, principally, is where the unorthodox military adventure began for Ferrell.

Between July 13, 1942, and early September 1945, the future highly regarded diplomatic historian went to war, but one could hardly tell this by the letters he sent home to his parents.⁶² The Army Air Force private made the point in one missive later in the war to his folks: "When you read about rear echelon troops, just imagine that I am behind them. I've never seen a German plane in action and never heard a bomb of any kind. I go to work each morning just like Dad goes to the bank." Perhaps to put a finer point on it, Ferrell added, "life here is easy." Beyond easy, soldier Ferrell's military service escaped that of routine simplicity.⁶³ The peripatetic private described military adventures beyond what most vacation-minded Americans could fathom. War or not, Ferrell had fun.⁶⁴

Young Bob's Air Detachment Group, part of the 9th Air Force Service Command, sailed first to Rio de Janeiro for a brief stopover, then encountered exotic cultural intrigue in India at Bombay and by train to the interior at Camp Deolali. Partiality to American ways was never far from his mind during a ten-day stay in India. A local newspaper captured this sentiment: "Bob Ferrell Describes India as Weird and Mysterious."⁶⁵ South Asia was no American Midwest. The newspaper reinforced the point with Ferrell as mouthpiece: the "natives are dressed in turbans and sheets for trousers and go barefooted the year round. Food is very scarce." Alarming too were Indian lifestyles, natives who had to live in huts on pennies a day and this to feed a family of about eight. Those who could not make it looked for money to borrow, which led to more trouble. After a few weeks of sightseeing, the news account stated that Pvt. Ferrell "was glad to get out." By December, his group shipped over to Egypt through the Suez Canal.⁶⁶

Once settled in Cairo (see Figure 1.1), in letters penned to family, soldier Bob shared ancient attractions throughout Egypt—the pyramids of course—and points of interest all along the Nile, even into neighboring Sudan at Wadi Halfa. As early as January 1943, Private Ferrell regaled his mom and dad with stories of the famed pharaoh tombs, and only a few months later, sent plenty of pictures with descriptions of "grand trips" cycling around them.⁶⁷ Foreshadowing the penchant for detail that would mark his future writings, the letters would often describe with exactitude the pictures enclosed. "The step pyramid at Sakhara," for example, fascinated the tourist soldier.

> This is the oldest of the pyramids and is falling apart, due to the inferior stone used in building it. The rocks here are merely [slags], approximately 5 inches thick. All the pyramids had a certain number of mortuary temples, and nobles' tombs surrounding them; many of these have been excavated. When last at Sakhara, they were still digging. Outside the picture to the right, are a couple of

Figure 1.1 Reflecting on his past, after retiring from Indiana University, Ferrell explained that cycling trips to the pyramids in Egypt during the Second World War turned his attention to history. *Source*: Courtesy of Carolyn Ferrell Burgess.

large shafts, perhaps 100 feet deep, in which the priest put the mummies from possibly this pyramid, when grave robbers began to become bothersome.[68]

Ferrell observed the social customs of local women in the same letter. Women's dress and behaviors held an allure to this bachelor. He noticed that "[t]he Mohammedan women" wore their hair so as not to draw attention from "outsiders," but big "nose pieces" contradicted the message. With veils and hoods, and "big baggy black dress, which comes down to the ankles," the women shared a certain anonymity. In comparison, the peasant girls "do not bother with the veil," only the black dresses, yet "are not troubled by them" in the summer heat. All are capable of "carrying things on their heads." The "young girls marry at about 15 or 16." In letters sent during May 1943, Ferrell expanded on various topics from Arabic funerals to habits of cleanliness. Back at the Army base, left with little to occupy himself, Ferrell was reading, even "studying" more, and no doubt expanding his knowledge of and interest in world history.

Beyond Cairo, the future historian found himself exploring much of what there was to see in historic Egypt. Luxor was a favorite spot, one he would revisit years later as a visiting scholar at the American University in Cairo.[69] As a soldier, traveling with Army buddies Franklin and Bennett, Bob explored the temples and kings' tombs and returned with souvenirs. Though only three days there, they "had a good time." One can certainly see the budding historian as Ferrell narrated the significance of Luxor to his parents, the once city "of Thebes . . . the capital of Egypt," this well before Christ. There were "several fine temples, mostly in ruins, but still worth seeing, a king's palace, two giant statues, and a lot of tombs." He could not overlook perhaps the favorite sight, that of King Tut's tomb, "the carvings and painting"; it stood out partly because it somehow escaped the fate of robberies.

Only months into his encampment at Cairo, a constant reminder of ancient civilization, Ferrell began to use Army connections to launch trips to other Middle East destinations. Not surprisingly given the Ferrell family's Christian piety, Palestine captured his attention.[70] By late February 1943, Ferrell spied Jerusalem and environs as the next tourist visit, targeting "the old city, Mount of Olives, Jericho, Bethlehem, Sea of Galilee, Nazareth, etc." Young Bob's good fortune came with the help of his boss, as he relayed, "Being a good friend of the Chaplain's, I'm sort of in on the ground floor of this trip business."

The Army assigned Ferrell as a clerk in the chaplain's office, where he proved himself exceedingly competent and hardworking. Running personal errands for his boss, however, likely accounts as much for the lowly private's pleasing relationship with the chaplain.[71] Bob simply had a winsome way with people, and he had fine-tuned skills as an organist, which he put to good use during Army base worship services. He produced religious activity bulletins, likely an aptitude learned in journalism tasks in high school and through preparing Boy Scout meetings and activities. In all, he fulfilled a variety of mundane but essential duties such as driver, Service Club manager, and supply and payroll clerk; his interactions with so many no doubt illuminated his personal warmth.[72] Only two months at post, Ferrell boasted to his parents that Captain Bradford, the 9th AFSC chaplain, recommended his promotion to corporal, and in less than a year, he added two stripes, telling younger brother June, "You can call me 'Sarge' now."[73]

After the first year of military service, Ferrell found himself well-positioned to explore cities bordering the Mediterranean—Alexandria, Bengasi, Tripoli— among other locales in North Africa, then on to those in the United Kingdom and western Europe (see Figure 1.2), with return trips to Palestine.[74] As with Egypt, the letters young Bob sent home read like a vacationer's travelogue. Bengasi had the look of its Italian conquerors, war-torn "modernistic buildings with a sort of Italian flavor." He and a friend arriving there by boat dipped into the clean, salty water of its coast for a swim; a sunburn was the result. The trip between Cireniaca and Tripolitania he described as nothing but desert, "where

Figure 1.2 Soldier Ferrell surveys the Mediterranean Sea in Nice, France, during the Second World War, c. 1944. *Source*: Courtesy of Carolyn Ferrell Burgess.

for miles, there is nothing to see but dirty, gravel like sand, littered with tin cans, a few burned out wrecks . . . [and] some kind of desert small, green bushes." Tripolitania, meaning "Land of the three cities," the future historian penned to his mom and dad, included Leptus Magna, Sabratha, and Tripoli; each had its allure.[75] Leptus Magna was "one of those old Roman [f]ormerly (Phoenician) cities." Delighted to have "a couple days in which to tour [Tripoli]," Ferrell noted. It was "the old Arab town, in which lived the pirates of the early last century, [but it] looks much like the old city of Jerusalem, dirty, crowded, stinking, narrow streets." The city's dietary practices left Ferrell aghast:

> Took a walk around the old city, which is very similar to Jerusalem. One sees them cut up meat practically on the sidewalk and throw into the narrow already stinking streets the pigs['] heads and anything else they have left over. In several places, they were baking bread—the flat pancake bread which the natives eat. The dough lay where the flies could help themselves first. An old black fellow had a long pole with a little round flat part at the end, on which he placed the dough and shoved it back into the oven. In town here, natives carry the stuff on flat box lids . . . all over town and sell it where they can. I saw one fellow whose bread had spilled all over the sidewalks. He was picking it up and putting it back on the tray. If you ever [saw] the sanitary state of the sidewalk . . . you would not want any bread.

Always ready with sardonic wit, Ferrell wrote of his travels in the former Italian stronghold: "From what I saw of Libya, which was most of it, except the desert part, which is most of it, the place is divided into two productive areas, Cirenaica and Tripolitiania. The rest of the country is good for nothing but the flies." The differences between these two sites, in Ferrell's mind, was irrigation or not, "rolling country," Roman ruins, and comparisons to his teenage hometown Waterville, Ohio, and environs. The Army Sergeant described the subsistence agricultural practices of farmers in Tripolitanian small towns: the land divided in small plots, arduous uphill water haul to ditches, buckets of water drained to reservoirs and then to plots, perhaps a cow, the daily grind. The Ferrell family's Depression era flight-to-farm living in the 1930s no doubt heightened the soldier's sensitivity to these conditions. Forty miles West of Tripoli stood more ruins, this in Sabratha. After the North African tour, Ferrell secured his first ever airplane ride back to the military base, "which was a lot of fun."

Tours of England and France awaited the peripatetic staff sergeant by mid-1944 through the V-E Day.[76] Red Cross clubs eased the burden of securing lodging. Ferrell shared his travels in England, highlighting the "cathedral and colleges at Oxford," the unique cathedral at the center of Salisbury, and Stonehenge in Amesbury. At Winchester, the remnants of a castle and its environs, the hospital at St. Cross, and "some nice-looking Elizabethan brick and timber work," also made the list of interest. Sixteenth-century Gothic-designed parish churches were part of the fascination, but Stonehenge was a disappointment in comparison to Egyptian ancient structures, and Winchester's abbey cluttered every available space with "hundreds of [plaques] telling of regimental battles, etc., etc." At Oxford, Ferrell paid six pence to an English-Speaking Union, "a British organization which tries to promote Anglo-American relations," to learn about the town. Aside from describing eighteenth-century wall paintings at the E. S. house, the tour leader engaged the group on the Christ Church cathedral, first begun as a monastery in typical fashion. Ferrell grew bored with the long-winded distractions and endless "dumb questions" posed by American soldiers and lack of tour progress and wandered off to explore on his own. Pressed to take the noon train back, he had to hurry through the sights. He enjoyed riding English trains. Although compartmentalized, the train seats by the windows permitted one to take in the countryside. He found "British landscape" preferable to the French, "in that everything is orderly and in its proper place."

Not long after the Germans had been chased out of Paris, but with several months of war left in Europe, Ferrell was exploring well-known travel spots in and around the capital city.[77] He also planned trips to London, Ireland, and Wales as part of the adventure.[78] Taking in the notable Parisian sights—the Louvre, Place de la Concorde, the Tuileries gardens, Notre Dame, among others—no doubt heightened the lure of history and led to comparisons. Observing exhibitions at the Louvre, he commented, "the only thing on display now is the Egyptian and Assyrian antiquities." Sharing "a K ration bundle of three cigarettes" with a museum guard "who looked especially cold," unexpectedly gained him admission to an out-of-the-way stairway entry, "where I went down and came into more exhibitions." Of course, given Ferrell's natural talents on keyboard, he could not pass up Durand, "the music store," just near the Louvre. The brisk cold pierced nearly every corner of his journey; it was January, after all. The Red Cross Club became his base of sightseeing operations and tours.

Beyond the sites near the Louvre, the Second World War soldier-tourist made his way to other well-known spots, narrating the journey for his parents: "After freezing slowly in the Louvre . . . [I] walked along the Seine, crossed onto the island where Notre Dame is . . . visited a little chapel which is in the Palais de Justice" [sic]. His telling of the story of "Louis XI" [sic], the acquisition of the "true cross . . . bought from some fellow in Palestine" brought a not unusual realist's remark: "The true cross business was a good racket in those days, and [I] think lots of people made their fortunes selling them."[79] From Notre Dame, it was on to "second hand bookstores," a stroll along the Boulevard St. Germaine, a visit to "the church of St. Clotilde, where Cesar Franck was organist for many years," a music composer to which Ferrell was drawn. A musician, himself, young Bob could not resist "bargains on French edition organ music" nor the Baedeker guide books so useful to inform a tourist of the historic significance of sites investigated, along with general books on architecture.[80] Young Bob planned to take future tours to Fountainbleau and Versailles conducted by the Red Cross. Sightseeing in Luxemburg and Germany came only months after the Germans surrendered.

Given Ferrell's embrace of world travel and history, it is hardly remarkable that he would later find himself a leading historian of American foreign relations. What is remarkable, with dominant stories of the Second World War conflict, is the ease with which soldier-cum-tourist Ferrell traveled through destinations in the Middle East, North Africa, the British Isles, and Europe from 1943 through the V-E Day. What, of course, one reads in the Second World War stories during Ferrell's jaunts to "parts unknown" is hardly that of this Sergeant's account.[81] While the Allies were attacking Italian forces along the peninsula off the Mediterranean Sea, this Army chaplain's clerk interrogated the landscape and cultures of North Africa. During the Battle of the Bulge, he whisked around celebrated sites in the United Kingdom. As Hitler's forces made their last-ditch push into Belgium and northeast France, Ferrell found it convenient, even if a little chilly, to take in the world's art masterpieces and architecture in and around Paris, seemingly untouched by the bloody casualties of the Second World War narratives. Though a lowly enlistee, this is quite a story, one missing from mainstream accounts.

NOTES

1. Letters to Charles Blankenship, July 8, 2006 and January 25, 2003 (in possession of Charles Blankenship, San Marcos, Texas); letter from Robert Maddox to Botzenhart, November 19, 1973; letter to Richard S. Kirkendall, February 26, 1973; letter to David S. McKellan, May 20, 1973; letter to Margery M. McKinney, July 23, 1973; letter to Holsti, September 1, 1973, Box 41, Lilly Library, Indiana University, Bloomington, Indiana. Gregory M. Pfitzer, *Samuel Eliot Morison's Historical World: In Quest of a New Parkman* (Boston: Northeastern University Press, 1991), 277. Into the twenty-first century, see Richard S. Kirkendall (ed.), *Harry's Farewell: Interpreting and Teaching the Truman Presidency* (Columbia: University of Missouri Press, 2004); Robert H. Ferrell, *Harry S. Truman and Cold War Revisionists* (Columbia: University of Missouri Press, 2006).

2. Index Card, Robert Ferrell's evaluation of candidates for the David D. Lloyd Prize associated with the Harry S. Truman Library; Ferrell wrote that Bruce Kuklick's entry *American Policy and the Division of Germany* is "revisionist" and "for that reason alone we really cannot give it the prize" (circa May–June 1974), Box 48.

3. Ferrell, *The Review of Politics* 36, no. 2 (April 1974), 323–326, Box 179.

4. *AHA Newsletter*, "Professor Schlesinger Replies," circa 1963–1964, Box 41.

5. Robert H. Ferrell, "Pearl Harbor and the Revisionists," *The Historian* 17, no. 2 (Spring 1955), 215–233; letter to George Brinkle, April 14, 1974; Robert H. Ferrell, "The Revisionist Historians," symposium paper, April 1974, Box 41.

6. Ferrell, "Pearl Harbor and the Revisionists," 215–233.

7. Callum G. Brown, *Postmodernism for Historians* (New York: Routledge, 2005), 3–6; Martha Howell and Walter Prevenier, *From Reliable Sources: An Introduction to Historical Methods* (Ithaca, NY: Cornell University Press, 2001), 103–109; see Mark Donnelly and Claire Norton, *Doing History* (New York: Routledge, 2011), for the multiple purposes of history in the ancient world and beyond, Chapter 2; Howell and Prevenier, *From Reliable Sources*, 14–15.

8. Ferrell details many of the arguments put forth against these revisionists in Ferrell, *Harry S. Truman and the Cold War Revisionists*, esp. Chapter One. The overlap is remarkable (given the dates the two were published) if one compares this account to Ferrell's Pearl Harbor and the Revisionists," 215–233.

9. Brown, *Postmodernism*, 27.

10. Ibid., 26–29.

11. Jonathan Dewald, "Rethinking the 1 Percent: The Failure of the Nobility in Old Regime France," *The American Historical Review* 124, no. 3 (June 2019), 910–932.

12. For two well-documented studies discussing interdisciplinary history, see David S. Landes and Charles Tilly (eds.) *History as a Social Science* (Englewood Cliffs, NJ: Prentice-Hall, 1971); H. Stuart Hughes, *History as Art and as Science* (New York: Harper & Row, 1964).

13. Letter to Stephen Kertesz, June 23, 1953, Box 44.

14. Letter to Ferrell from Stephen Kertesz, July 3, 1953, Box 44.

15. On Maddox and Handlin, see David S. Brown, *Beyond the Frontier: The Midwestern Voice in American Historical Writing* (Chicago: University of Chicago Press, 2009), 143–144.

16. For an excellent overview of this period, controversy, and context, see Richard J. Evans, *In Defense of History* (New York: W. W. Norton, 1999), 18–37.

17. Interview with Robert H. Ferrell, conducted by Elizabeth Glenn, transcript p. 42, November 3, 1994, Indiana University Oral History Research Center, Bloomington, Indiana (hereafter IUOralHistory).

18. Brown, *Postmodernism*; Donnelly and Norton, *Doing History*, 5.

19. Brown, *Postmodernism*, 6–31.

20. Interview with Robert H. Ferrell, by Glenn, 42, IUOralHistory.

21. Interview with Robert H. Ferrell, conducted by Steven Sheehan, February 13, 1998, IUOralHistory; Theodore A. Wilson, "Introduction: Individuals, Narratives, and Diplomatic History," in *Presidents, Diplomats, and Other Mortals: Essays Honoring Robert H. Ferrell*, ed. J. Garry Clifford and Theodore A. Wilson (Columbia: University of Missouri Press, 2007), 3–11.

22. Interview with Robert H. Ferrell, Sheehan, transcript p. 3. IUOralHistory.

23. History 103, December 6, 1940, Box 74.

24. Robert H. Ferrell BGSU grade card sheet, semesters January 25, June 10 and August 9 (all 1940), Box 74.

25. Letter to Ralph McDonald, January 10, 1952, Box 44.

26. Letter to Sumner Canary, January 17, 1966, Box 7.

27. See transcripts and note discrepancy in Ferrell's telling (e.g., minor in English and German) and letter to Mom and Dad (hereafter M/D), August 15, 1943, Box 74.

28. Letter to Robert C. Gallagher, September 19, 1952, Box 44.

29. Letter to Philip E Mosely, January 27, 1957, Box 43.

30. Note contrary evidence on "enlistment" draft board letter, in letter to Ferrell from H. A. Siphen (Chairman, Selective Service System, Local Board #23, Lucas County, Ohio), Box 74.

31. Interview with Robert H. Ferrell, by Sheehan, 3, IUOralHistory.

32. Letter to M/D, July 16, 1943, Box 74.

33. Letter to M/D, August 15, 1943, Box 74.

34. Letter to D. Gregory Badger (Field Executive, BSA, Cleveland), January 15, 1938, Box 74.

35. Letter to M/D, January 8, 1945, Box 74.

36. Letter to Sunderlin, April 28, 1951, Box 84 (among others to Sanderlin, May 9, 1979, August 16, 2001); letter to M/D, circa late July 1945 Box 74.

37. "The Key 1946," BGSU Key Yearbooks, *Book 20* (Bowling Green, OH: Bowling Green State University, 1946), 30.

38. Letter to Robert Gallagher, September 19, 1952, Box 44.

39. Ferrell, GRE (Graduate Record Exam), May 10, 1947, Box 84.

40. Ernest Ferrell Sr., *Stories I Want My Grandchildren to Know* (Columbus, OH: author, 1980), 69.

41. Interview with Robert H. Ferrell, by Sheehan, 3, IUOralHistory.

42. Ferrell Sr., *Stories*, 72.

43. Interview with Robert H. Ferrell, by Sheehan, 3, IUOralHistory.
44. "150 Additional Awards," *The American Magazine* 128, no. 3 (September 1939), 70.
45. *The American Magazine* 128, no. 1 (July 1939), 42.
46. *The American Magazine* 128, no. 4 (October 1939), 27.
47. Letter to M/D, December 25, 1944, Box 74.
48. Ferrell's Bronze Star Medal certificate, August 23, 1945, Box 74.
49. Elizabeth Duffy and Idana Goldberg, *Crafting a Class: College Admissions and Financial Aid, 1955–1994* (Princeton, NJ: Princeton University Press, 1998), especially pp. 73–84; Michael P. Riccards, *The College Board and American Higher Education* (Madison, WI: Fairleigh Dickinson University Press, 2010), 44–45; Peter Schmidt, "A History of Legacy Preferences and Privilege," in *Affirmative Action for the Rich: Legacy Preferences in College Admissions*, ed. Richard D. Kahlenberg (New York: The Century Foundation Press, 2010), 33–69.
50. Duff and Goldberg, *Crafting a Class*, 80.
51. Ibid., 82–84.
52. Leonard Cassuto, *The Graduate School Mess: What Caused It and How We Can Fix It* (Cambridge, MA: Harvard University Press, 2015), 33–43.
53. Schmidt, *A History*, 40.
54. Yale was an all-men's school at the time, thus gender comparisons were irrelevant.
55. Riccards, *The College Board*, 44–45; H. C. Allen, "Samuel Flagg Bemis," in *Pastmasters: Some Essays on American Historians*, ed. Marcus Cunliffe and Robin Winks (New York: Harper & Row, 1969), 204.
56. Letter to Ferrell from Leonard Lebaree, June 15, 1948, Box 74.
57. Lawrence Kaplan, "Robert H. Ferrell: An Appreciation," in *Presidents, Diplomats, and Other Mortals: Essays Honoring Robert H. Ferrell*, ed. J. Garry Clifford and Theodore A. Wilson (Columbia: University of Missouri Press, 2007), 316–317.
58. One document suggests that the Selective Service Board denied Ferrell's application to enlist, contrary to his telling. See letter, H. A. Sipher to Robert Ferrell, June 19, 1942, Box 74.
59. V-Mail, to M/D, December 31, 1942 and May 23, 1945, Box 74.
60. Letter to M/D, August 19, 1942 and "Monday Evening" (circa July 1942), Box 74.
61. Ferrell would later arrive at West Point Academy as a visiting history professor.
62. Letter to M/D, August 30, 1945, Box 74.
63. Letter to M/D, December 25, 1944, among other letters, Box 74.
64. Travel booklet, for itinerary, and see example letters to M/D, May 6, July 18, August 8, September 1, 4, and 9 (all 1943), Box 74.
65. "Bob Ferrell Describes India as Weird and Mysterious," (newspaper article, circa January 1943), Box 74; see also letter to M/D, December 25, 1942, Box 74.
66. Letter to June (Ferrell's brother, Ernest Jr.), December 27, 1942; postcard, Ferrell to Ernest Ferrell Sr. (Dad), December 8, 1942, Box 74.
67. Letters to M/D, April 13, May 6, and September 1, 1943, Box 74.

68. Letter to M/D, May 6, 1943, Box 74.

69. Letter to M/D, May 6, 1943, Box 74.

70. Letter to M/D, February 28, 1943, Box 74. Later, Sergeant Ferrell turned tour guide for Army buddies while revisiting Palestine and other sites and complained that travel can be difficult during wartime, "because transportation is erratic and crowded, and the hotel situation is tough. . . . [But we] didn't have too much trouble." By this time, Ferrell was enjoying flying to his destinations too. Letter to M/D, August 3, 1943, Box 74.

71. Letters to M/D, September 27 and November 25, 1943 and circa November 1942, Box 74.

72. Letters to M/D, September 27 and November 2 (V-mail) and November 25, 1943; July 7 and October 2, 1944; letter, Venna Patterson (American Missionary Society, Cairo, Egypt) to Edna Ferrell, October 18, 1943, Box 74.

73. Letter to M/D, February 8, 1943, and letter to June, August 5, 1943, Box 74.

74. Letters to M/D, July 2 and 4, August 3 and 17, September 6 and 14, (all 1943); June 20, August 26 and September 1 (letters #1 and #2), (all 1944); January 22, February 20, and March 11, (all 1945); letter to June (Ernest Jr.), March 11, 1945 (all Box 74).

75. Letter to M/D, July 3, 1943, Box 74.

76. Letters to M/D, June 20 and 24, August 26, September 1 (letters #1 and #2) (all 1944). For 1945 trips before the official end of war in Europe (May 8, 1945), see letters to M/D, January 22, February 20, March 11 (all 1945).

77. Letter to M/D, January 22, 1945, Box 74.

78. Letter to M/D, March 11, 1945, Box 74.

79. Ferrell is likely referring to the Sainte-Chapelle built by King Louis IX to house holy relics in the Palais de la Cite. http://www.visual-arts-cork.com/architecture/sainte-chapelle.htm.

80. Letter to M/D, November 19, 1944, Box 74.

81. "Parts Unknown" was the popular twenty-first century exotic travel show of the late Anthony Bourdain.

Chapter 2

Two Lovers

[H]aving both Lila and Lou 'on the string' makes me think or conclude that you are getting to be quite a 'Ladies Man'.

—Aunt Ocie Brown (Letter to Robert
Ferrell, September 8, 1953)

Lou is coming out here this spring for some of her vacation. . . . Trouble is that I'm all set to go and she is not. . . . Right now it would not take much bait from any line to bring me in.

—Robert Ferrell (Letter to Bob and
Kit Siller, February 1, 1953)

By the time Robert Ferrell came to Indiana University as an assistant professor in the fall semester 1953, he was a rising star in the field of history. Recognizing the merits of his first book, Yale editor Eugene Davidson looked forward to guiding the second volume, *American Diplomacy in the Great Depression*.[1] Davidson, as with other press editors (including Bernard Perry at Indiana University or Beverly Jarrett at the University of Missouri), would become both a good friend and publishing confidant to the young Hoosier historian, seeking him out as a consultant.[2] The IU position came partly due to his connections with Samuel Flagg Bemis, and their relationship also brought more opportunities to publish, including a secretary of state volume and a biography. Ferrell's professional network extended well beyond Indiana too as he served as a highly sought-after lecturer at more than a half dozen universities, including a Carnegie Visiting Assistant Professorship at Yale during 1955–1956 and year-long stints at the American University in Cairo and military academies, the Naval War College, and West Point. Several schools attempted to recruit him permanently.[3] At IU, Ferrell was coming into his own as a popular teacher and mentor.[4]

Yet the ambitious Ohioan-turned-Hoosier had reached an age where other personal agendas began to gain some attention. Early on, Bob did not have a wife to share in his success, even as there is evidence that the fairer sex found him desirable. Before heading to Bowling Green State University (BGSU), he enjoyed assuming the romantic role of Anthony to swooning classmate Cleopatra and Romeo to Juliet.[5] But that was kids' stuff no doubt, and thirty-year old Bob was no youngster in the summer of 1951 when he met a young girl (a Fifties-era term for a woman) at his cousin Christine's wedding to Robert Bryant.[6] The meeting was too brief to be of any moment at the time, but the two, Bob and Loueva (Lou), found themselves seated next to each other at a Thanksgiving Day dinner later that same year, likely orchestrated by Chris (i.e., Christine), to allow for more intimate exchanges.[7] Lou would recall the sit-down affair as a high point in her time with young men and as a reminder of how much she enjoyed Bob's companionship. They met at least two other times before the future Indiana scholar shared the relationship with his dad, the first time in Washington, D.C., while Ferrell worked as a research specialist in aerial targeting for an Air Force Intelligence unit in May 1952, and the following month on a rendezvous at Springfield, near Smith College.[8]

By the time Lou had made her presence to Bob of weightier concern, another young woman appeared on the scene to distract the first-year lecturer of history, this at Michigan State College (later university) in the fall of 1952.[9] Lila was a student of Ferrell's in an undergraduate American history course in his first semester there (see Figure 2.1). The attractive, young coed captured her teacher's attention, at least in part, because she wore a red dress, sat near the front by the window, and excelled at history.[10] Bob favored blondes as did Ferrell men generally, and Lila fit the mold. Lou and Lila were only two of several that the MSC history teacher would entertain during these early years, which raises the question whether in fact he had designs on any one woman or merely enjoyed the company of a variety.[11] But available correspondence throughout this period provides evidence that these two, Lou and Lila, were the primary foci of Ferrell's romantic interest from 1952 through 1956.

The Lou and Lila courtships represent, as did the episodes on how young Bob found his way to Yale and the anomaly of his war service, the postmodernist repartee against that of Bob's unitary, coherent, truthful approach to stories of the past. The extant evidence, particularly from Ferrell's correspondence, suggests that at least two stories vied for the truth, and even more, it is possible that one truth dominated at times against the other, depending on the volatility of his relations with either or both girls. The two competing stories documented in the letters are that Robert Ferrell was a playboy or that he was

Figure 2.1 Lila Sprout, a graduate of Michigan State College, had been a student in Ferrell's history course in the Fall, 1952; she worked as his office assistant in the Spring, 1953. *Source*: Courtesy of Carolyn Ferrell Burgess.

desperate, on his way to matrimony. Other evidence suggests too, at times, Ferrell played hard-to-get or was just too hard to please.

An added part of the intrigue highlighted in his engagement with these two love interests was their training and commitment to the profession of social work.[12] This adds more paradigmatic richness because Ferrell-type traditionalist historians were fighting a battle against an onslaught of social science disciplines (e.g., political science, sociology, psychology, statistical demography, economics, among other fields) that were muddying the boundaries and the distinctive contributions and outlook of formally trained chroniclers of the past.[13] American historians were also opening new avenues of interest and pursuing stories, those of racial and ethnic minorities and women (by women), that Ferrell's preparation and/or personal biases had dismissed. Ferrell found himself fighting battles on both professional and personal fronts: The ambitions of professional, career-oriented, future potential mates, and the interdisciplinary mix that underlay their career training, particularly sociology and psychology, set against its encroachment on the young professor's work.[14] A significant strand among these complexities, however, was a simple truth. Ferrell wanted a 1950s-era traditional wife, mother, and family caretaker, not a working professional equal.[15] As he wrote a friend and former history professor at BGSU, "Above all, I want just some common, ordinary person who will cook potato soup and talk sense. No cocktail parties and sophistication."[16]

Before turning to the main thrusts discussed here, in this era of the "Me-Too" movement, it is useful perhaps to address the potential for unwarranted accusation borne of the historical notion of presentism, that professors in the 1950s who engaged their students romantically were somehow unethical or predatory or unworthy of the profession, as the alarm is raised today. It is fair to say that while these relationships can be problematic to all concerned, the result in many cases, especially at mid-twentieth century, were long-lasting, reasonably felicitous marriages. To this point, an older history department colleague, Maurice Baxter, shared the following insights with Ferrell soon after the Yalie had joined the IU history faculty. Bob passed on the full context to Lila in a letter:

> Baxter saw me [Ferrell] coming out of a bookstore, and so brought me home in his car, after which we sat around and talked for a couple hours. . . . He turns out really to be quite a good person. He kept asking when I planned to go to Washington (for the American Historical Association meeting), so finally I broke down and told him that it was after you [Lila] arrived. This reminded him, he said of how he got married (not, he added, that he was suggesting such a thing to me). It seems that he picked his wife out of the junior—no, it was the sophomore class here [at IU], and married her when she became a senior. After that she took her M.A. in history and started work in the library. . . . The way he got acquainted with his wife was by playing bridge![17]

The chronological narrative of Bob's early-to-mid-1950s love life, its nod to postmodernist allegory, and the intriguing mixture of parallel professional antagonisms is the story told here. The conflicting disciplinary angst of these antagonisms was borne of the underlying expertise thought to make social workers something beyond amateur do-gooders and similar disciplinary confusions mucking up Ferrell's conception of the discipline of history.[18]

Few details remain of the first meeting between Bob and Lou during the summer of 1951 wedding celebration.[19] Reflections years later, however, reveal a restive attempt by the first-year history lecturer to learn more about his cousin's former roommate. What he came to discover in the initial courtship was perplexing yet worthy of pursuit.[20] Bob shared his thoughts and optimism with family, childhood friends and colleagues. His dad learned of the budding romance perhaps at first after his son borrowed a car to use on an outing with Lou. The oldest son wasted no time after the date, writing, "I don't know where I stand with this girl [Lou], although I would marry her if the chance presented itself."[21] Such boldness may have reflected some desperation, given his younger, only brother's success creating a family, and of course, the coming-of-age professor had arrived at middle age.[22] To friends Kit and Bob, Ferrell confessed that when Lou came to see him during a Christmas break in Washington, D.C., "I don't know where I stand [with Lou]," but that he "was all ready to go," yet she "was not."[23]

Lou certainly had qualities that recommended her to Ferrell as a first-class future wife. One gets the sense of this as the young MSC history lecturer introduced her to his dad.

> Her name is Loueva Pflueger (what a name!) and she comes from a very small town in Nebraska. She has an M.A. from Smith College in Massachusetts, a very good school—in fact, considered at the top for girls' schools in the East. . . . As for the social graces, she is the sort which could travel in any sort of company. She knows how to act in all occasions. . . . No smoking, no drinking; and a lukewarm Lutheran.

Lou's physique and age were less endearing ("rather tall and quite thin" and "26 years old"), and these along with occupational choice, a social worker ("a dead end for any girl . . . where [one] meets few eligible men"), marked her, in Ferrell's mind, as reaching the upper limit to find a mate or "be left out."

In their early exchange of letters, the history lecturer cum professor fumbled a bit in describing the desirability of social work.[24] The confusion as Ferrell described it stemmed from his belief that social work and by extension its workers were plying a trade long thought within the Christian duty to care for those less fortunate, yet social work training and professionals tried to dress themselves up in scientific garb. Recognizing social work as a "Christian calling," and "demanding some Christian principles to serve as fixed points for purposes of guidance," would demonstrate the unnecessary resort to finding best practice through science.[25] Of course, social work did have deep roots in religious efforts to ameliorate social conditions. Lou attempted to meet Ferrell half way: Nonjudgmental psychology had to be practiced within a sensible ethical framework.[26] By the end of 1954, Ferrell would learn a lot about the intricacies of social work from both Lou and Lila, and its demands came in conflict with what the rising star in history circles wanted from a potential mate. Part of the science of social work training, in practice, came from psychiatric consultants who coached social workers, most of whom were women that they must push beyond society-sanctioned roles. For Ferrell, this seemed to be the case with Dr. C. in Lou's training, requiring that she become "an emancipated female of the sort of which there are already far too many."[27]

Nearly six months after what Ferrell had uncompromisingly shared with his father, his desire to marry Lou, the second semester-MSC history lecturer reversed direction. His revised message to Lou sounded the alarm that there was no potential for a permanent relationship: "I believe our likes and dislikes and aspirations and general outlooks are so different that we could never hit it off together."[28] In the same missive, he continued, "we are such different people that for me friendship is the only logical conclusion" and that "we [must] adjourn seeing each other until perhaps this summer." Not surprisingly, Ferrell's sudden shift coincided with his interest in Lila, an MSC coed, whom he had come to know more intimately after taking her on as an office assistant in the history department.[29] But Ferrell was hardly finished with Lou, even as he shared with his dad, that he had sent her a "Dear John letter."[30]

Ferrell kept his brother Ernie (or June), among others, informed during the early developing romance between himself and Lou and Lila.[31] He certainly prided himself on capturing the attention of such a pretty girl, Lila, while sharing her picture with others ("the pleasantries of East Lansing life"); Lou, contrarily, was tall and thin, and this required some defensive remarks. Lila was a decade younger than her favorite MSC history lecturer; Lou, only six years his junior. History teacher and Lila relished traveling to big cities, Chicago and Detroit; she enjoyed cooking for him; Lou did not. As Ferrell coyly mused when introducing Lila to his long-time friend, Waldo, "my office assistant here has been doing some assisting at the apartment—frying pork chops for hungry history teachers, making popcorn, reading books to history teachers with tired eyes, running around the apartment with green shorts, etc. etc. Lila is quite the girl."[32] A month later, he was bragging that by ten o'clock, Lila had cooked "up some steaks . . . [wearing] blue shorts . . . and time passed quickly, without thinking of eating." In the same letter though, Ferrell admitted that there was a "confusing situation in Springfield, Mass. which I have to look at in August." This, of course, was his continued interest in Lou. But, again, to friends Bob and Kit, after the Spring semester at MSC had ended, Bob shared: "my present research assistant . . . is staying around working . . . and what time she has to spare, she spares it in my apartment wearing red shorts. Ummm."[33] Both Lila and Lou studied psychology and sociology to prepare for their careers caring for the underprivileged, yet Lou relished the opportunity to expound social science theories, whereas Ferrell underscored that Lila "never talks in the psychological jargon which we both detest."

There was likely more to the delight Bob took in Lila, beyond, as he stated, "her obvious talent," rooted in their shared experiences growing up and hardship.[34] She helped out as a farmer's daughter near Quincy, Michigan; he, on a farm during stretches of the Great Depression after his father lost a banking job. In Ferrell's words, Lila "came from the farm; her father, Earl Sprout (a typical country name) raised cattle in . . . Coldwater, Michigan. She . . . never had a great deal of help in getting through college. Her father paid her tuition now and then, but that was about all, and Lila earned the rest."[35] Lou possessed a more refined set of social and intellectual skills that likely fit better with Ferrell's educated set of family members.[36] Unlike the Ferrell family,

Lila was the only college attendee among her immediate family and smoked and drank.[37] But Bob and Lila both knew something of earning one's way through hard work. The two also shared a common language of evangelical Protestant faith (the Church of the Nazarene and that of the Methodist), if not the devotion, while Lou had ties to Lutheran traditions. Conventional institutional religion, whether based in church doctrine, ritual, or in evangelical fervor, carried little weight with any of them, and Bob was noticeably disenchanted with church members' hypocrisy.[38]

By mid-summer 1953, Ferrell sent a letter to his brother's family, making comparisons between the new love interest, Lila, and the Smith College graduate Lou, reinforcing some points of distinction between the two.

> Lou was a very nice girl in many ways, but she was chuck full of psychological jargon and fake sociology, and she also had a lot of false ideas about living in general: she disliked cooking; at one time more than hinted that I might turn her into a 'domestic' (lord, I wouldn't do that to anyone!); whereas Lila likes to cook, can cook excellently, and there's nothing I like better than to sit down to one of her pork chop dinners. As for vital statistics, Lila is a very pretty blond, about 5'5.

The difficulty, to Ferrell, with either Lou or Lila was that they were not ready to quit the professional track nor take on the family role that the rising history scholar had for them.[39] Lila rejected the low-level job prospects Bob had found for her before coming to Bloomington; the pay would not meet livable standards; the work would not satisfy her; and she could not likely "pass a typing test."[40] It took little time for Lila to reconsider joining him. By the end of summer 1953, she left Bob for Detroit and a job at the State of Michigan Department of Social Welfare.[41] Lou would move closer (than Springfield, Massachusetts) to the newly ensconced IU history assistant professor but stop well short of Bloomington, perhaps thinking that she could lure him back to his boyhood hometown of Lakewood, a suburb of Cleveland.[42] Breaking away from work to visit their suitor was difficult due to the overwhelming load that social workers engaged. Lila shared that she could not come for a planned weekend as thought due to the busy scheduled "contact day," when "clients" came by to complain about their checks, etc.[43] Ferrell believed such absences created a hardship impossible to overcome.

Cousin Christine's husband Robert Bryant, a graduate student in theology, counseled his cousin-in-law after trouble appeared between Ferrell and Lou, partly at least stirred by her commitment to social work.[44] The MSC history lecturer had proposed marriage to Lou in February 1953, but he did not get the response expected.[45] Instead of a gushing yes, Lou hesitated, "all tied up in psychological doubts and inhibitions and all mixed up in what her future would be or ought to be." Without allaying her beau's ego, Lou headed to a conference of psychology lectures in Cleveland, then to a Smith College cocktail party. No affirmative message arrived as Bob waited. Then Lou turned down the possibility of a New York get-together with Ferrell because she had to attend professional seminars that crowded the weekends. Ferrell felt he was "being made a fool of" and wrote several letters to Lou calling the whole thing off. Now, perhaps he was reaching out to his cousins for affirmation and advice.

The problem, as Bryant (and Christine no doubt) saw it, was several-fold. Lou's mix of professional training and personal insecurity contrasted with that of the research historian's; Lou's work focused on a Freudian orientation, from a psychological and/or psychiatric perspective, on analysis of inner conflict, on dealing with personal problems. This training was a break from the narrow upbringing that Lou had experienced growing up, and it required some caution, on her part, in seeing relationships and the world in optimistic, overly simplistic and uncomplicated terms that Ferrell's words seemed to suggest.[46] Bryant also described the women's changing professional expectations that Lou likely felt uncertain Ferrell would appreciate her professional training as a "psychiatric social worker." To Bryant, Ferrell had to readjust his thinking about the role of wives and respect their professional choices. Requiring wives to be cooks, seamstresses, and household managers, with no consideration of their professional aspirations was an outdated way of thinking.

After more than a year passed, little had changed between the Hoosier historian's outlook on courtship intentions and that of his girls, Lou or Lila. While arranging a trip to see Bob at IU toward the end of her social work service, Lila wrote: "Forgot while talking with you I would be out in the field all day. Thought this morning I may be able to get back to the office but presently I am at the [Detroit] Welfare offices and see that the two cases I have to read are pretty fat." Along with large caseloads, there were investigations yet to be finished and "reinvestigations," at least nine of which were "due at the end of the month."[47] In another note, sharing her hectic life as a social worker, Lila relayed that she had put in her resignation at the welfare agency and was preparing to come to Bloomington, close to Christmas:

> Everyone is rather disappointed I signed the [resignation] papers. . . . It's leaving a lot of work for the remaining workers. I'll have to do 23 reinvestigations besides the 12 applications before I leave. Today . . . I talked on the phone or in Intake all day so there is nothing done. Just more troubles—address changes, budget changes, special investigations, supplement checks, conferences, etc.[48]

Even with Lila's departure from the State of Michigan job, she communicated ambivalence about joining Bob permanently. Now firmly ensconced at IU, he was having none of that, restating an "ultimatum" given her about his timeline: "I've already held forth . . . that I won't wait any longer than the end of the first semester of school here [in Bloomington]."[49]

As Ferrell grew increasingly uncomfortable with Lila's reticence to reunite, letters flew back and forth, many from Lou to Bob.[50] Unlike Lila who shared the practical side of her social work trials, Lou reflected on the theoretical. Annette Garrett, a former Smith College teacher of Lou's, had come to Cleveland to speak on the "current trends in social work."[51] Lou responded positively to the message:

> They're finally realizing its senseless to wallow around in a lot of sexual and unconscious [Freudian] material unless you can involve the ego to do something about it. That is now known as 'management' as against the old 'treatment.' You have to help people control themselves, and in many of our situations there is danger of homicide. My latest client is in this spot.[52]

By this time, however, Ferrell had become firmly entrenched in opposition to psycho-social theories, what they could offer to social work, and as part of the larger constellation of social sciences and their application to history.[53]

Ironically, Ferrell's belief that social work in the 1950s remained in the Victorian era a philanthropical paradigm (a dutiful Christian endeavor) underscored his ignorance of, and/or disregard for, what had transpired in the field during the twentieth century. Long before the future historian would meet either Lou or Lila, universities had created dozens of accredited social work programs across graduate and undergraduate schools in the United States, and their foundation was based on "scientific knowledge and research," along with field work investigation, new techniques and technology, and increased focus on race and gender.[54] Freud's psychoanalytic theory provided a scientific base, and Lou's letters to Ferrell clearly reflected this.[55] Addressing immediate client needs and potential resources also were priorities as was mastering organizational insights, group dynamics, aspects of social policy, and research. A social work research journal, *Social Service Review*, began publishing studies by 1927 to improve practice.[56] Balancing the broad interests of clients and public needs and expectations was (and is) crucial to social work success, and thus, the earliest academic instruction included a mix of economics, sociology, scientific methods and statistics, and labor and industry, all of which could be brought to bear on social issues and reform.[57] To underscore the point, the American Social Science Association's efforts beginning in 1870s were instrumental in promoting the study of social problems and their remedies, central to the social work mission.[58] Adherence to public expectations and aims would become more pronounced as state and federal governments dictated through programs and funding the ends to be served.

At mid-century, Lila wrote her Bloomington beau about overstuffed casework files and overwhelming numbers of investigations and reinvestigations at the State of Michigan Department of Social Welfare.[59] This was evidence of the scientific method applied in social work.[60] To do such work, she and Lou prepared for a wide variety of tasks that awaited them through an eclectic set of program requirements. For example, to be admitted as a social work graduate student at Smith College, Lou completed "at least twenty semester hours in the social and biological sciences," including "studies in sociology, anthropology, economics, government, history, and in related fields . . . psychology and physiology."[61] Lila had majored in both sociology and anthropology as an undergraduate at MSC. Psychoanalytic terminology such as "transference" based on client "identification" with a social worker and feelings of security and trust were examples of foundational concepts.[52] The evaluation of results often centered around attainment of "satisfactory adjustment" and length of case work completion. Ferrell's potential mates fit the dual tracks that aspiring social workers could take at the time. Lou completed a graduate degree; Lila, a baccalaureate. First track graduates headed principally to the private, nonprofit work world; Lila, as with others in the second track, found work at a public welfare agency.[63]

But early on, experts questioned the legitimacy of social work as a profession, that it lacked "definite and specific ends," or "a clear line of demarcation about [its] respective fields."[64] In this, Ferrell and his tradition-bound colleagues studying U.S. history also signaled some internal discomfort by the 1950s and beyond. The respectability afforded emerging social sciences and their imprint on the methods, theoretical perspectives, and the work of historians caused part of the alarm. Social scientists engaged a broader critique of the past, encompassing a wider swath of voices heard, a diverse set of purposes served, and conflicting epistemological perspectives.[65]

As an approach to knowledge creation, empiricism drove the modernist conception of history (1800–1960), including Ferrell's.[66] More specifically, as historians have elaborated, it is

> a simple, common-sense method of objectivity and fact-collection in which all knowledge has to be proven before it can be accepted. . . . It relies solely on experience (or observation and reading) of knowledge. When combined with inductive reasoning, it allows the scholar to move from particular bits of knowledge (cases) to generalizations (conclusions).[67]

These conclusions required "consistency" about what happened in the past. Writing the historical narrative was central and completed the process of constructing history. To maintain disciplinary respectability, the narratives had to pass muster with fellow historians (peer review), then be subjected to further scrutiny with colleagues who revisited the topics. As differences arose among historians, "relevant facts" and "plausible explanations" were evaluated and resolved. Professionalism was judged on the competent capacity to engage these processes.[68]

The rise of the social sciences and their application to history creation met with fierce opposition among Ferrell and modernist allies.[69] The disagreement was rooted partly in disputes over what was considered credible historical knowledge and theoretical frameworks and partly over what should be the goals served by historians. Sociologists, political scientists, among other social scientists, focused on identifying and understanding rules that explained human behavior. These rules of behavior or generalizations would permit the development of models of the past, to explain, predict, and/or prophesize. Such purposes were antithetical to Ferrell's beliefs, which encompassed the 'reality' of uniquely situated individual action, potential for heroism, human agency, and contingency as powerful forces directing and helping explain historical events.[70] This, aside from the topical foci, likely underlay much of his repudiation of collegial proponents of Marxist history, the new social and cultural historians, and social work experts relying on Freudian theory.[71] Sociology has been identified as the core of the social sciences, and thus, it is hardly surprising that Ferrell and colleagues treated it with such scorn.[72] The IU historian's attitudes toward the social and behavioral sciences may also explain why IU political scientists ignored Ferrell's expertise in presidential history despite his successful scholarship well beyond his courtship phase—this in studies on Harry Truman, Woodrow Wilson, and Calvin Coolidge, among others.[73]

Strands of criticism directed at social work as a profession overlapped with those aimed at historians. One of the earliest critics of the former, Abraham Flexner (1915), identified six essential criteria to the work of physicians, lawyers, engineers, among others, that signified professional status: "intellectual operations with large individual responsibility," the work "rooted in science and learning" and toward "a practical and definite end," delivery of "an educationally communicable technique," tendency toward self-organization, and an increasing shift toward altruism.[74] Social workers lacked at least two qualities according to Flexner; first, they were primarily mediators between client needs and ultimate problem-solving agents (e.g., medical issues require referral to a doctor), and second, they lacked clearly defined goals.[75] One might add that social workers disagreed over proper training, theoretical perspectives, and practices and/or emphases.[76]

The social work mission was so broad that its practitioners had to draw on a wide range of outside professionals and complete a wide diversity of curriculum choices.[77] Like nurses, social workers were "collaborators" at best, more often dependent on recognized professionals to observe, reflect, and decide ultimate needs and take action.[78] The myriad spheres of social work—juvenile delinquency, mental health, single mother/out-of-wedlock children/family welfare, medical care, homelessness, child care/protection, labor strife, the impoverished, disability, and more—covered such a wide array of specialized knowledge and skills that establishing a clear disciplinary boundary was also unachievable. Thus, as in the case of Lou and Lila, training reflected a broad selection of fields, from economics to sociology, psychology, cultural studies, ethics, religion, medicine, and so forth.[79] Conflicting theories tied to different social science areas also complicated any unity on purported definitions and causes of, or remedies to, social problems.[80] Ideological commitments led workers to pursue different goals: Were social workers to help maintain the existing social order or emancipate the downtrodden? Were they to care for or facilitate control over clients?[81]

Joseph Helfgot noted that sociologists' ideas contrasted with those of psychologists' or cultural anthropologists' regarding the need to address "individual adjustment," larger issues of workplace discrimination and unequal compensation, "rites of passage," "masculine identification," or a constellation of "culture of poverty" personal/community inadequacies, in planning a 1950s Mobilization for Youth federal program.[82] Lack of political power blocked any attempt to facilitate "opportunity structures" rooted in one of the three-pronged social science solutions to the youth problem, juvenile delinquency. Social work mental health services were grappling with differences in the "medical perspective" and what would come to fruition decades later labeled the "ecological" treatment of mental illness, the first with attention to external signs while the latter incorporating the individual's environment and departing from Freudian or Eriksonian "linear, sequential or stage theories."[83] Government regulations that reflected pro-business, paternalistic, and racist norms, particularly after the Second World War, undercut social worker autonomy or agency in implementing research-based practices.

One must only follow the evolution toward professionalism, topics, and purposes of twentieth-century American history scholars to arrive at the parallels to social work disciplinary-boundary ambiguities and internal conflicts. Historian H. Hale Ballot noted that in the 1950s, "very little American history that was written before 1900 is current to-day . . . and that after 1910 men of the elder school began to be outmoded."[84] Furthermore, these earlier works were "big narrative histories," and "the aim . . . was to produce good citizens and competent public servants, rather than scholarship." The early products came from those trained in law, philosophy, and sociology. Interestingly, not long into the so-called American Century, the new breed of U.S. historians (empirically trained) continued to share their turf with interdisciplinary interlopers. By the time Ferrell began his work at MSC, historians were witnessing even more change: the broadening landscape and purposes that scholars of the past sought to explore or re-explore (often with ideological motives rooted in social theories), the rise of social science disciplinary expertise drawn on, and the increased attention to non-elites or disadvantaged populations (e.g., women, ethnic minorities, economically marginalized).[85] Even social workers without historian credentials—ironically, given Ferrell's love life—have written credible narratives of the evolution of social work and education and social welfare policy and women.[86]

By the time the Yale-trained diplomatic scholar landed at Indiana University, he was long acquainted with the writings of native Hoosier historian Charles Beard, and it is likely too, he knew something of the assortment of Midwestern-rooted researchers who were revolutionizing the path and foci of the historians of the United States.[87] Beard, of course, proposed that the economic interests of the founding fathers motivated the passage of the U.S. Constitution, removing George Bancroft's halo from the nation's first leaders and the idealism that lit democracy's narrative. He synthesized multiple biographies as method, a novelty. His original use of 1790 documents of the U.S. Treasury Department and accusation that national financial interest groups—not "We the People"—led to the critical successful convention negotiation with Southern plantation owners plowed new ground. He proposed too that economic interests underlay the development of the first political parties. Beard was president of both the American Historical Association and the American Political Science Association well before Ferrell was paying attention to history. Once settled into his studies on American foreign relations, the future IU historian did not miss the respected history leader's critique of President Franklin Roosevelt, including allusions to FDR's unconstitutional actions and lying to the public or Congress, arguments that Ferrell found unappealing and likely unsupported by the data.[88]

Aside from Beard's innovative influences, historians from the Midwest and beyond were also overturning expectations of their colleagues, employing interdisciplinary investigations, social science theories, or quantitative and other original techniques and perspectives. James Harvey Robinson, an Illinoisan, guided scholars to use the knowledge of the past to improve society. Though well-grounded in scientific history methods, he focused more on causes of past events (not merely description), and in this, he drew on multiple social sciences, including anthropology and psychology ("animal, child, and social"). Unlike Ferrell, Robinson widened the scope of history beyond the political, constitutional, and military. Iowan Carl Becker infused his history work with "psychological" analysis of people without paying much attention to the record of events; the value of history, in his thinking, was moral not scientific; it opened the portal to self-discipline through broader understanding, greater sympathy, and an emboldened willfulness. James Malin concentrated on local community studies in past farming practices, "ecological" history "from the bottom up," likely a first among colleagues. A native of North Dakota, he may have come to understand the challenges of farming experientially, beyond climate and geography, before identifying capital requirements as essential to permanent occupancy on the Plains. Unlike Beard, Malin professed that historians could approach an objective reality in the facts, existing outside the mind of the observer; to him, history-making was an intellectual enterprise, not to be applied.

Hailing from Wisconsin, Frederick Jackson Turner, much like Beard, reoriented decades of scholars to embrace his proposed relationship among democracy, free land, and the North American frontier. The fuzzy nature of central concepts confused as much as enlightened, but the appeal of his interpretive framework lay in economic determinism, nationalistic pride, and ethnocentric theory; his edict—historians should not disparage the United States. Explaining the influences of the "frontier" fused disciplinary ideas from geography, economics, and social psychology. The frontier signified various ideas: a region, the cutting-edge encounter, a process leading to the white man's evolution. Along with Turner, one could add historians of the new disciplinary approaches with roots outside the Midwest—Warren Susman, focusing on American culture; historian/sociologist W. E. B. Du Bois, who worked to counter middle-class white male dominance with African American narratives; Louis Reichenthal Gottschalk's generalizations on revolution and in history writing generally; or social historian Herbert Gutman's interest in capturing the experiences of "ordinary people who built the United States." J. Franklin Jameson is worthy to note too, perhaps as bookend, to the others described above, due to his relentless organizing efforts on behalf of history as a profession, even beyond his work that characterized the American Revolution as partly borne by social changes.

Perhaps most critically, the history field's shifting approach to epistemology also put Ferrell on the defensive. Postmodernism was likely the most radical shift within historical circles witnessed by the Hoosier scholar and his traditionalist colleagues. Its challenge to history is connected to a string of twentieth-century language theorists.[89] Leaping over the theoretical synthesis, Ferrell witnessed one of the end results—a philosophy of knowledge relying on the "social construction of reality," which dismissed the possibility of a science of knowing and opened a pandora's box of heretofore marginalized voices to be heard and topics to be explored. The postmodernists' philosophical wave smashed against the modernist shore creating a stir among historians such as Ferrell as alluded to in chapter 1.

As to professional methods, not philosophical underpinnings, had the upstart IU diplomatic scholar investigated the "initial process" of the "social work case method"—including the first client interview and concomitant resort to other family members, search for further insights and sources, and careful weighing of the evidence gathered and its interpretation, the overlap with the historian's task would have been unavoidable.[90] Both social workers and historians relied on widely practiced methods (if not theoretical stances or end purposes) within their respective fields. For Lila and Lou, that meant casework, intake, investigations (or "social diagnosis"), and reports.[91] Ferrell also could point to agreement among historians regarding history standards surrounding "human observation, experience, testing of authenticity, verification, corroboration and presentation for judgement."[92] Bob's love interests no doubt stood firm in dismissing their suitor's slights partly due to the solid foundation of their training and field work rooted in casework management. Ferrell's early success with scholarship made him, perhaps, more confident (or overly defensive and thus cocksure) than he should have been in haranguing colleagues who differed with him on the new ways of approaching the study of the past and "new" social science expertise infusing it. He, no doubt, felt the pangs of battles on two fronts, both personal and collegial.[93]

Ferrell won plenty of professional battles, if not the war, throughout his career. He authored and edited sixty books, many of which came after his retirement from Indiana, this well beyond the postmodernist push into the history profession mainstream. While social scientists certainly have also made their appearance permanent as historians' bedfellows, overcoming whatever resistance traditionalist historians have provided, the Hoosier storyteller's academic offspring, perched on twenty-first-century academic roosts, have continued to crow allegiance to the "Ferrell approach."[94] Aside from allegiance to empiricist roots, the successful presidential, diplomatic, and military scholar's work paid homage to Samuel Eliot Morrison's literary flair and provided engaging narrative. Also, to his credit, perhaps acknowledging the importance of the new social history, his final book, *Unjustly Dishonored*, honored a poorly treated U.S. African American soldier division that fought during the Great War.

Whether Ferrell, at any one time, was a playboy, desperate, or just hard to please or placate (i.e., to make someone less angry or hostile), depended more on the rollercoaster ride that exemplified his love life, particularly through those early years at Michigan State and Indiana University. His matrimonial-courtship past is best told by the mercurial Ferrell himself in many letters left to us. The letters sent back and forth to family, friends, colleagues, and of course, Lila and Lou, suggests that Ferrell was all three (playboy et al.), but primarily desperate to find a mate. He had arrived at two potential brides that suited his fancy at one time or another, all the while just having fun perhaps with Kathleen or Nerena, among others, only until he could negotiate a marital agreement with the most favorable social worker. Two letters, one from Aunt Ocie to her nephew, spoke to Bob's playboy persona: "[H]aving both Lila and Lou 'on the string' makes me think or conclude that you are getting to be quite a Ladies Man."[95] To his brother's family, Ferrell noted: "I had just about given up hope—not of finding someone, for there were always plenty of people around, but of finding someone suitable in every sense of the word. Marriage in the ordinary way is not attractive, and I'd rather be single." Strangely, Ferrell had signaled the end with both Lou and Lila within a year that he married one of them. In the autumn of their relationship, at least four years into "dating," on September 30, 1955, Bob wrote to Lou: "there is no possibility of us ever getting together"; and to Lila, in the same month, he proclaimed: "This is really, then, the end, and I am determined that nothing further will occur between us."[96] Nevertheless, Lila acquiesced and became Mrs. Ferrell before a year would pass. The allegorical postmodern irony, of course, is that the Hoosier historian's matrimonial partner would symbolize, in part, the fight he found in the profession of history, professional women coming of age, and eventually, writing themselves into Ferrell's and the American story.

NOTES

1. For a list of Ferrell's book publications (minus *Unjustly Dishonored*, 2011), see Robert H. Ferrell. *Contemporary Authors Online,* 2018. *Biography in Context,* http://link.galegroup.com. Accessed September 24, 2018, p. xiii.

2. Letter to Gene, January 31, 1998; letter to "Evie" [Eugene Davidson], September 21, 1998, misfiled under File January–February 1998 (#2), all Box 58; letters to Gene, July 2 and July 13, 1994, Box 25; letters to Bernard B. Perry, September 22, 1955 and March 11, 1959, Box 72; and July 20, 1960, Box 73; and January 6, 1963, Box 18; memo to Bernard Perry, February 19, 1964 (on Ferrell's H.S. History Textbook project), Box 77; letter to Ferrell from Beverly Jarrett, August 14, 2001, Box 95.

3. In a letter to Howard Lamar, June 26, 1970, Box 10, Ferrell noted that Gaddis Smith's reunion with Yale opened the offer of a professorship at Duke, but Ferrell used it as a bargaining chip to earn full professor at IU.

4. "Favorite Profs," *IU Alumni Magazine* (Fall 2013), p. 11, Box 207 (and related letter to Ferrell from Becky Batman [IU Alumni Association], February 24, 2014, Box 207); letter to Dad, February 11, 1954, Box 46; letter to Ferrell from David E. Ellies (Dean's Office, Arts and Sciences), February 19, 1998, Box 58.

5. See yearbook notes, Milton High School (MHS), May 4, 1938, Box 74.

6. Letter to Ferrell from Lou, August 16, 1955, Box 72; letter to Dad, October 6, 1952, Box 44.

7. Ibid.

8. Ibid.

9. Letters to Dad, August 27, 1952 and October 6, 1952; letter to Bob and Kit [Siller], October 26, 1952 and May 30, 1953; letter to Pete, September 15, 1953; letter to Waldo Pratt, May 13, 1953; letter to Lou, March 8, 1953; letter to Aunt Ocie Brown, September 8, 1953—all Box 44; letter to Samuel Bemis, June 27, 1955, Box 72.

10. Letter to Charles [Blankenship], February 20, 2002, File December 2001–January 2002 (misfiled), Box 97; letter to Flo and June, April 29, 1953; see also Lila's graded History 105 course assignments/tests.

11. For example, in letters to family and Lila, Ferrell noted, "The new girl, Kathleen . . . , I took her out to dinner" or "I am taking Nerena to dinner this Friday night."—see letters to Dad, December 2, 1953, Box 44, and to Lila, February 22, 1955, Box 72, respectively.

12. Loueva Pflueger, social worker, family services, *Lakewood (OH) City Directory* (Cleveland Directory Co., 1955), 519 (at Lakewood Public Library); Lou also listed as a "casewkr" in *Springfield, West Springfield, Longmeadow Directory, 1953* (Springfield, MA: The Price & Lee Company, 1953), 744; Lila Sprout is identified as a "social worker" on her death certificate (Bloomington, IN: Indiana State Department of Health, 2002); letters to Dad, October 6, 1952 and to Lou, January 1, 1953 and January 17, 1953; letter to Flo and June, July 12, 1953; letter to Ferrell from Lou, "Tuesday" (circa January 1953); letter to Bob and Kit, October 26, 1952 (all in Box 44).

13. Evans, *In Defense of History*, 27–28; Donnelly and Norton, *Doing History*, 40–41, 57–58.

14. Letter to Lou, January 1, 1953, Box 44; letter to Ferrell from Lila, circa October 1954, Box 72.

15. Letter to Lila, August 6, 1953; and to Waldo [Pratt], May 13, 1953 (all Box 44); letter to Flo and June, July 12, 1953, Box 74; and see endnote 17.

16. Letter to the Nordmann's [Mr. Nordmann, a history professor at BGSU, and his wife], February 1, 1953, Box 44.

17. Letter to Lila, August 6, 1953, Box 44.

18. Letter to Flo and June, July 12, 1953, Box 44; Leslie Leighninger, *Creating a New Profession: Beginnings of Social Work Education in the United States* (Alexandria, VA: Council on Social Work Education, 2000), p. 67; Landes and Tilly (eds.), *History as a Social Science*; Hughes, *History as Art and as Science*.

19. Letter to Ferrell from Lou, August 16, 1955, Box 72; A local newspaper recorded the wedding, listing Loueva Pflueger as "maid of honor" and Robert Ferrell as organist; see "Emily C. Rentsch Bride Saturday of Rev. Bryant," *Derby Evening Sentinel*, August 13, 1951.

20. Letter to Bob and Kit, October 26, 1952, Box 44; see also letter to Aunt Ocie, February 28, 1953, Box 44; letters to the Nordmann's, September 10 and December 22, 1952, Box 44.

21. Letter to Dad, October 6, 1952, Box 44.

22. Letter to Aunt Ocie, February 1, 1953, Box 44.

23. Letter to Bob and Kit, February 1, 1953, Box 44.

24. Letter to Lou, January 17, 1953, Box 44.

25. Ibid. Importantly, Ferrell made clear that the Christian framework so thought to guide social workers would not include "the crude sense of the evangelists and the tub-thumpers . . . [that is] learn[ing] the ways of the righteous." Ibid.

26. Letter to Ferrell from Lou, "Tuesday" (circa January 1953), Box 44.

27. Letter to Lou, September 10, 1952, Box 44.

28. Letter to Lou, March 8, 1953, Box 44.

29. Letter to Bob and Kit [Siller], May 30, 1953, Box 44.

30. Letter to Dad, December 2, 1953, Box 44. The most telling letter that puts in perspective Bob's juggling Lou and Lila came to friends Bob and Kit, June 30, 1953, Box 44: "My Springfield pal and I have been having all sorts of correspondence and even some visitation, but nothing has developed to date. . . . The reason for all this dalliance is probably my present 'research assistant,' Miss Lila Sprout, who just

graduated from 'MSC' this winter. . . . What time she has to spare, she spares it in my apartment wearing red shorts. Hmmm." See also letter to Bob and Kit, July 12, 1953—Ferrell relays, "As to the love life, that is a vast and complicated affair . . . I'm going to . . . New Haven, via Springfield"; letter to Lou, September 6, 1953—Ferrell plans for rendezvous with Lou at a hotel in Springfield; see also stayovers in his apartment, letters to Lou, October 10 and October 17, 1954; and to a colleague, Pete, Ferrell wrote: "I've been going with a couple of girls but there is no information of any moment yet." September 15, 1953, Box 44.

31. Letter to Flo and June, April 29, 1953, Box 72; see also letters to Waldo on Ferrell's new office assistant and apartment activities, or to others about admiring colleagues (e.g., Professor Hogue, etc.).

32. Letter to Waldo [Pratt], May 13, 1953, Box 44; letter to Waldo [Pratt], June 23, 1953, Box 44.

33. Letter to Bob and Kit, May 30, 1953, Box 44.

34. Letter to Samuel Flagg Bemis, June 27, 1955, Box 72—Ferrell wrote: "I 'discovered' her obvious talent three years ago at Michigan State. . . . There is no pretense, and unlike the movie star Grace Kelly, Lila is a real country girl. She is intelligent, but not super-sophisticated."

35. Letter to Flo and June, April 29, 1953, Box 44; Obituary, Hilda F. Braatz, May 10, 2009, *East Lansing Journal* (accessed October 24, 2018 at https://www.legacy.com/obituaries/lsj/obituary.aspx?page=lifestory&pid=127106013).

36. Letter to Dad, October 6, 1952, Box 44; see Ferrell, Sr., *Stories I Want My Grandchildren to Know*, 127–133.

37. Letter to Waldo, Jan, Baby Will and Snoopy, June 17, 1960: "Hope that Lila hasn't drunk all the beer in the icebox." Letter to Nordmann, January 24, 1957, Box 43: "Lila and I downed five free whiskey and sodas at the Yale meeting [of AHA]."

38. Bob's daughter Carolyn shared that their family did not attend church services as she grew up. Organ playing was the incentive that put him in a church setting; email, Carolyn Ferrell to author, June 11, 2018.

39. For example, Ferrell wrote: "I wish you could come down quickly, so I can have a decent meal." And, "I'm up to your doings tonight; doing a washing. The first machine I put a dime in refused to work and got hot and something began to smell, like a burning motor; I didn't do anything to it really; so I unplugged it, and spilled water all over the laundry room to the disgust of a couple of women, and then made the other machines work, except that I put too much soap in them and it ran all over the floor too. I'm some mechanic, don't you think?" See letter to Lila, August 3, 1953, Box 44. Days later, he shared with Lila, "My cooking is rapidly going from worse to worser. Tonight it was hotdogs and some hash cooked in the skillet. The hash turned out very greasy and almost inedible, and together with the hotdogs has ruined my appetite. I'm presently drinking orange juice to drown out the taste, but not very successfully. Coming down soon?" Letter to Lila, August 4, 1953, Box 44. Letters to Lila often identified secretarial, waitress, or administrative jobs as those Ferrell would try to find for her when she planned to come to Bloomington; see for instance, August 1, 1953, Box 44.

40. Letter to Ferrell from Lila, August 6, 1953, Box 44.
41. Letter to Dad, December 2, 1953, Box 44; letter to Ferrell from Lila, October 1954, Box 72.
42. Letter to Ferrell from Lou, April 6, 1953, Box 44.
43. Letter to Ferrell from Lila, circa October 1954, Box 72.
44. Letter to Ferrell from Robert Bryant, March 20, 1953, Box 44.
45. Letter to Chris and Bob, March 17, 1953, Box 44.
46. Ferrell responded to one of Lou's introspective letters, attempting to help her work through her next career/personal move: "psychologists always have to run in a mother-complex, or whatever they call it" or "screw-ball techniques . . . of theoretical social work." See letter to Lou, April 6, 1953, Box 44.
47. Letter to Ferrell from Lila, "Thursday pm" (circa September 1954), Box 72.
48. Letter to Ferrell from Lila, "Monday night" (circa December 1954), Box 72.
49. Letter to Lila, January 15, 1955, Box 72. Despite this warning, Ferrell would continue to see Lila, and another 'break-up letter' would follow by September 1955, followed by more courting. See for instance, letter to Lila, Sept 25, 1955, File May–December 1955, Box 72 ("This is really, then, the end, and I am determined that nothing further will occur between us. Please do not write, for I will not read any letter; nor will I take telephone calls," then Ferrell's letter to Aunt Ocie, December 14, 1955, Box 43, noted Lila and Bob with each other during his visiting professorship at Yale, 1955–1956.
50. By this point, Ferrell had made it clear there was no future with Lou. A good example came after many love letters from Lou to Bob, the result of which was the following reply: "there is no possibility of us ever getting together," See letter to Lou, September 30, 1955, Box 72.
51. Letter to Ferrell from Lou, "Sunday" (circa May 1955), Box 72.
52. Ibid.
53. By the 1950s, historians had discredited an example of this in Sir Lewis Namier's emphasis on Freud; see Evans, *In Defense*, 27–29.
54. Leighninger, *Creating a New Profession*, v; Diana M. DiNitto and C. Aaron McNeese, *Social Work: Issues and Opportunities in a Challenging Profession* (Needham Heights, MA: Allyn & Bacon, 1997), 18–22. Lena Dominelli has reviewed the arguments in the social work community between practice as an art or as a science; she advocated for both. See her *Sociology for Social Work* (London: Macmillan Press, 1997), 68.
55. Martha Morrison Dore suggested that Freudian-rooted "psychiatric social work" casework theory was being challenged by proponents of a functional approach at the New York School of Social Work (later Columbia University School) in the 1930s and 1940s; see her "Clinical Practice," in *The Columbia School of Social Work: A Centennial Celebration*, ed. Ronald A. Feldman and Sheila B. Kamerman (New York: Columbia University Press, 2001), 128–132.
56. See its website at https://www.journals.uchicago.edu/journals/ssr/about accessed November 16, 2018.
57. Leighninger, *Creating a New Profession*, 11, 20, 23, 28–30; see also Smith College School of Social Work (1950s) faculty specialties (e.g., clinical psychology,

medicine, law, psychiatry, cultural studies, economics, social case work, child psychiatry, etc., online at https://archive.org/details/smithcata4950smit/page/n373 (accessed November 11, 2018). By the early 1950s, Columbia University's School of Social Work, a model for others, required all students to study content covering "growth and development, psychopathology, medical and social problems of illness, and the socio-cultural basis of individual and community life." See Alfred F. Kahn, "Themes for a History: The First Hundred Years," in *The Columbia School of Social Work: A Centennial Celebration*, ed. Ronald A. Feldman and Sheila B. Kamerman (New York: Columbia University Press, 2001), 24; Joseph H. Helfgot reported that the United States since the Second World War had "seen an enormous expansion in the use of research," including the study of "domestic problems," and social science research had become widespread by the end of the 1940s. Federal government spending on it increased many times over beginning in the 1950s. See his *Professional Reforming: Mobilization for Youth and the Failure of Social Science* (Lexington, MA: Lexington Books/D.C. Heath and Company, 1981), 14–15.

58. According to Alfred F. Kahn, by 1876, Johns Hopkins University would develop "a new type of social science school . . . [whose professors] carried out social investigations, used [the] research as a basis for teaching, and documented findings." An early Johns Hopkins's PhD graduate, Amos Warner, compiled "the new studies" in "the first social work text." See Kahn's "Themes for a History," 10, 13–14. There is a discrepancy as to which college offered the first social work program. See ibid., 9–12 and Smith College, Springfield, MA, claims at https://sophia.smith.edu/ssw100-history/ (accessed November 10, 2018).

59. Letter to Ferrell from Lila, circa October 1954, Box 72.

60. Leighninger, *Creating a New Profession*, 66–84 (esp. p. 68). It is important to note that Lila's academic social work preparation included completing an undergraduate degree with majors in Sociology and Anthropology; see *MSC Yearbook* (Lansing: Michigan State College, 1953), 348; Lou completed a graduate program in Social Work (per email to author from Nanci Young, Smith College [Springfield, MA] archivist, November 2018, and an undergraduate degree in sociology from Midland (now University) in Fremont, Nebraska; see Midland College yearbook, 1948.

61. See the *1948/1949 Bulletin of the Smith College School of Social Work* (Northampton, MA: Smith College, 1948), 16–17; provided by Nanci Young, Smith College archivist, November 14, 2018; see Lila Sprout, MSC Yearbook, 1953.

62. Lena Dominelli has elaborated central sociological concepts for social work (e.g., "status, power, roles, authority, legitimacy, institutions, organizations, responsibility, rights, relationships and division of labor" in *Sociology for Social Work*, 51, 59–67.

63. DiNitto and McNeese, *Social Work*, 19.

64. Leighninger, *Creating a New Profession*, 44; DiNitto and McNeese, *Social Work*, 10–11.

65. Evans, *In Defense*, 18, 23–24; for the debate in Ferrell's circles, see *The Truman Period as a Research Field: A Reappraisal, 1972*, ed. Richard S. Kirkendall (Columbia: University of Missouri Press, 1974).

66. H. Hale Bellot, *American History and American Historians: A Review of Recent Contributions to the Interpretation of the History of the United States* (London: The Athlone Press, 1952), 1–25; Brown, *Postmodernism for Historians*, 12–18; Donnelly and Norton, *Doing History*, 35–39; Evans, *In Defense*, 14–17; see also John Barker's discussion on Leopold von Ranke, *The Superhistorians: Makers of Our Past* (New York: Charles Scribner's Sons, 1982), 145–175.

67. Brown, *Postmodernism for Historians*, 16–17; Evans, *In Defense*, 31–32; for a more elaborate overview, see Donnelly and Norton, *Doing History*, 33–39.

68. For greater elaboration of the historian's task, especially "interpreting source materials" and the "use of sources to make inferences," see William Kelleher Storey, *Writing History: A Guide for Students* (New York: Oxford University Press, 1996), 31–38, 59–74.

69. As will be discussed in the final chapter, Ferrell's approach to history also drew on history as art/literary accomplishment; see also Wilson, "Introduction," 3–4.

70. Ibid., 3–11.

71. Brown, *Postmodernism for Historians*, 19. See Chapter One herein, endnotes 1–7; see letter to Lou on Freud and documents (letter and Diary entry) criticizing the hiring of faculty that focused on gender history (e.g., Joan Wilson at IU in 1981); letter to Jim, June 9, 2011, also Ferrell diary entry, April 13, 1981, pp. 1–2, Box 216. Evans, *In Defense*, 27–28.

72. Letter to Kertesz, June 23, 1953, File 7, Box 44; letter to Ferrell from Stephen Kertesz, July 3, 1953, Box 44.

73. Letter to Ken Duckett, January 30, 1999, Box 58.

74. Leighninger, *Creating a New Profession*, 39–44.

75. An example of this is in Helfgot: social workers in the Mobilization for Youth program initiated an effort to "alter the opportunity structure" (i.e., provide economic or educational opportunities/programs for the young to succeed) that it had no power to implement; see his *Professional Reforming*, 52.

76. DiNitto and McNeese, *Social Work*, 10, 20–21.

77. Kahn, "Themes for a History," 20–24; more than likely both Lou and Lila specialized in the division "working with individuals and families," and perhaps within a department of Social Casework, family and child. See for example, Smith College's graduate social work program attended by Lou in the 1950s, accessed November 11, 2018 at https://archive.org/details/smithcata4950smit/page/n373.

78. Leighninger, *Creating a New Profession*, 42–44.

79. Smith College's graduate social work program in the 1950s, accessed November 11, 2018 at https://archive.org/details/smithcata4950smit/page/n373.

80. Mimi Abramovitz, *Regulating the Lives of Women: Social Welfare Policy from Colonial Times to the Present* (Boston, MA: South End Press, 1996), 315–329; Martha Morrison Dore identified several intra-social work paradigmatic conflicts (e.g., diagnostic versus functional, emphasizing human agency and rooted in psychodynamic theory, and ecological theories); see her "Clinical Practice," 125–128, 137–140.

81. Leighninger, *Creating a New Profession*, 52.

82. Helfgot, *Professional Reforming*, 3, 43–55.

83. Robert L. Jackson, *The Clubhouse Model: Empowering Applications of Theory to Generalist Practice* (Belmont, CA: Wadsworth/Thomas Learning, 2001), 20–31.

84. Ballot, *American History and American Historians*, 7–8. See also Evans, *In Defense*, 27–28.

85. See Brown, *Postmodernism for Historians*, 40–48, for an elaboration of this theme (e.g., "concentration on the lives of ordinary people . . . women, peasants . . . working classes, ethnic minorities and the poor" or "the use of alternative sources" or "writing social and economic rather than political and diplomatic history." Several of the more well-known examples include Marxist, Annales, and postcolonial schools of history. Ferrell characterized as historically insignificant "Indians and gender . . . in diplomatic history"; see letter to Garry Clifford, February 27, 1998, Box 58.

86. Abramovitz, *Regulating the Lives of Women*; Kahn, "Themes for a History."

87. This review relies heavy on Lucian Boia (ed.), *Great Historians of the Modern Age: An International Dictionary* (New York: Greenwood Press, 1991), 715–781. Ferrell joined the Mississippi Valley Historical Association once he arrived at Indiana and successfully helped to bring its publishing entity to Bloomington.

88. Ferrell, "Pearl Harbor and the Revisionists," 215–233.

89. According to Callum Brown, Ferdinand de Saussure (1857–1913), Roland Barthes (1915–1980), and Michel Foucault (1926–1984); Foucault, a philosopher, theorist, and historian, is most credited for the origin of postmodernism, arguing that "knowledge is socially constructed by different ages" and that postmodernists had to "dismantle" earlier centuries social constructs including discourses on gender, race, mental health, and so forth; see Brown, *Postmodernism for Historians*, Chapter Two.

90. Leighninger, *Creating a New Profession*, 68–69; also on page 80, Leighninger draws on the ideas of Mary Richmond, a leading advocate for advancement in social work in the early twentieth century, who noted that "the art of diagnosis does not consist merely in gathering together a great many facts, but in coordinating those that one has been able to collect, in order to reach a clear conception of the situation" and in evaluating "the evidence" as to what has "been accepted or rejected and why, what inferences have been drawn from these accepted items and how they have been tested."

91. DiNitto and McNeese, *Social Work*, 71–75; Martha Morrison Dore noted that by mid-century, "of thirty-one full-teaching faculty listed on the [New York School of Social Work] roster in the 1955–56 General Announcement, fourteen were identified as Casework faculty," with the rest divided among Group Work (5), Research (4), and Community Organizing (1); See her "Clinical Practice," 132–136.

92. Historian Callum Brown noted, "To be a good historian, it is thought you have to be good in empiricist method," and further, "this method of doing History is broadly what all academic and professional historians aspire to the world over." See his *Postmodernism for Historians*, 21–22; see also ibid., p. 25: "Even if the *consequences* of empiricism are challenged, postmodernists most certainly do not reject empiricist methods. Like all historians the postmodernist needs empiricist method for the essential skills, and any student of History *must* learn and deploy them."

93. It is fair to say that Ferrell learned to adjust along the way, in part; his final book, *Unjustly Dishonored* (2011), addressed the unjust reputational damage suffered by African American troops after their brave fighting in the Great War.

94. Wilson, "Introduction," 3.

95. Letter to Ferrell from Aunt Ocie Brown, September 8, 1953, Box 44.

96. Letter to Lou, September 30, 1955, and letter to Lila, September 25, 1955 (both Box 72).

Part II

BEGINNINGS AND SCHOLAR-ACTIVIST

Chapter 3

Ferrell in the Making

To portray Robert Ferrell in hues greater in depth and nuance than graduate school pursuit, war service, or matrimonial courtship, it is possible to reach back to early years and geographical origins, to beginnings, even underlying layers of rock. Birthplace and era, neighborhood environs, religious allegiances, boyhood activities, among other signposts that would define the Hoosier historian are documented. These provided the geological formations mixed with personality that crystalized into Indiana University's distinguished historian. What lay behind the public Ferrell were attachments to family traditions and values, sensitivity to metropolitan Cleveland complexity and northern Ohio rural simplicity. To understand Truman, the Indiana storyteller intoned, one must know the man and his times, and this lesson is as applicable to knowing the president's most prolific biographer. This chapter reveals something of the realities that shaped his worldview.

One can almost see a young Bob Ferrell stepping out the door of the split-level home that his family (see Figure 3.1) shared with others at 12955 Emerson Avenue, then turning up the street northward along Nicholson Avenue toward Lake Erie, and finally across the broad boulevard at Clifton and into the door at Taft Elementary School.[1] Built in 1927 to accommodate a surging northeastern Lakewood population, Taft was the closest school to home as Ferrell approached his sixth birthday. In the Cleveland suburb of Lakewood, where Ferrell lived through most of his early years, Taft Elementary was just one of six primary schools named after Ohio-born presidents; the others were Grant, Hayes, Garfield, Harrison, and McKinley in order of election succession.[2] Harding Junior High, named for the twenty-ninth president, would complete the list of those that the Buckeyes could call their own.[3] Other local schools at the time—Lincoln, Roosevelt, Madison, and Wilson—would also reflect the tradition of celebrating notable chief executives, and Horace Mann

Figure 3.1 A young Bob Ferrell, second from left in the first row, sits at a gathering with his mother's (Rentsch) family in New Philadelphia, Ohio. Ernest Ferrell Sr. and Edna are second from right, top and middle rows, and favorite Aunt Ocie is seated middle row far left. *Source*: Courtesy of Carolyn Ferrell Burgess.

Junior High no doubt underscored taxpayer's commitment to the famous New England education reformer's promotion of public education. Thus, early on, school options of youthful families reflected what historian Andrew Cayton professed was a sense of "public culture" among native Ohioans.[4] Young Ferrell was surrounded by what defined a strand of his scholarship years later, presidential studies.

The future Indiana historian also had easy access to the Lakewood Public Library that seemingly could not keep up with the needs of its residents, expanding twice with the infusion of $150,000 in 1922, then twice as much only two years later.[5] The diversity of activities hosted by the library was another mark of New England culture grafted onto northern Ohio and into the Ferrell family ethos.[6] Other influences of that region included a belief in small-town participatory government, religious commitment, educational aspiration, attitudes of racial equality and human dignity (anti-slaveholding), and patriotism. These linkages to the northeastern United States came from its original settlers by way of Connecticut's divestment of pre-American Revolution territory known as the Western Reserve. After acquiring much of this land, the Connecticut Land Company sold the property to newcomers, and many of its leading pioneers represented northeastern ideals.[7] An agent of the Land Company and surveyor from Connecticut, Moses Cleaveland, a Yale law school graduate, helped to establish the area, including the misspelled city named after him. In 1797, Lorenzo Carter from Rutland, Vermont, brought a sense of permanence to what would become Lakewood. Two New Englanders, Dr. Jared Kirtland, likely the area's most celebrated citizen for his work in geology, medicine, and law, and Franklin Reuben Elliott, collaborated in horticulture. A Yale-educated missionary minister, Joseph Badger, brought evangelical zeal. By the 1820s, the Methodists had established the first of several mainline Christian denominations; the Baptists and Congregationalists followed.[8] In these early years, taverns and log-cabin-whiskey drinking was met with religious pushback led by New Yorker Datus Kelley, "the first temperance man in the district," a struggle that would last into the following century. James Nicholson, from Chatham, Massachusetts, married Betsey Barthlomew—a transplant from Waterbury, Connecticut—and traded his homestead for 160 acres at the future site of Lakewood, then purchased more, and began farming the area that would blossom into vineyards and orchards across the city. These were some of the roots of Bob Ferrell's upbringing, continued more than a century later as his parents worshiped as Methodists, farmed, earned college degrees, and frowned on alcoholic indulgence.

Settlers created the township of Rockport, the progenitor of Lakewood, in 1819, and several decades later, round-trip rail service to Cleveland led urbanites to its rural environs.[9] A student of local history noted that a passenger train service known as the "Dummy Railroad" chugged along toward the town of Rocky River, a get-a-way vacation spot for city dwellers 20 miles west of Cleveland. The train tracks running through Lakewood east to west marked the boundary between working-class neighborhoods to the south and middle-class residents to the north, the site of Ferrell family homes (see Figure 3.2). Less than a mile further north stood another dividing line, Lake Avenue, which sheltered the community's elite that had come long before the Ferrells to enjoy elaborate estates near Lake Erie. As the years passed, later-day Lakewood—between the big city and Rocky River—was spied as a congenial location to call home for those looking to escape urban congestion, what Ferrell Sr. would boast was cool, clean air from the lake. Interurban streetcars such as the Lake Shore Electric Line (see Figure 3.3) made possible the switch from Cleveland homestead to the western suburb for Ernest Sr. and Edna, the future Indiana historian's parents.[10] The present-day Lakewood United Methodist Church (LUMC), built in 1912 along Detroit Avenue (originally the "plank road"), led services that young Bob would attend with his family, just beyond a mile from home.

The excitement of economic progress surrounded Bob Ferrell in his early years before his family felt the sting of the Stock Market crash. Lakewood quadrupled in size from 15,181 to 70,509 residents from 1910 to 1930.[11] Robert likely sensed the growth up close on Sundays, as fellow LUMC attendees mushroomed to 4,306 by 1930.[12] New homeowners could expect to pay soaring prices for lots at $2,500 per acre. A local boom in natural gas production

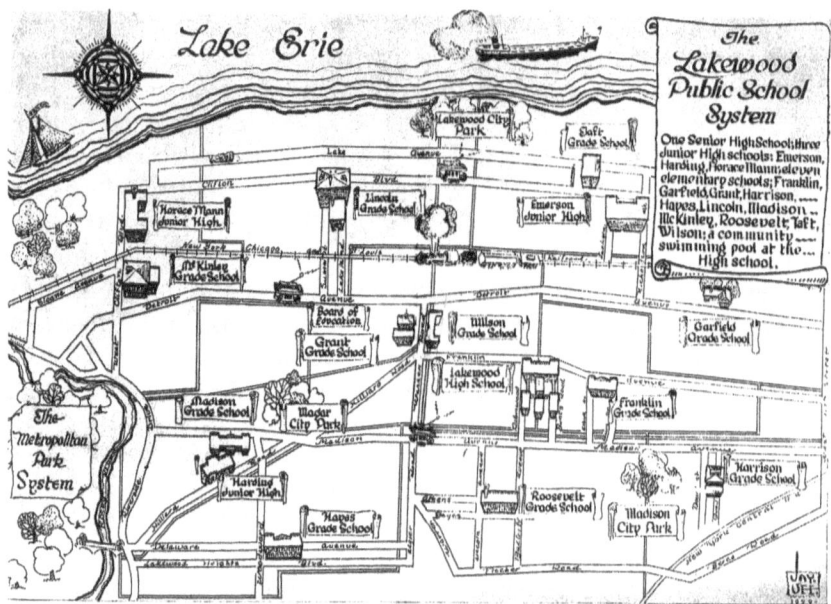

Figure 3.2 The Ferrell family lived in the neighborhood near Emerson Junior High (top right), initially at 12955 Emerson Avenue, then at 1312 Ramona Avenue. Lakewood Public School System Map, 1929. *Source*: Margaret Manor Butler, *The Lakewood Story* (New York: Stratford House, 1949).

put money in the pockets of citizens and city coffers for a short while, but white-collar workers such as Ferrell's parents, commuting from the big city, provided the long-lasting support and vision for what the community would become. Ferrell Sr. worked at the Guardian Bank in Cleveland, among other banks, and Edna taught school.[13] They both had graduated, in fact had met, at Wooster College just 70 miles south and moved to the city afterward. Edna's sister, Verna, and her husband Ivan Meggitt, the relatives Ferrell would address in letters as "Auntie and Uncle Ivan" during wartime, attended Old Stone Presbyterian Church. Edna and Verna were twin sisters, and the two along with chosen beaus enjoyed the cultural benefits of urban living.[14] The families must have remained close as Bob continued to attend Boy Scout Troop #67 meetings sponsored by the Meggitt's church whose spires were dwarfed by surrounding office buildings near the center of Cleveland. Verna and Ivan later joined Ferrell's family in Lakewood. Stalwart Republicans, they brought their politics with them, knocking on doors in the neighborhood to convert and cajole the uninitiated to vote for GOP candidates.[15]

Depression-era economics pushed the Ferrells to relocate at the beginning of 1932, and with this, to expand the perspective of their eldest son. Bob,

Figure 3.3 The Ferrells often rode the interurban street cars that they boarded only blocks away on Clifton Boulevard. *Source*: Cleveland State University Archives.

along with younger brother Ernie Jr. ("June"), found himself a few hours to the west, in rural Custar, Ohio, on a farm, and attending Milton Township Rural School, several miles from his new home.[16] Another family move, just up the road, put him at Waterville High School the last year, where he would further cultivate his literary, musical, and boy-scout-leadership skills. Nevertheless, Ernest Sr.'s chaotic job changes permitted Bob to return to Lakewood and attend the junior high named for the celebrated American writer, Ralph Waldo Emerson, and Emerson's famous essay "The American Scholar" portended what this young boy would become.[17] With all these experiences in Lakewood and Cleveland, economic surge and bust, city-to-farm relocation, Milton Township and Waterville schooling, Methodist services, northern Ohio conservatism, family Republican circles, and parent and extended family input, one can point to the influences that would shape the perspective of the future Indiana historian. Bowling Green State University and world war also would contribute, as would Yale. But the early years likely made the most lasting impressions. With all this, the subtext to Ferrell's words and deeds becomes visible.

Ferrell's parents sowed many of the seeds of the future historian's commitments and historical biases: patriotism and constitutional defense, ethical zeal, belief in truth and factual reality, right and wrong, defense of capitalism, and common man sensibility.[18] Letters Ferrell sent from the warfront display the love of the son for both Ernest Sr. and Edna, yet the attention that the Second World War Staff Sgt. Ferrell devoted to his father's First World War tales demonstrated the interest and respect that sons reserved for elder doughboys (see Figure 3.4).[19] Ferrell Sr. relayed long after the Great War ended that "American soldiers . . . had come to save [France] from invaders."[20] Just out of high school, Ernest Sr. had found himself stationed in the midst of what historian Ferrell years later would characterize as the deadliest battles for Americans in the war, Oise-Aisne and Meuse-Argonne.[21] As soldier-father shared it with his son, on June 13, 1918, he "marched on board" the British ocean-liner *Olympic*, arrived to England, then shipped to Le Havre, France, and traveled by train and truck through a series of cities and encampments, ready to meet the atrocities of German warfare. Ferrell's was no ordinary war service. Rejected as an infantryman ("many times on the march the entire company

Figure 3.4 Ernest Ferrell Sr. (far right) in training at Camp Sherman, near Chillicothe, Ohio, for medical duties in the First World War. *Source*: Courtesy of Carolyn Ferrell Burgess.

would be out of step but me") and as a mule skinner, Ernest was reassigned to shoulder the medical duties for incoming wounded, more than 1,000 soldiers in a single day and nearly 10,000 over a period of months. Death was all around. Robert must have relished his father's telling of the histrionics of battle: artillery shells exploding, French and German aerial dogfights, bombed out bridges and buildings, barbed wire entanglements. At some point, Ernest Sr. contracted diphtheria, and in the confusion of war and lost military records, the brass reassigned him as a "casual," detached from any given billet or unit for months. With some luck, he reunited with the 332d field hospital company and celebrated war's end, returning home August 3, 1919.

Given Ernest Sr.'s war stories and soldier camaraderie, camp lifestyle, soldierly discipline and uniform, marching, medals, and lifetime friendships, it is hardly surprising that young Bob Ferrell would be attracted to the Boy Scouts. The scouts imitated soldier-like rules and routines (camping, marching, exploring, meritorious achievement with badges) and offered the same opportunity to develop lifetime friendships.[22] The Boy Scouts also mirrored beliefs and values central to American patriotism, reinforced by his father's value system.[23] Showing extraordinary commitment to scouting ways, beliefs, and values, Bob earned Eagle Scout designation by the age of fifteen, gaining eagle palms with additional merit badges thereafter, and served as a leader into his later teenage years.[24] Boy Scouting historian Benjamin Jordan found that the Boy Scouts of America (BSA) diverged some from Victorian era, race-based insularity that reflected Ferrell's parents' rural Ohio roots, and thus, broadened his perspective.

Jordan explored the guiding principles, practices, and expectations that encompassed boy scouting in the 1920s and 1930s, Ferrell's era.[25] The BSA served two larger societal goals at the time: to cultivate young boy's ways of thinking to fit the needs of modern, bureaucratic work and to counter the threats to traditional authority (well-placed white males) originating from women, minorities, immigrants, and the economically and rural disadvantaged.[26] In transforming boys to "right thinking and acting" men, so the underpinning philosophy went, the organization had to guide them through a series of psychological adolescent stages and a recapitulation of earlier periods of racial development—from "beasts to infant cavemen, Native American hunter-gatherers, feudal Knights, and self-assertive pioneer settlers," at which point then, they would arrive at the moment of "cooperative, democratic, white Americans," according to theorist G. Stanley Hall in his Child Study Movement.[27] Boys were thought to possess both good and bad character traits, and scouting activities and achievements were thought to lead its members through these stages productively, "habituating" the positive traits. Inferior traits (e.g., selfishness, individualistic, impulsive, intolerant, chaotic) enveloped young white, middle class boys among others excluded from the scouts, and thus, working through the recapitulation stages with the right guidance brought the appropriate cultivation of altruism, cooperation, self-control, tolerance, and organization to achieving scouts. Ferrell followed the usual path, initially gaining Tenderfoot status by February 1935, then Second Class, First Class, and finally Eagle Scout with extra palms, a level reached by only a small percentage of scouts (see Figure 3.5).[28] Ernest Sr. served as one of Troop #67's leaders throughout Ferrell's time as a scout, and younger brother Ernie Jr. also followed the path to Eagle Scout, much to the delight of his father.[29] Ernest Sr. gave credit to scout training for his boys' success in life.

Within the mantra of Boy Scout ideals came a peculiar way of thinking toward so-called "inferior races"—women and minorities, foreign nationals, among others. These groups were thought incapable of mastering the "advanced" racial character traits that came with Boy Scout membership and activities. Whether these prejudices carried over to Ferrell's historical thinking is impossible to tell, but there are traces that follow the logic. The Indiana historian later dismissed the importance of Indian history in Idaho, upstart gender and other social histories, and New Left history.[30] His scholarly

Figure 3.5 Ferrell (second from left) achieved Eagle Scout honors by the age of fifteen through the Boy Scouts of America, Cleveland Council #440. *Source*: Lilly Library, Indiana University at Bloomington.

interest in the African American troop experience in the Great War came only late in Ferrell's life, well after retirement.

BSA laws also are worthy of note since they reinforced values that Ferrell absorbed from other sources, family, church, school, and father's shared corporate and military experiences. Jordan's analysis has demonstrated the deeper meaning of these laws exemplified in Boy Scout culture; that is, in BSA guides and activities and within the context of the early twentieth-century.[31] For example, we might examine the first, second, and seventh laws (to be trustworthy, loyal and obedient), taken together, which oriented the member to respect lines of authority, not to lie or cheat (particularly consequential in the performance of duty), and to show allegiance to Scout leaders, parents, home, and country. These all helped to teach the scout to work within a corporate hierarchy. Being untrustworthy was the singular misbehavior that could lead to one's dismissal from scouting. The eighth and ninth laws, to be cheerful and thrifty, applied principally to work task completion, within the new, less autonomous, bureaucratic order. Being cheerful and thrifty helped members to avoid the destructive tendencies in street life, mass entertainment, or attitudes and actions of striking laborers. Thriftiness also meant saving money in a bank account, "the only law necessary to advance in scouting."[32] The fourth and eleventh laws, to be friendly and clean, were geared primarily to draw like-minded peoples together while separating scout members—generally white, male and middle class—from those labeled "inferior." The tenth law, to be brave, pushed the scout to "stand up for a just cause" (especially if unpopular) or for a disadvantaged person, showing "moral heroism."[33] To be reverential, the twelfth law encouraged the scout to show respect for, and participate in, religious or church activities (e.g., lawn mowing, ushering, attending services) and be tolerant toward other mainstream faiths.

As several of these BSA laws demonstrated, scouting overlapped with young Bob's religious ties and beliefs. The Boy Scout Oath required "Duty to God and Country," and the Scouts relied on congregational sponsorship and infrastructure of various denominations, for example, Methodists or Presbyterians.[34] Ferrell's family was Methodists. Historian John Wigger has chronicled the expansion of Methodism in Ohio, which "quickly outstripped growth in nearly every other state or region."[35] Just decades before the Ferrell family moved from Cleveland to Lakewood and to Methodist Church membership there, the denomination dominated church establishments and adherents among all religious groups in Ohio, with 2,115 buildings and 272,000 more self-identifiers. Denominational leaders denounced slavery early on, and Ohio became a refuge for southern-based abolitionist church members. The United Brethren Church took the same stance; Orlando Ferrell, grandfather to Robert, had organized a United Brethren Church in Custar, Ohio, Ernest Sr.'s birthplace.[36] The Methodists and United Brethren overlapped in their commitment to equality and temperance, and the title "United Methodist" was born from the fusion of the two evangelical congregations.[37] Fighting against slavery, however, did not equate to feelings of African American and white, middle class camaraderie. Northern Ohio churches remained as segregated or more so than the denomination's followers in the South. Nevertheless, historian Ferrell, with Methodist ties, would denounce racist attitudes of university leaders well into the mid-twentieth century, and he and brother Ernest Jr. would take pains to hide any indulgence in alcohol.[38]

Wiggins has described Ohio Methodists as "more politically active than just about anywhere else in early-nineteenth-century America."[39] Jeffersonian-Republicans made up the greatest proportion of voters. Its ideology equated the institution of widespread agrarian society with optimal democratic government as investment in property would assure political independence and freedom and provide a reason to participate. This played well in Ohio, a state with high rates of land ownership; Ernest Sr.'s father Orlando Ferrell owned seven farms by the time the son came of age in the late 1800s.[40] With just such a political orientation, and projecting a concern for the common opinion of the electorate, Methodist leader, Edward Tiffin, defeated Ohio territorial governor and Federalist Arthur St. Clair, and future Methodist-Republicans gained prominent offices at high rates.[41] Republicanism and Ohio became more intertwined with the cause of abolitionism, defending the Union against the rebel slaveholder South and patriotism beyond the Civil War. As the decades passed, the GOP also embraced business and banking interests.[42] These issue stances resonated with Ernest Sr., who worked in banking, served in the First World War, affiliated with Methodists, and had strong attachment to rural ways of thinking.

Ernest and Edna were attracted to Cleveland nearly two decades into the twentieth century, and thus, had traveled well beyond their rural settings culturally and otherwise. The issue of slavery was a distant memory no doubt but patriotism, temperance, and political bossism tied to big city machines and ethnic diversity still divided the electorate. Irish and German Catholics found their way around prohibition (as did some Methodists and military men) and worshiped outside of a Ferrell-familiar protestant catechism.[43] Other immigrants, particularly eastern and southern Europeans (Poles, Slovaks, Russians, Italians, etc.) had flooded into Cleveland and into certain sectors in its suburbs such as the "Bird's Nest" in south Lakewood as its industrial base expanded. They spoke and learned a variety of languages much to the chagrin of Americanization proponents.[44] Young Robert, growing up near Cleveland, enjoying its cultural attractions and diversity and feeling the crunch of economic dislocation embodied in the Great Depression in his teens (and sensing the usefulness of the federal government), may have been less enamored of his parents' political Republican calculation as were others living around Cleveland during the Democrats' rise to national power in the 1930s.[45] He embraced courses in German, studying it as a minor in college.[46] In fact, Ferrell may have been conscious of the city's tilt away from the GOP as historian George Knepper noted, "Cleveland and most northern cities have been dominated since the 1930s by the ethnic-labor-black vote that formed much of the old 'Democratic coalition.'"[47]

Frank J. Lausche's ascent to political prominence in the 1930s and 1940s reflected the changing circumstances of young Ferrell's world even with Ohioans' continued attachment to conservative politics.[48] In the midst of Cleveland diversity and as a Slovenian Catholic, Lausche championed the cause of immigrants but sought to clamp down on organized crime and guard the public treasury. A nominal Democrat, he willingly crossed party lines to support Republican candidates and causes. Appointed, then elected, to Cleveland judgeships in the 1930s, Lausche was unsparing in shuttering gambling operations, ordering raids on clubs, and spearheading campaigns against recalcitrant sheriffs who refused to act. He denied pay raises to city workers in an election year and proved himself honest by quitting as judge before running for mayor. Showing independence from Democratic machine bosses, Lausche refused to fire Elliot Ness at the request of a former Cleveland Mayor and Democratic county chairman. Ness was a Republican who fought unrelentingly against mob bosses and gangsters.

Though removed to the Custar family farm by his early teens, Ferrell could not have missed newspaper reports from Cleveland and Columbus extolling the virtues of the unorthodox and independent former Mayor-turned-Governor of Ohio, Lausche. Editors at the *Cleveland Plain Dealer* and *Cleveland Press* praised the independent-minded governor. Aside from endearing personal qualities to conservative Buckeyes—penny-pincher, county fair mixer, straight-arrow, Lausche defied labor leaders by sidelining strikes, in part, to supply soldiers during wartime, even losing labor-union backing thereafter. He obliged his own pay cuts as Cleveland Mayor and later as Governor. Long at odds with the Democratic Party, at all levels, his gubernatorial victory in 1944, even as the state of Ohio went for Republican Thomas Dewey over President Roosevelt, brought offers of campaign finance help from the national party, which the candidate declined.[49] Caught in postwar domestic economic difficulties and Soviet communist blame-gamesmanship, he would lose the governor's office in the Republican landslide in 1946 only to regain it the following term (and several more), campaigning across the state with President Harry Truman. Ohioans continued to support him due to his no-tax stance, even as it led to a deterioration of government services.

By the time Lausche had won the Cleveland mayoral race, Ernest Sr. had made strides in the banking industry, and he no doubt, must have admired this conservative Democrat who embodied frugal attitudes toward government and taxation and who led moral campaigns against gambling and the criminal element including the illegal liquor industry that went with it. Robert was imbibing lessons in penny-pinching as his dad headed off to the Cleveland Guardian Bank, likely on the Clifton Avenue branch of the Lake Shore Line's interurban streetcar, then to the Brotherhood of Locomotive Engineers National Bank (B of LE) after switching jobs.[50] These were heady times in the financial industry, leading up to the market crash, and Ernest Sr. had a birds-eye view of the problems partly made clearer due to night-school training received at the American Banking Institute. He had moved up from "savings teller" at the Guardian to branch manager of the Standard Trust Bank (the reorganized B of LE), and the role provided a much broader perspective of missteps within banking at the time.[51]

As Ferrell Sr. described it, Standard Trust corporate mismanagement and inefficient administrative practices wasted branch resources and attempts to improve efficiencies were ignored. Bank employees were neither trained well nor capable of training. The bank encouraged small depositors to open accounts, even as checking accounts did not retrieve costs through service charges. The president, a union man, and other top officials, lacked banking experience. Most damning, as the stock market careened downward, the bank was overleveraged with declining values of stock secured against loans and could not meet depositors' needs. From the start, Ferrell Sr. had warned his bosses that the branch, at Broadway and Fifty-Fifth Street, was in the "bootlegger section of Cleveland," and since he neither smoked nor drank, would not be a good fit.[52] They assured him he was just the conservative banker they needed there to use care in granting loans, and not surprisingly, Ernest Sr. boasted that eighty percent of loans he approved were paid back. A bookkeeper who embezzled funds for years at the branch added to the difficulties. As problems mounted, the Broadway extension was closed, and Ferrell Sr. transferred back to the main branch, where bank examiners would put the Standard Trust Company and Robert's dad out of work by the end of 1931.

It is difficult to judge what effect any of this would have on a ten-year-old Ferrell, aside from the immediate insecurity of uncertain family income, estrangement from local school friends and Cleveland environs, and new lifestyle and schooling near Ernest Sr.'s inherited farm just south of Custar. Robert continued his Boy Scout activities, joined by his younger brother. He was thrust into new chores: fixing up the farm house, painting the outside, wall-papering and adding paneling to the dining room, planting oak trees, and frequently filling a tub in the "milk-house" with cold water from a well to keep food cold.[53] He faced a new set of schoolmates, more isolated surroundings, and long distances from home to school. Nevertheless, the Ferrells were encouraged by extended family still living in the area where Ernest Sr. had lived as a child. Once grown, Ferrell's younger brother claimed that the farm years during the depression "taught him . . . how poor people had to work." Ernest Sr. added that farm living "taught Bob and Ernie Jr. what it was like to live on a small income without modern conveniences" and "the value of a dollar."[54] Years later, Ferrell shared with his daughter only that he remembered wringing the necks of chickens for dinner during his farming days.[55]

In spite of losing his Standard Trust position, Ernest Sr. returned to banking "for two longish periods during the 1930s," this back in Cleveland with the Reconstruction Finance Corporation (RFC).[56] Bob and family had to endure a fatherless home for several years through the work week and many times on the weekends for five-week intervals as Ernest Sr. returned to Lakewood alone, moving in with in-laws Verna and Ivan while he performed the duties of bank examiner. A government agency, the RFC, provided loans to closed banks, secured principally by real estate mortgages. Those that were able, then, reorganized and began anew, paying off depositors. The RFC laid off part of their workforce, including Ferrell's dad, but then rehired him for 18 months, at which time young Bob rotated back to Lakewood to attend high school for the first two years, then transferred to Waterville High to graduate after Ernest Sr. became the President of Waterville Bank (see Figure 3.6). One can speculate whether such economic uncertainties, both in the wider economy and at home, may have prompted more reflection from young Robert on the precarious nature of capitalism or Republican pro-business attitudes. Years later, letters he sent after coming to Indiana as an historian revealed that he was, as Ferrell himself put it, "what is called a liberal Democrat," and it is possible that these earlier boyhood times eased the transition from self-professed–Taft Republican to Adlai Stevenson (and beyond) Democrat.[57]

An added layer of intrigue and its potential impact on young Robert during the 1930s was the turmoil embroiling the citizens of Toledo over the improprieties surrounding their financial institutions, just up the road from Custar. It is hard to fathom that the reports would not have caught the attention of the Ferrell family, given Ernest Sr.'s occupation and the widespread media coverage.[58] News on the misdeeds continued through 1937, when the last gasp of litigants' efforts to hold bankers and others responsible fell on deaf judicial ears.[59] Historian Timothy Messer-Kruse has written a case study on the era and banking crisis, using Toledo as a counterpoint to the stereotypical images of the causes and/or effects of the Great Depression and the financial world's role in it. While mainstream textbooks well beyond the event pointed to bank runs or independent economic events or declining income and prices as precipitating events, popular news stories of the times (when Toledo banks were failing) captured a very different culprit. Whether in conservative media outlets such as the *Saturday Evening Post* or more liberal, the *Nation*, the reports of villains in the Toledo "Smart Money" scandal were directed at bankers and their unsound money practices, "not [at] a depression which engulfed

Figure 3.6 Ferrell (top center) graduated from a rural area high school located hours to the West of Lakewood and Cleveland environs. *Source*: Waterville Historical Society.

well-managed banks." Even more, Messer-Kruse found that for the years 1930–1932, "the largest single year's loss of deposits for any of the twelve Federal Reserve districts was that which occurred in 1931 in the Fourth District," including all of Ohio, and that the Fourth District's misfortune "was due largely to the contribution of Toledo, which alone accounted for three-quarters of the district's losses."[60] President Roosevelt called Toledo's banking crisis "the worst . . . of any city in the nation."

Poorly run Toledo banks and corrupt bankers were not minor players nor were they alone in the financial-failure complicity. Messer-Kruse detailed the parts played by the area's real estate industry and Toledo municipal-bond decision-makers over a twenty-year period, beginning with poorly designed subdivision platting and concomitant mortgages, land lots proffered as collateral for bank loans, and related mortgage-bundling scams.[61] Intertwined with misjudged valuations for loan guarantees were overlapping interests of the banking directorships—well-connected family members, city and state officials, and real estate and other industry leaders that relied on the bank's loans or who gained from the association with banking officials (e.g., Henry Close, Raleigh Mills, Ira Fulton, George Jones, among many others).[62] Toledo banks were infusing their loan collateral portfolios with company stocks of their own directors. Banks were not auditing adequately their real estate valuations against market conditions or loans. Businessmen-turned city officials, who might have fought for the public good, had been corrupted by their own interests in banking-related decisions over annexation, rezoning (glutting the market of lots and homes), and allowable bonded debt. Under Republican control, the State of Ohio Banking Department ignored its own financial regulations and did not impose fines on widespread improper or illegal behavior. The Ohio Bank paid undeserved dividends; the Commercial Bank grossly overvalued its Liberty Funds; the Security-Home Bank manipulated accounts to hide losses; the Guardian Bank maintained secret accounts to avoid paying thousands in taxes.[63]

There is reason to believe that Ferrell's dad, Ernest Sr., would have known something about these specific wrongdoings and the politics associated with bank closings and attempts to reorganize and reopen or liquidate during the Great Depression. Troubled Toledo banks were spending extravagant sums of money building branch facilities while performing poorly financially, just a short distance away from where his close relatives lived. These same banks may have had to draw on cash reserves of neighboring banks, perhaps reaching toward Custar or Cleveland, as other banks did under Federal Reserve requirements.[64] During the financial crisis, three of Toledo's four largest banks sought to acquire loan guarantees from RFC to reorganize and reopen through the same unit Ferrell Sr. worked, though at a later time.[65] Most importantly, Ernest Sr. served as a bank examiner for the RFC in the middle of the Toledo imbroglio, which gave him privileged information to the sorts of shenanigans such big banks were indulging, with the aid of prominent, wealthy industry leaders and public officials in northern Ohio. Regardless of personal scruples, a lowly bureaucrat such as Ferrell likely would have had to follow the wishes of higher-ups, such as Republican party boss Walter Folger Brown, W. W. Knight, a member of the Federal Reserve Board for the region, and/or Henry Thompson, a member of the Toledo Trust Bank and member of the RFC loan group for the Cleveland district covering Toledo. Messer-Kruse has detailed the duplicity surrounding the efforts of Toledo's Ohio Bank to borrow RFC monies, regain its footing, and reopen, and RFC's Thompson's (among others') obstructive role in this. The crux of the theory was that Toledo Trust Co., a competitor to other Toledo banks, sought to block reopening banks such as Ohio or Commerce Guardian to gain market position, and did so successfully. This left Ferrell Sr. and others the task of liquidating the assets of the remaining banks, reviewing all the unscrupulous banking practices, and divvying up payouts. As Messer-Kruse noted, "Like the bank failures themselves, the bank liquidations were characterized by insider favoritism, class privilege, and political patronage" to the great disadvantage of "humble depositors," who in turn, "recovered a small fraction of their savings."[66] The media blitz surrounding the whole industry would have been unavoidable, especially as ordinary citizens were losing their funds to banking insiders who were capitalizing on restricted information to make a potentially salvageable financial crisis even worse. Interestingly, two decades later in historian Ferrell's first semester at Michigan State College, he had to teach U.S. economic history. What he came to know about banking practices in the Great Depression may help explain why Professor Ferrell did not say much about his father's role in banking to the present author.

Regardless of the Toledo bank scandals during the Great Depression, historian Andrew Cayton wrote that toward the last half of the nineteenth century, Buckeyes, as Ohioans began to label themselves, were increasingly obsessed "with personal as well as public improvement."[67] Public improvement depended on developing one's character. This tradition continued into the next century in the Ferrell's case. As young adults, Ernest and Edna switched from farm living in Custar and New Philadelphia, respectively, to Wooster College, studying to improve themselves and find greater opportunity.[68] Edna would become a school teacher at Milton Center Township then in Euclid, Ohio, a suburb of Cleveland. After joining the Lakewood United Methodist Church, she led Sunday School classes.[69] Ferrell Sr. noted that attending college was "the greatest ambition of my early life," but even as a youngster, he found opportunities for character development through learning each facet of farming, abstaining from "alcohol or tobacco in any form," and reading from the book *Bible Stories for Young Children*. Later, he extolled the values he adopted from the Bible: "it is more blessed to give than [to] receive" or "a good name is more to be desired than great riches."[70] Building character while serving a larger cause came as he joined the Army, attending to those injured in the bloodiest American battles of the Great War. The experience heightened his sense of pride in country. Returning to civilian life, Ernest rejected the easy transition to farm life offered by his father and instead cultivated his financial talents, partly through attendance at evening classes at the American Banking Institute and by pursuing increasingly more responsible bank positions. Edna and Ernest also improved themselves by taking advantage of Cleveland's cultural events and institutions after they graduated from college. Robert Ferrell, their first son, came along a year after their marriage, and a few years later, the Ferrell family, along with another son, replanted themselves in Lakewood, joining the Methodist church there. Ernest Sr. took on roles as Boy Scout leader and bank examiner for the RFC during the Great Depression, providing additional avenues for personal and public improvement. He found that scout lessons reinforced what others had taught him (e.g., "do a good deed daily, be prepared, success comes through hard work"). From Rotary Club slogans, he noted, "service above self" and money must be earned.

Robert Ferrell absorbed many of his parents' lessons, values and biases, rooted partly in northern Ohio culture. He took advantage of school opportunities, then plied the gains to teaching, mentoring, and authoring dozens of books; he cultivated his musical talent and shared it throughout his lifetime in private piano lessons and public forums, at churches, colleges, and military events. After Pearl Harbor, he donned a military uniform and went off to war, just as his father had done decades before, and this patriotic zeal followed him as a scholar when colleagues questioned United States' motivations. One might speculate on the beliefs he derived from Methodist church services, family socialization, and scouting. As a Hoosier historian, he berated southern colleges for racial discrimination and Ivy League schools for their antidemocratic elitism. His biases were positive and negative, of course. There is evidence that Ferrell indulged in alcohol, both with Lila and colleagues, and coached his brother to keep such dalliance from their father.[71] Generally, he believed women had a special role in the home, serving the husband and family, and not in professional pursuits.

Plenty of episodes underscore Ferrell's biases, including several alluded to during his matrimonial courtship or as will be noted in his political and professional activism. Yet a particularly useful example is the confrontation that Sergeant Ferrell had with his superiors while serving in the Second World War. The future historian described it in a letter to his parents at the time.[72] While Ferrell was creating a Jewish New Year's celebratory bulletin cover, several chaplain officers tasked the young soldier to drive them on an errand. One of these superiors, Officer Fagan, was entertaining two others at the military base. What might have been thought to be official business turned out to be a whiskey run for the visiting officers. As Ferrell explained it, the drive was merely the distance of "a block and a half" and "90% of the time was spent waiting for these three fellows." But this request, piled on top of other "personal errands" that he had had to endure, hit a nerve. Sgt. Ferrell claimed that he sternly told the officers that "as of today, [he] was through running personal errands, that [he] was not used to this sort of work, and [that he] didn't come into the Army to do it." The incident, when seen through the lens of Ferrell's early years, takes on added meaning: Eagle Scout Ferrell objecting to ethical improprieties; that is, requiring an enlisted man to perform a nongovernment job on the government's time and dime. The Ohio, Jeffersonian-Republican Ferrell had to put up with so-called superiors interrupting his more-worthy pursuits without a legitimate purpose. The antiliquor-Methodist Ferrell pushed to buy alcohol. The Boy Scout Ferrell following the BSA tenth and twelfth laws, raising objections to injustice and showing tolerance to mainstream faiths.

One can make too much of any singular life episode and its ties to the socialization of young Bob Ferrell. Yet once ensconced at Indiana University, the Hoosier historian no doubt felt the impact of growing up in predominantly Republican Lakewood, then rural Custar, in the conservative state of Ohio, while experiencing the diversity of big city, Democratic Cleveland. He and brother Ernie Jr., no doubt, had heard their parents' favorite Biblical admonitions and the Methodist's appeal to human equality, temperance, serving others, and the role of hard work in good living. Ferrell had lived through the volatile economic times of the Great Depression, and this brought home the values Ernest Sr. passed along on living frugally and being sympathetic, even empathetic, to others not quite so fortunate. His father's war service, then his own, taught lessons about patriotism, self-sacrifice, and larger causes. Boy Scout lessons, camaraderie, and laws broadened his perspective, while reinforcing others, perhaps attitudes toward "inferior" groups and the need to care for them. As Ferrell himself would agree, the history of his early years could not predict later thoughts and actions, but it provided a framework to understand who he would become and how he would engage the historian's craft.

NOTES

1. Lakewood's Emerson Junior High had offered primary school classes until Taft Elementary opened on January 24, 1927, due to the growing population in the northeastern section of the town. Margaret Manor Butler, *The Lakewood Story* (New York: Stratford House, 1947), 210.

2. Butler, *Lakewood Story*, 210, 212, 222; Ferrell Sr., *Stories I Want My Grandchildren to Know*, 68–69.

3. E. George Lindstrom, *Story of Lakewood, Ohio* (Lakewood, OH: author, 1936), 89; Butler, *Lakewood Story*, 195–197. Both U.S. presidents named Harrison, William Henry and Benjamin, had ties to Ohio, but the state served only as a birthplace to Benjamin.

4. While Cayton weaves the concept throughout his book (and Ohio history), in short, he described "public culture" as an environment that instilled Ohioans with the desire to rise above base natural instincts and to develop civility and industry and to actively participate in government. Andrew R. L. Cayton, *Ohio: The History of a People* (Columbus: The Ohio State University Press, 2002), 2; see also Kenneth Wheeler's discussion of "a culture of usefulness," in "How Colleges Shaped Public Culture of Usefulness," in *The Center of a Great Empire: The Ohio Country in the Early Republic*, ed. Andrew R. L. Cayton and Stuart D. Hobbs (Athens: Ohio University Press, 2005), 105–121.

5. Butler, *Lakewood Story*, 195–197; Lindstrom, *Story of Lakewood*, 103–104.

6. Lindstrom, *Story of Lakewood*, 36; Butler, *Lakewood Story*, 10, 15–18, 29, 123.

7. Butler, *Lakewood Story*, 10, 14–15, 22, 35–36, 81, 94; Cayton, *Ohio*, 29–30; Lindstrom, *Story of Lakewood*, 9. Carol Poh Miller and Robert Wheeler wrote that "in 1860, the majority of Clevelanders were still transplanted New Englanders and other native stock." A large percentage were also German and Irish, which brought some cultural clashes with Methodist protestants over alcohol consumption and Catholic allegiances and traditions. Carol Poh Miller and Robert Wheeler, *Cleveland: A Concise History, 1796–1990* (Bloomington: Indiana University Press, 1990), 72.

8. Butler noted that the Swedenborgian church was the first; see his *Lakewood Story*, 55–56, 225.

9. Butler, *Lakewood Story*, 26. Aside from travel by boat along Lake Erie and Rocky River, city dwellers came by wagon on the "plank road" (now Detroit Avenue) or by train on the Rocky River Railroad, also known as "the dinky" or "Dummy." By 1981, the dinky line was sold to the Nickle Plate, which ushered in the era of street cars. Lindstrom, *Story of Lakewood*, 45–51, 71–72, 91, 125; Butler, *Lakewood Story*, xv, 45–48; H. Rodger Grant, *Ohio on the Move: Transportation in the Buckeye State* (Athens: Ohio University Press, 2000), 112–114, 135–136. Interview with Martha Gubernath, Lakewood United Methodist Church, July 2018.

10. Ferrell, *Stories*, 68–69; Lindstrom, *Story of Lakewood*, 47; Butler, *Lakewood Story*, 137–139; Miller and Wheeler, *Cleveland*, 51, 70, 102; Thea Gallo Becker, *Images of America: Lakewood* (Charleston, SC: Arcadia, 2003), Chapter Three, especially, p. 57.

11. Lindstrom, *Story of Lakewood*, 50–51.

12. "Remembering the Past: Celebrating 125 Years, LUMC, 1876–2001," compiled by Henry J. Holtz for Lakewood United Methodist Church (hereafter, LUMC), (unpublished, circa 2001), 14, 19, 21, 25. The LUMC began as the East Rockport Methodist Church in 1876, an important distinction since Methodists were more aligned with the evangelical tradition during Ferrell's youth. Furthermore, the Cleveland Methodist District's "1941 Official Record and Yearbook" proclaimed that its "emphasis . . . was on evangelism." Ibid., 26; Butler wrote that the Lakewood Methodist Church of Ferrell's early years "was rated the second largest in the country," see *Lakewood Story*, 227.

13. Ferrell Sr., *Stories*, Chapter 5.

14. Ernest Sr. described outings to theatre, movie houses, the Cleveland Art Museum and Zoo, and Wade Park; ibid., 57–59.

15. Letter to Lou, June 29, 1953, Box 44.

16. Ferrell Sr., *Stories*, 64–65. The records of various activities and classmate notes, including as solo pianist during intermission at a school play, tie Bob Ferrell to Milton High School; see pamphlet/playbill to "A Crazy Mix-Up," January 1, 1938, or a note to Ferrell from "Juliet," a classmate, May 4, 1938, Box 74. Notes for a family photo album provided by Ferrell's daughter, Carolyn, provided the following account: Ferrell attended Taft Elementary from kindergarten through fifth grade, then 1932–1934 at rural Milton Center after a brief six months at Bowling Green, Ohio, then back to Lakewood for schooling at Emerson Jr. High and first two years of high school at Lakewood H. S., then back to Custar farm for a year at Milton High, eventually ending at Waterville High School.

17. "Ralph Waldo Emerson," in *The Norton Anthology of American Literature: Volume I*, ed. Nina Baym, Ronald Gottesman, Laurence B. Holland et al. (New York: W. W. Norton & Company, 1989), 931–943. Lakewood's Emerson Junior High was named after the American writer, Ralph Waldo Emerson.

18. This account of Robert H. Ferrell's family history relies principally on Ferrell Sr., *Stories*. Other sources corroborate basic factual claims in the account of the immediate family (e.g., see Robert H. Ferrell birth certificate, Cuyahoga County, OH; *Tidings* 19, no. 48 and ibid., 27, no. 46 (Lakewood, OH: Lakewood United Methodist Church, April 10, 1925, 4; and April 19, 1935, 3; Robert H. Ferrell mss., Lilly Library (including early years, Box 74).

19. See Ferrell's Second World War letters, Box 74.

20. Ferrell Sr., *Stories*, 41.

21. According to Ferrell Sr., the Army awarded him three medals for battlefield service, in a "'defensive sector,' Oise-Aisne, and the Meuse-Argonne," ibid., 53. For recounting of war service, see ibid., 28–53; Robert H. Ferrell, *America's Deadliest Battle, Meuse-Argonne, 1918* (Lawrence: University of Kansas Press, 2007). Ferrell also edited several volumes (e.g., a diary and memoirs) detailing the dangers of trench warfare and mustard gas, and the vagaries of combat.

22. John Storey, Robert Blouch, and Daniel Cook are several examples; Blouch lived a few houses down from Ferrell at 12950 Emerson Avenue. See Troop #67, "Application for Renewal of Troop Charter, Boy Scouts of America" (Cleveland BSA Council #440), February 7, 1935; January 29, 1936; February 12, 1937; and February 9, 1938. Several letters document the close relationship among these boys, Ferrell mss., Box 74.

23. Ferrell Sr., *Stories*, 135–137.

24. Ibid., 80; "These Eagle Scouts Guests at [Cleveland] Council Dinner," *The Cleveland Press*, circa Fall 1956, Box 74.

25. Benjamin Rene Jordan, *Modern Manhood and the Boy Scouts of America: Citizenship, Race, and the Environment, 1910–1930* (PhD Diss., University of California San Diego, 2009). Jordan's work has been published under the same title by the University of North Carolina Press, 2016.

26. Jordan, *Modern Manhood*, 71.

27. Ibid., 73–75.

28. Troop #67, "Application for Renewal of Troop Charter, Boy Scouts of America," (Cleveland BSA Council #440), February 7, 1935; January 29, 1936; February 12, 1937; February 9, 1938.

29. Ferrell Sr., *Stories*, 80.

30. For instance, Ferrell denigrates the value of a fellow scholar's research because it focuses on the Shoshone Indian tribe in northern Idaho; see letter to Tim [Herbert Hoover Presidential Library staff], May 25, 2011, Box 84; in a diary entry, Ferrell raised concerns over a faculty recruit, Joan Wilson, who concentrated on gender history using social science theory; see April 13, 1981, pp. 1–2. See both in Ferrell mss., Lilly Library, Bloomington, Indiana.

31. Jordan, *Modern Manhood*, especially, pp. 85–118.

32. Ibid., 98.

33. Ibid., 118.

34. See endnote 204 (Troop #67, "Application for Renewal") and *Tidings* Vol. 20, No. 20 and Vol. 27, No. 39 (Cleveland, OH: Lakewood Methodist Episcopal Church), September 25, 1925, 4, and March 1, 1935, 3, respectively. The Lakewood Church sponsored Troops #60 and 177. Ferrell's Troop #67 was sponsored by the Presbyterian Church.

35. John Wigger, "Ohio Gospel: Methodism in Early Ohio," 62–104, in *The Center of a Great Empire: The Ohio Country in the Early Republi*, ed. Andrew R.L Cayton and Stuart D. Hobbs (Athens: Ohio University Press, 2005), 62–63.

36. Ferrell, Sr., *Stories*, 23.

37. Cayton, *Ohio*, 38–39, 71–72. The building of the Custar United Methodist Church in Ernest Sr.'s hometown is engraved with United Brethren, Evangelical United Brethren, and Methodist origins.

38. Letter to Auntie and Uncle Ivan, March 9, 1961, Box 17; letter to Murph, Marion, Karl, and Stephen, February 25, 1952, Box 84; letter to Bob and Kit, July 12, 1953, Box 44; letter to Chris and Bob, September 15, 1953, Box 44; letter to Frank [History Professor at MSC], December 1, 1955, Box 43; Ferrell credits Midwest university democratic attitudes against Ivy League school elitism.

39. Wagner, "Ohio Gospel," 66;

40. Ferrell Sr., *Stories*, 5. Local historian George Grill noted that "Lakewood is one of the Republican Party's strongholds" in Cuyahoga County and in the State of Ohio, see "Introduction," Lindstrom, *Story of Lakewood*, n.p.

41. Wagner, "Ohio Gospel," 68–71; Cayton, *Ohio*, 4–8.

42. George W. Knepper, "Ohio Politics: A Historical Perspective," in *Ohio Politics*, ed. Alexander P. Lamis (Kent, OH: Kent State University Press, 1994), 1–17.

43. Cayton, *Ohio*, 194–200; see also Lindstrom, *History of Lakewood*, 67–68, on the issue of prohibition and Cleveland's attempts to annex Lakewood.

44. Employment at the National Carbon Company, and the nearby housing it supported, attracted many of these immigrants; see Butler, *Lakewood Story*, 228–230; Miller and Wheeler, *Cleveland*, 100–103.

45. Brian Usher, "The Lausche Era, 1945–1957," in *Ohio Politics*, ed. Alexander P. Lamis (Kent, OH: Kent State University Press, 1994), 18–41, 21.

46. Transcript of Robert H. Ferrell, Bowling Green State University, 1947.

47. Knepper, "Ohio Politics," 3. The Republican Party came to dominate Ohio politics—as it did nationally—by 1896, then came the Great Depression; ibid., 5.

48. Usher, "Lausche Era," especially 18–38.

49. According to Brian Usher, Roosevelt lost Ohio in 1944 by 11,500 votes, while the same year Lausche beat his Republican opponent Mayor James Garfield Stewart by 108,000. Ibid., 23.

50. Ferrell Sr.'s banking history is drawn from his unpublished book, *Stories*, especially chapters four and six. Ernest Sr. also noted that during Robert's early years, the family had no car, and that his, Ferrell Sr.'s, Army years had taught him "not to want expensive things," and that "a good name is better than great riches." During his family's Lakewood years, they paid expenses in cash, used streetcars to avoid using a car, and avoided vacation travel. Through farming and investments in the 1930s, the Ferrell family saved "more than three thousand dollars," ibid., 56, 73–74.

51. According to Ferrell Sr., the B of LE reorganized as a state bank at a time when Republican-controlled state government eased regulations on bank practices. See Ferrell Sr., *Stories*, 62, and Timothy Messer-Kruse, *Banksters, Bosses, and Smart Money: A Social History of the Great Toledo Bank Crash of 1931* (Columbus: The Ohio University Press, 2004), 41–44.

52. Ferrell Sr., *Stories*, 63.
53. Ibid., 71, 77.
54. Ibid., 80.
55. Email to author, July 3, 2018.
56. Ferrell Sr., *Stories*, 78–79, and Chapter Six.

57. Letter to Taft, April 9, 1951, Box 84; letter to Art [Ekinch, SUNY-Albany], December 8, 1969, Box 7—Ferrell described himself as "a liberal Democrat;" see also letters to Eugene Davidson [Yale University Press Editor], October 30, 1952, Box 44; to Sir John [Pratt], November 3, 1952, Box 44; to Marion, November 5, 1952, Box 44; to Lou, June 29, 1952, Box 44; to Chris and Bob [Bryant], September 15, 1953, Box 44; to Jan and Waldo, October 21, 1960, Box 73; to Dad, July 21, 1960, Box 73; also in a letter to John Stewart, January 12, 1999, Box 58—In childhood recollections, Ferrell noted that he was in agreement with FDR policies, including protecting labor.

58. Messer-Kruse, *Banksters*, 2–3.
59. Ibid., 148.
60. Ibid., 5, 8.
61. Ibid., 11, 13, 22–23, 37–38.
62. Ibid., 14, 19, 44–45, 49, 70, 80–81, 91–92.
63. Ibid., 45–46.
64. Ibid., 52–54, 58.
65. For an overview of the facts surrounding this, see ibid., 103–110.
66. Ibid., 109–110.

67. Cayton, *Ohio*, 80–81. The nickname Buckeye derived from the omnipresent "horse chestnut" tree within Ohio. Ibid., 81.

68. Ferrell Sr., *Stories*, 10–11, 54, 57–59, 67. The Ferrell family found itself pursuing what historian Andrew Cayton has described as Ohio middle-class respectability, which translated to attaining better living circumstances and socializing with the church crowd while avoiding taverns; "[respectable residents] read books, practiced the piano . . . and talked with other descent people;" and they began attending college. See Cayton, *Ohio*, 87–88.

69. "Tidings," 19, no. 48, LUMC, April 10, 1925, 4; "Officers and Teachers, 1936–37: Lakewood Methodist Church School," LUMC, "Sixtieth Anniversary" [bulletin], December 6, 1936, np; Ernest Sr. also taught Sunday School; see letter to Ferrell from Ferrell Sr., June 1952, Box 44.

70. Ferrell Sr., *Stories*, 135.
71. Letter to Dunbar, September 24, 1957, Box 1.
72. Letter to Mom and Dad, September 27, 1943, Box 74.

Chapter 4

Dear Senator Taft
"Heads Ought to Roll"

I am not an admirer of President Truman . . . but I do think that in regard to MacArthur's politicking the Senate should side with the President.

—Robert H. Ferrell (Letter to Senator
Robert Taft, April 9, 1951)

Robert Ferrell was an activist as scholar, teacher, and private citizen. In books, he called for constitutional change so that presidents and their physicians could not easily hoodwink the nation during its leaders' incapacity to execute the duties of office. He castigated military brass for unfairly tarnishing the reputation of an African American Division fighting the fiercest battles in the Argonne Forest during the Great War. He advocated for President Harry Truman's historical place among highly ranked chief executives and longed for American citizens to engage foreign policy more realistically.[1] Aside from scholarship, Ferrell organized efforts to oust a Big Ten university president and to subvert an executive secretary of the Organization of American Historians.[2] While building a reputation for teaching excellence at Indiana, he joined forces with colleagues and the Eli Lilly Foundation to improve precollegiate history instruction.[3] Part of the task included traveling throughout the state, observing classes, and interviewing school personnel to understand better the causes of what he argued were inadequately prepared students that took up seats in his courses. The history teaching improvement campaign also encompassed providing rigorous coursework for committed teachers and laying out the problems to be addressed by public schools and university-level schools of education and history departments in a book-long call-to-arms. Long before finding a place in academia, the Yale history student pressured home-state Senator Robert A. Taft of Ohio to correct the deplorable actions of an Army general in the recruitment of reserves. Ferrell had harsher words for Taft a few years later due to the Senator's support for another renegade Army general, Douglas MacArthur.

Of course, playing the role of a strong advocate, whether it was Ferrell as scholar, teacher, or constituent in private life, raises questions about his approach to history and objectivity, an ideal that possibly never warranted the attention it received, for various reasons, but still lingers in the minds of history teachers and students alike.[4] Part of the confusion over producing objective history has been clarified by historians who approach the topic from at least two vantage points: the first focuses on methods of source identification, collection, analysis, and interpretation (the empirical method) and the second turns on more philosophical issues, for instance, whether in fact any person can investigate the/a past unencumbered by personal identity, background, or ways of thinking structured by language ("discourse"), or even more, whether any relic of the past can reflect the past or merely be an intermediary of it.[5]

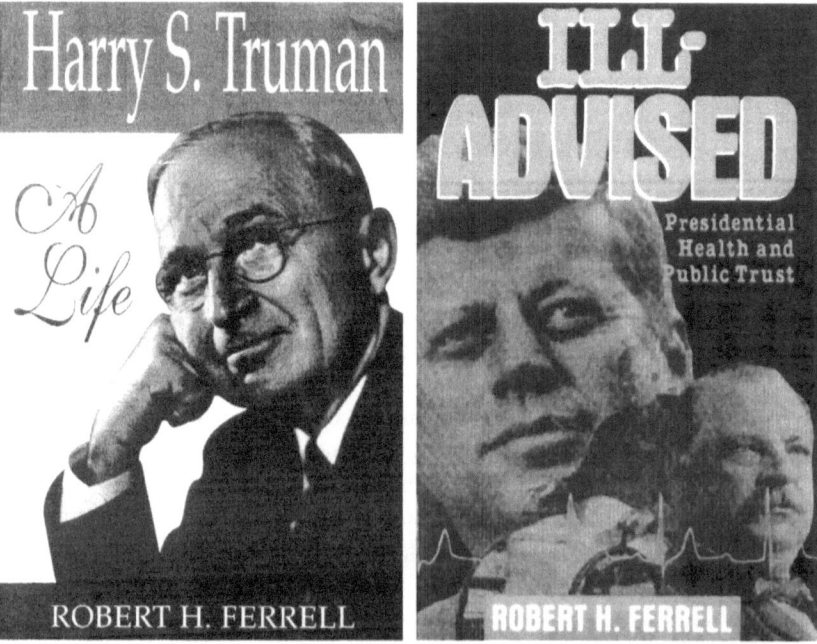

Figure 4.1 Ferrell wrote or edited fourteen books on Harry S. Truman, including *Harry S. Truman: A Life*, and several books on other presidents, including *Ill-Advised*, which investigated presidential medical coverups at historical crisis points to the detriment of the nation. *Source*: The University of Missouri Press. Copyrights © 1996 and 1992 by the Curators of the University of Missouri.

Some experts suggest those who interpret the past can reach some level of objectivity on methods (or protocols) but to little result because what can be discovered or recounted eludes accurate depictions of the past. They say, the past is gone and only its "surrogates" remain.[6] Moreover, bias encompasses every new generation due to changing values, contexts, claims on historical legitimacy and purpose. Even the concept of historical objectivity itself was borne of an era that has passed, some have argued.[7]

Ferrell, activist or not, structured his historical efforts in line with acceptable protocols of fellow practitioners, but unlike some postmodernists, he believed that what was discovered could represent an accurate essence of the past with a measure of objectivity, point to a right and wrong, and apply to contemporary problems.[8] History and hope could rhyme.[9] Until the latter part of his career, the Hoosier historian also focused his attention principally on elites inhabiting political, diplomatic, and military topics. Given this orientation, it is fair to say that Ferrell's historical writings did not escape a host of postmodernist or others' critiques of objectivity. Nevertheless, aside from several of his struggles discussed below (e.g., the fight with Army brass over reserve recruitment or the shake-up of state-wide history instruction), his engagement with Truman and presidential medical malpractice demonstrated historian Ferrell as both desirably objective and desirably not so.

A review of excerpts from three Ferrell publications provides a glimpse of his approach to history, and even more, to the "conventional" standards of historical objectivity.[10] There is no intention in this study to be comprehensive, only to highlight objective criteria as applied. The first two works, *Harry S. Truman and the Modern American Presidency* and *Harry S. Truman: A Life*, explored Truman from cradle to grave (see Figure 4.1). The third publication, *Ill-Advised: Presidential Health and Public Trust*, examined several cases of serious presidential illness that also crippled the nation with virtually no warning to the public at critical times. The Indiana historian's expertise on Truman is widely acknowledged after years of traveling to and staying months in Independence, Missouri, the site of Truman's home and presidential archives. As Ferrell tells us, his focus on the Truman record came after a thoughtful chief archivist at the Truman Library and his assistant diverted the Indiana scholar's attention to a newly released set of handwritten diary entries by the late president, this in PSF Box 333, which led to the highly celebrated edited volume, *Off the Record: The Private Papers of Harry S. Truman*. His now familiar biographer edited Truman's autobiography the same year.[11] Another set of Truman letters to wife Bess Wallace Truman came to Ferrell's attention too, "over twelve hundred" of them by Ferrell's count, opening up insights into Truman's world before he found himself replacing President Franklin D. Roosevelt.[12] These early works opened the way for Ferrell's several books on the president from Independence.[13]

A call to Ferrell from a former graduate student at Indiana is what led him to a cache of primary sources of Eisenhower's medical malpractice "coverup," this at the president's library in Abilene, Kansas.[14] Eisenhower's case occupies the majority of Ferrell's *Ill-Advised*, and alone, provides plenty of fodder for analysis on historical method and objectivity. The by-now Truman expert had researched other presidents who had had illnesses, some unexplained, as he relayed in the book he wrote on President Woodrow Wilson, years earlier.[15] The tip-off on presidents Harding's and Roosevelt's medical issues likely came from other former students.[16] Both presidential source discoveries for the books reviewed here came seemingly out of nowhere, and as empiricists claim, history was thus there to be "discovered."[17] True enough, but postmodernists might wave the male, White-Anglo-Saxon-Protestant (WASP) red flag as to the foci of Ferrell's research, and of course, each topic reflected political, top-down history.

Before reviewing Ferrell's treatment of Truman, one might consider the parallels in the two men's lives that likely drew each to the other and perhaps to writing a more generous history.[18] Both had similar talents and interests (See Figure 4.2). As young boys, both learned to play the piano, then continued to do so throughout life; both loved history (and wore glasses) and thought there were lessons from history that could inform contemporary decisions; both experienced, one might say, ordeals shifting from city to farm life, Truman from Kansas City or Ferrell from Cleveland; both knew something of banking, teenage Harry as teller, Ferrell as son of a banker; both sipped the wine of fundamentalist religious creeds, Baptist and evangelical Methodists; both were labeled with family names, Truman after his two grandparents, Soloman and Shipp, and Robert "Hugh" Ferrell after a cousin with missionary parents. There was good reason for their attitudes supporting democratic equality borne from soldiering in wartime and religious inculcation: Captain Truman in the Great War and Sergeant Ferrell in the Second World War. A shared understanding of patriotism and loyalty likely emanated at least partly from a belief in their nation's purposes in the two world wars and coming-of-age in the so-called American century; both had leadership qualities and followings. Both experienced the pain at a relatively young age of losing a parent: Harry his father and Bob his mother. And of course, both were WASPs. They were different too of course, especially in career trajectories, but both could boast of accomplishments that outweighed any detours to getting there. It is fair to say that they shared some level of mutual admiration and conviviality with one another.[19] In this, Ferrell may have seen a lot of himself in the president about whom he was researching and writing. Certainly, one could identify in Robert Ferrell himself many of the traits that he attributed to Truman. All this might be the first complaint postmodernists would lodge that objectivity would elude any fair assessment of Truman's "greatness" by Ferrell.

Figure 4.2 President Truman and Robert Ferrell shared many characteristics, experiences, and recreational outlets. Both enjoyed playing the piano. From his teenage years, Ferrell passed on his musical expertise to others including granddaughter Amanda. The Ferrell-Truman similarities may have been a source of bias. *Source*: Courtesy of Carolyn Ferrell Burgess.

Another point to consider is the process by which the Indiana biographer likely affixed on Truman as a worthwhile focus. Ferrell, no doubt, learned of the thirty-third president's efforts while researching and writing a book on American diplomatic history and another on George Marshall.[20] As the Indiana historian admitted in an introduction to *Off the Record*, however, it was the chance introduction to newly opened diaries, interrupting an unsuccessful search for materials on Truman as a First World War soldier that put Ferrell on to learning deeply about the president's full life and White House years. Ferrell's father had fought in the war "to end all wars" or its equally well-known sobriquet, the war "to make the world safe for democracy." Ernest Sr. had tutored his son on a patriot's view of President Wilson's war. He shared war's bloody scenes and American battlefield contributions at Chateau Thierry, Oise-Aise, Argonne, then near Verdun, during the last half of 1918.[21] The drama stayed with Robert perhaps due to Ernest's tales of the continuous storm-like roar of the war, constant German flyovers, artillery maneuvers, and exploding shells. He learned of his father's erratic and dangerous adventures after the confusing separation from his unit, this during a bout with diphtheria and then assignment as a casual. The future Truman historian referenced his soldier-father in war letters sent from overseas three decades later.[22] It is fair to say that Ferrell Sr. influenced his eldest boy to think positively of an American president who shared the patriotic call-to-arms, one who had his own war stories.[23]

Whether or not the overlapping experiences and characteristics of Truman and Ferrell colored the Indiana historian's thinking, one cannot miss his overwhelmingly positive treatment of the president in the Modern American Presidency series book if one scores the content with pluses and minuses alone. Of course, neither low nor high ratings, in themselves, signal historian bias or objectivity according to the profession's conventional criteria (see Tables 4.1a and 4.1b).[24] Nevertheless, it is worthy to note that Ferrell framed the future president's mediocre trajectory, nearly to age forty, as more the result of bad breaks than bad character, decision making, or behavior.[25] Possible entrance to West Point and success at business ventures—in zinc or lead mining, oil-field leases, or the haberdashery—all were foiled by events and economics beyond Harry's control seemingly, except for joining the Army, which would be one of three prerequisites, as Truman told Ferrell, to excel in government; the remaining requisites included experience in finance and farming.[26] Ferrell gave Truman high marks for implementing advanced crop techniques and his hard work, from pre-dawn to dusk. Even as the future president faced investment disasters and business bankruptcy, this only provided evidence that Truman was honest, true to his commitments, and willing to pay off bad debt.[27] Captain Truman's war service enabled him to demonstrate natural talent for leadership, business savvy, organization, even bravery, and to succeed in the

Table 4.1a Examples of Professional Criteria Established as Checks on Historical Account Objectivity

Provides evidence that supports and refutes the work
Establishes facts from the evidence
Presents account in a detached manner
Serves to explain as function or purpose
Situates the narrative within the discourse of historians using citations
Balances controversial assertions with explanation
Interrogates sources with regard to import, imputation placed on them by other historians, perspectives of the originator, the function of the document served, situated meaning with regard to other sources of the period, authenticity and reliability

Mark Donnelly has emphasized that his and co-author, Claire Norton's, "intention was simply to summarize some conventional ideas about what historians do and think they are doing," but that the authors "[do not] endorse these views." Email to author, January 28, 2019.
Source: Mark Donnelly and Claire Norton, *Doing History* (London: Routledge, 2011), especially pp. 59, 73, and chapter 6.

Table 4.1b Examples of Professional Criteria Established as Checks on Historical Account Objectivity

Demonstrates an on-going past and present dialogue
Takes "large-view perspective"
Describes interconnections that display larger meaning within history
Avoids "conformity to an imagined future" (e.g., Bolshevik Revolution's long-term outcome)
Selects evidence not guided by a provisional desired conclusion
Is guided by sources without prejudice
Makes explicit the nature of the historian's guiding hypothesis
Integrates multiple perspectives

Source: Richard J. Evans, *In Defense of History* (New York: W. W. Norton & Company, 1999), especially chapter 8.

world of local politics, with some help from political boss Tom Pendergast. Truman's entanglement with the Pendergast machine, its graft, and corruption, seemed merely to help his biographer show traits of loyalty, honesty (Truman went along with patronage not graft), and political intelligence.

Truman continued to receive praise from Ferrell for his service as "Senator from Pendergast," but the man from Independence's record had some blemishes once he began shouldering presidential responsibilities. The Missouri senator fought for the public interest against errant railroad companies and corrupt defense contractors and supported FDR's New Deal programs. Loyalty, trustworthiness, and honesty were Truman attributes, according to Ferrell, and these helped him to secure re-election without the Kansas City political machine. Even putting Bess, Truman's wife, on the payroll received not criticism, but praise, because the rationale was to pay off early life debts. Yet, Truman scored poorly on his part in significant policy issues: dropping the atom bomb ("he made the decision . . . with insufficient forethought") or impatiently stepping in to regulate postwar prices and labor disputes, likely leading to the Democrats losing legislative control. More positively, in the role of Truman apologist, the Indiana historian pointed to the president's unwillingness to lead by way of public opinion, to his insistence on decision-making based on right or wrong calculations, and to his support of African American civil rights. Defending Truman, Ferrell alludes to the difficulties of the times, the misfortunate timing of taking on the Supreme Court, and more broadly, to a country that did not understand the enlarged role necessary for government. Ferrell smiled on the president for creating a postwar security system, including the Truman Doctrine, Marshall Plan, and North Atlantic Treaty Organization. The presidential historian devoted a full chapter, all glowing, to Truman's success in reorganizing and repurposing the Executive Office, its structures, procedures, and staff norms.[28]

Aside from recognizing Ferrell's partiality toward Truman across his life span in both private and public spheres in some general sense, an application of objectivity as described by history professionals provides a different lens to evaluate the presidential biographer's bias. As noted earlier, picking Truman as a topic likely resulted from a commitment to political, diplomatic and/or military interests, which aligns with a Rankean (or modernist) stance toward legitimate history and sources. Moreover, personal attraction to Truman's characteristics and commitments, not unlike those in many ways of Ferrell or his father, likely figured into the calculation. Examining a few examples from dozens or perhaps hundreds of possibilities provides a glimpse of the Ferrell approach to conventional standards of historical objectivity. Another Truman biography of Ferrell's, *Harry S. Truman: A Life*, is the focus here, with professional historian's objective criteria in mind.[29]

In one passage, Ferrell described Truman's decision to join the army during the First World War. The reason, the biographer argued, was that the future president responded to President Wilson's call for patriots and not out of hope for personal gain.[30] In explaining the assertion, several conventional criteria of historical objectivity were represented. Ferrell demonstrated interconnections that displayed larger meaning in history, avoided "conforming to an imagined future," identified evidence that would refute a desired conclusion, established facts from evidence, evinced a detached manner of presentation, used explanation as purpose, and situated meaning in regard to other sources of the period, as described in the following examples.[31] Ferrell identified the use of letters to Bess from enlistee Harry that showed the latter's ignorance of "the carnage on the front—the killing by machine guns, artillery, and poison gas" and his lack of understanding of "submarine issues" or of the senseless lives lost on torpedoed ocean liners. The president's autobiography pointed to Wilson's stirring call for soldiers to fight for democracy, liberty, and human rights. Ferrell quoted Wilson's rationale for war, which aligned with Truman's memory. An added context piece eliminated another possibility, that Truman would not have been drafted at the age of thirty-three; this and the fact that he was a Jackson County farmer made him "an unlikely candidate for the draft," but that as a member of the Missouri Guard, volunteering seemed to him the thing to do. One cannot evaluate, as readily, if Ferrell interrogated Truman's letters to Bess for the function they may have served, a sign of objective balance. Given the multiple purposes of letters, Truman may have desired to go off to war to prove bravery to Bess yet sought to avoid arguments she may have provided against it, especially the dangers he might face.

Another biographical episode, Truman's election to the U.S. Senate in 1934, turned on his support from Tom Pendergast, who Ferrell argued, dominated the entire state of Missouri politics at the time.[32] Again, one can see the historian's nod to conventional standards of historical objectivity. The account, as told, begins with stories of the ribbing Truman took once in the Senate, as "bellhop" or puppet for Missouri's Edgar Bergan, cited in Jonathan Daniels's *The Man from Independence* or Richard Miller's *Truman: Rise to Power*. In the next few pages, Ferrell lays out the foundation through examples as to Pendergast's grip on power, this through a variety of sources and stories—from the Missouri Governor of the time, Guy B. Park's archival papers; *Kansas City Times*; James Aylward's oral history (among others'), interviews with Colonel William Jr. Southern, Truman's "My Impression of the Senate," Lyle Dorsett's scholarship on *The Pendergast Machine*, Truman's letters, and so forth. In these sources, the reader learns how by 1934 Truman's chance at the Senate was made possible only because Pendergast had already locked up the State through presidential-nomination sleight-of-hand, legislative-gerrymandering bottle-necks, and governor payback. Ferrell then turns to "Boss Tom's" gift to the future president, alluding (without attribution) to *Plunkitt of Tammany Hall's* classic lines, the machine boss was only "seizing his opportunities." Truman was hardly the optimal or first choice of Pendergast, we learn, coming only after more than a dozen or so had been pushed aside for various reasons. Even more, Ferrell then provided solid evidence as to why those around Truman thought he should not be considered: "Nobody knows him. . . . He's an ordinary county judge . . . not known outside Jackson County." The "Boss men then ticked off reasons he would be electable—a former soldier, a Mason, a Baptist, a long-time local activist." But the ultimate feather in his cap, as Ferrell quotes the Pendergast men's claims: "We're in a position to do it because we have all the contacts. We know all the politicians in this state. . . . They're all our friends and they're willing to go along."

Pendergast, so it appeared, was the gatekeeper to Truman's Senate seat, but Ferrell also gave credit to the future president's agency in the matter; that is, getting over the primary hurdle, and this is where the author pulls out more devices from the historical objectivity toolkit. Biographer Ferrell identified several facts rooted in the evidence as to why Truman was not likely to rise to the occasion, for example, Pendergast's angst over road construction contracts awarded by "his candidate" and penchant for election manipulation or obstacles arising from seemingly more competitive candidates. The difference in the contest in the end, aside from Pendergast, was Truman's indefatigable "endurance," and here again, Ferrell is ready with examples from multiple sources: the candidate driving to "60 county seats" throughout the state, making speeches, shaking hands, claiming to represent all Missourians, enlisting powerful state politicians and employees to the cause, overcoming opponents throwing dirt. A big part of Truman's advantage, he came to learn, was all the county judges he knew and his acquaintances with so many state legislators and senators, especially those outside of the two big cities. Ferrell raised counter-arguments; the two leading state newspapers did not endorse the Independence candidate. Then he explained these facts away: the papers' past behaviors, telling lies so many years, led rural Missourians to vote for Truman. Ferrell concluded with facts on the history of machine-controlled, city-vote fraud in Missouri and across the nation, from Pendergast's time to more recent, to suggest this last trick (not so unusual) put him over the top. Pendergast's candidate won the general election handily mostly due to a weak Republican opponent, the story told in multiple latter-day history accounts.

Ferrell employs similar techniques to counter bias in his account of presidential malpractice. For example, he investigated President Eisenhower's controversial medical treatment leading up to and surrounding the elections in 1952 and 1956.[33] The initial medical cover-up claim is the focus here. Ferrell's essential conclusions, after sifting through the evidence, were that Eisenhower had two heart attacks in 1949 and that his personal physician, Dr. Howard McC. Snyder, covered it up to protect his patient's political fortunes. The contrast in historical treatment of this episode with the historian's presentation on Truman is striking, not so much in his approach to objectivity as to his efforts, seemingly, to refute his hypothesis, then to conclude it happened with the thinnest reeds of evidence.

Ferrell's efforts to refute his own hypothesis are everywhere apparent, and in fact, except for his strongly stated belief that there was a cover-up (a failure of objectivity), they might lead one to reject his proposition. The president's cardiologist in 1953, Dr. Thomas W. Mattingly, one could say, was Ferrell's leading and best witness, though he experienced none of the events first-hand. In his own research, Mattingly believed the president and his personal physician, Snyder, conspired to cover up Ike's heart attacks. Another artifact, the president's abnormal EKG produced in Key West in April 1949, following an illness two weeks prior, could in Ferrell's mind be tied to a heart attack. Snyder is the villain of sorts, but this is where the investigation gets fuzzy since it turned more on the lack of a record, where Ferrell (and others) think there should be one, of seemingly misplaced or discarded medical records, or stashed away personal files, without which the historian attempts to make the case.

The plausibility of Ferrell's account relied on a few additional artifacts. First, the reader learns that Eisenhower's family had a history of "hypertensive cardiovascular disease, cerebrovascular disease, and coronary disease" (which incidentally Ike's parents overcame at least till their eighties; and of course, the president refused to die until after his presidency). Second, the military hero had a "Type A personality," driving him to compete relentlessly (working overtime), to smoke immoderately (four packs a day during the war), and to eat too fast. Climbing the ranks quickly, Ike found himself at odds with superiors, which might have provoked blood pressure and heart troubles. Nevertheless, Ferrell continued to remind us through the narrative that from early to later years, there is little to no evidence of cardiovascular-related issues, factual claims that refute the health problems he suggested came to Ike in 1949. Other factors perhaps too hard to estimate causing heart problems, but salacious enough to share, were the rumors of infidelity and companion "heartache" with Mamie Eisenhower, then the frustrating appointment as Truman's Chairmanship of the Joint Chiefs of Staff. Aside from a few medical conjectures, there was evidence that a physician, Colonel Charles L. Leedham, at a medical conference boasted that at some point between 1947 and 1950, "he [had] treated Eisenhower for a heart attack," as the story was told by fellow attendee, Mattingly. Ferrell went with Mattingly's theory that Leedham had been sworn to secrecy about the event, had recognized the breach, and Leedham thus would share no more. Perhaps it was an illegitimate boast initially.

Early in Ferrell's analysis of Eisenhower's medical issues, the Indiana storyteller paused, pulled back, and placed the controversy within larger historical points (e.g., the case of President Lyndon Johnson's "major heart attack, when medical science could better treat such conditions," and just the opposite with the case of FDR). To make the incidents of credible historical import, Ferrell surveyed the difficulties facing the country at the time, and by extension, facing its presidents. He concluded that perilous world conditions underscored the danger of electing a leader predisposed to disability without the public's knowledge. Trickling out are Ferrell's nods to objectivity such as taking a "large-view perspective," establishing facts from the evidence, acknowledging facts that support and refute desired conclusions, situating the narrative within the discourse of historians using citations, balancing controversial assertions with explanation, among a host of others under the category, interrogating sources.

That Ferrell explained his topics or argued points strewn with anecdotes and examples infused with what some historians have identified as marks of historical objectivity does not, of course, signify that what he wrote was not positive or negative in the ordinary sense; that is, merely assigning merit to a person, event, or argument. Rather it signals a sensitivity to criteria that, some historians agree, demonstrates respect for the process of investigating and writing about the past. We learn convincingly from Ferrell that Truman fought in the First World War because his country called and that he won a Senate seat with Boss Pendergast's help and through his own agency. Ferrell applied historical protocols that make readers believe it. In the case of Eisenhower's health issues, the evidential trail and overly confident conclusion leave more room for doubt.

Ferrell showed his advocacy skills beyond scholarship decades prior to pushing for constitutional reform in the wake of presidential medical malfeasance or for Truman's place among the great presidents. His argument was with top military brass, Major General Edward F. Witsell in the Department of the Army's Adjutant General's Office. The Adjutant General was responsible for soliciting applications for the Officers' Reserve Corps, and Witsell was in charge of the operation. In July of 1949, the Adjutant General's Office put out Circular 210 to recruit "History Specialists," among other billets, for the Reserve Corps. Ferrell had taken a master's in history at Yale by this time and was working to complete the PhD. This along with his status as a war veteran, he believed, greatly improved the chances of gaining an appointment.

The application process took hours of time, leg work, and some cost as Ferrell noted in one letter.[34] Applicants had to fill out various forms (i.e., WD AGO 170, DA AGO 643A, and Form 88, including undergoing a physical examination), take an intelligence test, seek recommendations, and endure an interview at an officers' board. This all resulted in a letter from Witsell notifying Ferrell that his application had been rejected "due to the lack of an assignment vacancy in the Army Security Reserve suitable for [his] qualifications."[35] Ferrell wrote Senator Robert Taft to complain, having earned three degrees, including a master's at Yale with prospects to complete a dissertation for the doctorate. He protested that the Army should not put out circulars soliciting applications for specialties in which it has no assignments available, sending out form letters that say as much. The New Haven Officers Board had told the Yale student he possessed the needed qualifications at the interview. The dejected Yale compatriot of Taft, a Yale man himself, requested that his home state U.S. Senator pursue why the application was denied.[36]

After some bureaucratic delay and back and forth among Taft, Witsell, and Ferrell, Witsell's office responded that Ferrell's original application had been forwarded to the Director of Intelligence for consideration. That office did not recommend Ferrell based on his qualifications. His application was then forwarded to other sections, but no suitable assignment existed. Witsell elaborated that the qualifications listed in the directive for which Ferrell applied were the minimum, and his education and experience did not meet the needs of the Department. The responses to the directive greatly exceeded the needs, and therefore, the vacancies no longer existed.[37]

What happened next would define why Ferrell found his way to the top of the history profession. Unwilling to accept such an unsatisfactory note from Witsell, the facts were laid out to highlight the wayward thinking of the Department of the Army.[38] Not overlooking Taft's helpfulness in the process, the future historian thanked him for his "stick-to-itiveness," his dogged follow up, then turned his attention to the problem, the most recent reply from Witsell, to wit, the response to the Army's directive "greatly exceeded expectations." Ferrell critiqued the Army for its lack of diligence in researching how many history bachelor's, master's, and PhD's were awarded, 9,245, 1,085, and 162, respectively, in 1949, all easily obtainable through the

American Historical Association at the Library of Congress. As importantly, he wrote, "[S]everal thousand people like myself [have] wasted perhaps fifteen or twenty thousand hours of time filling out reams of applications, taking examinations, and undergoing physical examinations and interviews" due to the ignorance of a subordinate in Witsell's office. "It seems to me that certain *heads ought to roll* in the Department of the Army's Adjutant General section" (italics added).

While Ferrell did not obtain the position he sought, he must have found some measure of satisfaction at the release of a new Army policy, "Reserve Program Curbed: Specialist Officer Appointments Limited by Army."[39] The first sentence stated, "The Army limited today its program for appointing professional and technical specialists in the Officers Reserve Corps." The new Army list did not include History Specialist. Witsell's final justification for denying the future Yale PhD a Reserve Officer billet very likely served as a harbinger for Ferrell's unhappiness with his Air Force Intelligence work the first year after earning his PhD; that is, incompetent bureaucrats.[40]

Ferrell's struggle over the military reserve appointment reminds us that he approached the past, even recently completed, with an interesting admixture of objectivity and public- and self-interest. The in-training historian at Yale complained that the Office of the Adjutant General did not seem to care about the facts nor apply them usefully to recruitment. Identifying the "relevant" facts demonstrated the clear logic that led to the appropriate conclusion. The wrong way of recruiting candidates could be corrected. Understanding the past was applied to future decisions—typical Ferrell, an activist who pursued objectivity colored with principle.

Ferrell's activism hardly stopped at what some might describe as the mundane issue of recruitment for the Army reserves. In a strange twist of irony, the future Truman biographer and defender mailed a letter to Taft at the height of the Korean War, April 1951, asserting, "I am not an admirer of President Truman . . . but I do think that in regard to MacArthur's politicking the Senate should side with the President."[41] The nation had witnessed General MacArthur's Army drive the North Koreans out of the south, but Truman and MacArthur disagreed publicly over expanding the war against the Chinese communists. Asserting his power as Commander and Chief, Truman dismissed the popular general. Taft, with his eyes on the presidency and popular sentiment, took MacArthur's side.

The April letter was followed by more that would presage the historian's political path well beyond these years.[42] The soon-to-be-Yale-PhD graduate shared that MacArthur had overstepped his "province as a military commander" and that he treated the President condescendingly. Ferrell's rationale found its root in "American constitutional practice," civilian leadership over the military. Especially alarming was the act of his Senator, "proposing to parley with the general, right over the heads of the Administration." Ferrell had some misgivings about how Taft would react to the letter, as he (Ferrell) hand wrote to himself at the bottom of his copy of the note: "Taft said over the radio yesterday that his mail was running 500 to 1, in favor of MacArthur."

The Ohio Senator found another letter from Ferrell less charitable.[43] The nearly graduated historian admitted "certain feelings of distress" on two matters: First, he complained again that Taft "had championed the general's cause," and second, that Taft "had testified in favor" of an Ohio Republican member of the House of Representatives "whose guilt was transparently clear from the beginnings of his prosecution." Walter E. Brehm, the House member, was convicted of campaign contribution violations. Given the previous form-letter controversy with Major General Witsell, it is puzzling that Taft replied to Ferrell with a "form letter."[44] The problem of course was that the Senator's mailbox overflowed with "opinion regarding the MacArthur situation." Enclosed with the reply came a copy of Taft's speech submitted to the U.S. Senate, April 27, 1951, titled "American Policy in the Far East: How Do We End the Korean War?" By the following year's presidential election, Ferrell was "rooting for Adlai Stevenson," the Democratic nominee for president.[45] Other political activity suggests the budding historian remained in the Democratic column.[46]

Ferrell's preoccupation with foreign policy grew from his experience in the war and as a scholar of diplomacy. Yale University Press published his book, *Peace in Their Time,* in 1952. A meeting with a former Assistant Secretary of State to Frank Kellogg, William Castle, introduced the Yale graduate student to the inter-sanctum of high-level government conversations, personnel, and motivations through a diary.[47] The Castle connection and written reflections helped produce the first two books. In addition, working under the tutelage of Samuel Flagg Bemis at Yale, Ferrell became an expert on secretaries of state and the workings of United States' emissaries overseas. The second book, *American Diplomacy in the Great Depression,* came out in 1957. Two years later, the Indiana University professor gained enough recognition to find himself producing a widely adopted textbook, *American Diplomacy: A History.* Within the following decade, he was attending the inauguration of President Kennedy and discussing the intricacies of American involvement abroad with fellow historians and providing insight to government officials.[48] The topics covered a wide range and included plenty of controversy: limitations on nuclear power, condemnation of the Vietnam War, Israel-Arab boundary settlements, Egyptian authoritarian rule, anti-colonization movements, among others. As a measure of Ferrell's commitment to clarifying issues in American foreign relations, he co-founded The Society for Historians of American Foreign Relations (SHAFR) and served to edit the U.S. Department of State's Foreign Affairs series.[49]

Ferrell's political activism affixed as naturally on state efforts to educate citizens. Obtaining an initial teaching appointment at Michigan State College (MSC) in 1952, he turned his attention, aside from scholarship, to at least three foci: college students and how they were served, colleagues and how they measured up, and administrators and how they worked (or did not) to improve education. Weeks before the semester began at MSC, Ferrell took aim at his new employer and its charges noting, "The head of the history department . . . is a real live stuffed shirt . . . and his department is not really a good one, although the people are nice. It is about Bowling Green [State University] all over again."[50] The comparison of course to his own alma mater underscored the purportedly deficient undergraduate training, teaching, and faculty who were "asleep intellectually," producing not much scholarship since opening its doors.[51] To another colleague, he added, "the faculty here [at MSC] is an undistinguished bunch. . . . [Y]ou know what sort of situation develops, where the uppermost members of the department grew up with the ag school and the smaller fry came in during the easy times of 1946–1948."[52] Offered more money to stay at Michigan State, Ferrell chose what he considered a better history department and school. Years away from the initial post at MSC, the Indiana historian came back to complaints about unqualified PhD faculty, including colleagues in the IU History Department, who did little or no research nor contributed to or knew about the professional literature.[53] In his mind, to mentor PhD candidates or teach beyond public school levels, one should have already produced scholarly works, books principally, and continue to do so. Scholarship reinforced good teaching; the two were not mutually exclusive.

The fault for poor faculty hiring, school resource duplication, inadequate libraries, and more, partly lay at the feet of university administrators, according to Ferrell.[54] History department heads, deans, vice presidents, and presidents all came in for criticism. The MSC's history department chair perhaps represented the background of some of what was wrong at all levels. Hired during the Great Depression, hanging on to the job was the priority, and this meant "efficiency over imagination."[55] Reflecting on his past year in East Lansing, Ferrell told a Notre Dame colleague that he planned to take the Bloomington job at Indiana University, so he could teach diplomatic history. The future Hoosier historian complained that "The School here [at MSC] has an agricultural-school tradition, and the administration is now full of plodders who came here during the [D]epression and are exceedingly status conscious and rather timid."[56]

Administrator decisions to grow campuses brought about problems. Too many upstart so-called universities across the state of Michigan in Ferrell's view could not provide the libraries sufficiently stocked to support research activities. There seemed to be an alarming trend of schools locating nearly fifty miles from one another, depleting state resources. The well-positioned University of Michigan had to put up with Michigan State nearby and with other underqualified schools such as Western Michigan Teacher College and the transformed "city college in Detroit," Wayne State.[57] The Indiana professor's opinions stood unchanged decades later, as President Sumner Canary received Ferrell's critique on a wide array of issues including the lack of quality history faculty and the scholars needed to recruit PhD students to establish a program.[58] Indiana University administration at the highest levels also had failed, in this academic's mind, in numerous ways. Presidents Myles Brand and John Ryan garnered the most criticism.[59] Ferrell accused Brand of destroying the work of former IU President Herman Wells on campus, leaving "IU in shambles," and charged Ryan with academic fraud and administrative ineptitude—overbuilding the campus, increasing salaries irresponsibly, and producing a dissertation that very likely included plagiarism and very little if any of Ryan's ideas.[60] Ferrell claimed that it "took four years" to oust him.[61]

The ultimate campus focus of Ferrell was his students and each week he grew more alarmed. He concluded that high schools across Michigan and Indiana were failing to teach history. Consequently, one of his greatest efforts was to address the problems with student preparation for college courses. Some of this he did by tailoring instruction to meet student needs, underscoring higher expectations, and correcting poor writing, the most time-intensive activity. In his mind, there was little doubt that students were not getting the education they needed prior to entering their basic history courses at MSC or elsewhere. During the first year of teaching in East Lansing, Ferrell wrote to his good friend at Yale University Press,

> I'm constantly amazed and annoyed at the lack of preparation furnished by the local high schools. The kids come here knowing virtually nothing and expect that their experience here will be an extension of that in high school. I'm making some of them put their noses into the textbooks, which is a brand new experience.[62]

Later he would find similar issues with Hoosier students in his courses at Indiana University.[63] Instituting weekly quizzes and rigorous grading were short-term solutions, but the long view had to encompass working with public schools, and the opportunity for this arose after gaining experience at Indiana toward the end of the decade in collaboration with colleagues under a Lilly Endowment grant. By the end of the 1950s, the IU History Department under James Byrnes leadership secured a grant from the Lilly Endowment to improve the preparation of Indiana high school history instruction.[64]

The Lilly funded "Program in American History at Indiana University" was directed initially for American History teachers throughout the State of Indiana, and for the purposes, in Ferrell's words: "to shake up high school teaching."[65] More than 100 teachers took part in the three intensive summer sessions in Bloomington. Creating off-campus reading programs and a "basic list" of American history books for high schools to consider putting on their shelves came with the push to improve.⁶⁶ As part of the newly introduced "home reading" course, history teachers were engaging twelve "selected titles," writing thousand-word critical reviews, engaging one-on-one with IU faculty, and demonstrating marked improvement.⁶⁷ As part of the "shake up," the Lilly Endowment also underwrote efforts to measure the pulse of the state's schools. Indiana University History Department colleagues fanned out across the state, conducting more than 200 taped interviews with program fellows, teachers, and administrators, observing teachers in action, and surveying school library shelves for history books. With great energy and optimism, Ferrell served for a time as the Director of the Lilly Teaching Program.⁶⁸ He travelled the length and breadth of the state from South Bend, Mishawaka, Goshen, and Ft. Wayne, to Kokomo, Indianapolis, Georgetown, and New Albany.⁶⁹ The Indiana historian documented his concerns on site visit reports: poor book selection, poorly informed and unmotivated history teachers, disengaged students, nonacademically focused principals and administration officials, inactive parents, hands-off school boards, and negligent history departments at universities.⁷⁰ Historians, in Ferrell's estimation, needed to reclaim their gatekeeping role over credentialed teachers sent out to high schools, a proposal that would presage his battle with schools of education, including that at Indiana University.⁷¹

The work to improve college preparation did not stop with high schools. Ferrell's efforts also reached into teacher education programs, including Indiana University's.⁷² After making enough noise, IU appointed the young professor to a committee at the 9th Indiana Teacher Education Workshop, chaired by Wanonah G. Brewer.⁷³ The focus of the workshop was to evaluate teacher education. The Hoosier historian had experienced the poor performance of too many of the IU School of Education students in his courses, later finding their way to graduation, teacher certification, and in front of public high school students.⁷⁴ Ferrell registered his alarm with a colleague, James Koerner, who had studied the problem of schools and poorly educated American teachers.⁷⁵ The immediate difficulty, as Ferrell shared it in his letter to Koerner, was with an IU Associate Dean in the School of Education who should not be promoting "low quality" teacher candidates who had "below average (C-) marks in history." Rigor was at the heart of the Lilly Teacher Program, of course, including reading twelve books a course and writing 1,000-word essays on each across three summer sessions.

Ferrell was also engaged with Indiana legislators to reconfigure teacher education with the aim to reduce college of education requirements. Indiana state representative David Thayer received a full accounting of what was going on and what needed changing.⁷⁶ Ferrell sought out Thayer because he led a Study Commission on Teacher Training and Licensing that was conducting hearings "allowing arts college graduates to teach in the State of Indiana without taking education courses." As history professors do, Ferrell educated Thayer on the history of teacher training, noting that at one time there were no requirements, and that schools of education had unfortunately begun to dictate what courses certified high school teachers had to complete to find themselves in a classroom. The course requirements had unnecessarily ballooned to 18 hours with an accompanying "undue amount of practice teaching," all of which "had been subtracted from the content requirements of a college degree." There was little doubt in this historian's mind that several hours of preparation were useful to prepare history teachers, but training had gotten out of hand, to the detriment of history content knowledge. As prelude to what would become standard fare in alternative teacher preparation programs in the twenty-first century, Ferrell recommended to Thayer that students should be permitted to gain a "temporary license" and begin teaching with an arts and science degree while completing a few education requirements.

The times were ripe for advocates of teacher education reform. Ferrell was aware of those pitching new ideas (or seeking to refocus on former ideals), for example, Koerner or Arthur Bestor, who presented a paper at the American Historical Association's conference in December 1952 titled "Anti-Intellectuals in the Schools."[77] Bestor published several volumes reflective of the push, including *Educational Wastelands: The Retreat from Learning in our Public Schools* and *The Restoration of Learning*. In a letter inviting Koerner to speak to his Lilly Program students, Ferrell recounted the lessons of another education reformer of the era, Morris Janowitz, a University of Chicago sociologist. Ferrell found Janowitz's arguments convincing, given his school observations throughout the state of Indiana. Four valid complaints stood out in Ferrell's mind: the fractionalized nature of school systems; the need for better teachers; educational problems ignored by schools of education; and the unwillingness of schools of education to apply statistical analysis to problems. Ferrell no doubt showed his personal angst surrounding IU teacher "educationists" by disparaging dissertations produced by education school doctoral students and voting against a prominent IU School of Education professor's (Howard Mehlinger's) promotion to professor of history.[78] He also joined an American Historical Association committee that sought to promote higher standards among history programs nationwide, but its recommendations fell on deaf ears, and the effort folded.[79] After retiring in 1988, Ferrell must have looked back on his efforts with some disillusionment, both in reigning in an ever-growing College of Education and its control over teacher candidate requirements and his attempts to limit the growth, even reduce the number, of what he considered to be illegitimate history doctoral programs through an AHA committee. Neither project led to results.[80]

Ferrell likely approached teacher education advocacy much like he did the other areas of his activism, with some degree of bias, perhaps rooted in personal indignities suffered (a rejected Army Reservist) or in his early family and institutional socialization (overlapping characteristics with the young Harry Truman) or in some idealism about the way things ought to be (preparing school teachers as scholars). One might speculate that there was some discord sowed in early experiences as he moved through the BGSU school of education courses as a music education major. The semester before going to war, he found himself with grades of C and D in school "observation" and "student teaching."[81] Upon return to the BGSU campus, education courses continued to deflate his more stellar record, with a C and B in student teaching and teaching vocal music. Witnessing poorly performing history students in his history courses years later as an IU history professor, then finding those same students going off to teach high school, likely added to his angst. Ferrell had to advocate for better ways.

An historian as activist is hardly a unique phenomenon, and bias is part of the human condition.[82] Some professionally trained storytellers have been captured by a commitment that seeks to correct civil-rights wrongs, and in doing so, produced more positive versions than warranted of what history teaches in op-eds.[83] Others have founded organizations for women (Gerda Lerner), produced evidence to prosecute school districts in desegregation cases (John Hope Franklin), and taken part in civil disobedience campaigns. Still more have written "new left" manifestos, participated in campus protests, publicized illegal behavior of university officials, and organized and led efforts to abolish nuclear weapons.[84] Historian Arthur M. Schlesinger Jr. advised and wrote speeches for Adlai Stevenson and John F. Kennedy, among others, all in the cause of American liberalism.[85] Ferrell certainly had his biases. There are, however, boundaries for trained historians, according to conventional criteria, producing "accounts of the past that reflect complexity, subtlety and nuance."[86] The evidence suggests that Ferrell sometimes adhered to conventions of historical objectivity and sometimes did not.

NOTES

1. Robert H. Ferrell, *Ill-Advised: Presidential Health and Public Trust* (Columbia: University of Missouri Press, 1992), 163; Ferrell, *Unjustly Dishonored*, 89–90; Robert H. Ferrell, *Harry S. Truman and the Modern American Presidency* (Boston, MA: Little, Brown and Company, 1983), chapters ten and eleven; Robert H. Ferrell, *Peace in Their Time: The Origins of the Kellogg-Briand Pact* (New Haven, CT: Yale University Press, 1952), 265.

2. Letter to Ted, January 15, 1999; letter to Ken Duckett, January 30, 1999, Box 58; letter to Arthur A. Ekirch Jr., October 1, 1993—Ferrell organized the opposition through the OAH ballot (See also attached letter to Ferrell from Ekirch, September 6, 1993); letter to Gene M. Gressly, October 1, 1993, Box 25 (see also attached letter to Ferrell from Gressly, September 8, 1993); letter to Charles Blankenship, April 7, 2003 (in possession of recipient).

3. See letter to Manning M. Pattillo from Robert F. Byrnes (IU History Department Chair), December 17, 1959 [and attachment—six pages on the program], Box 73; Travel Voucher Requests, June–July 1963, Box 77.

4. The following discussion relies heavily on the following works: Brown, *Postmodernism for Historians*; Donnelly and Norton, *Doing History*; and Evans, *In Defense*.

5. See Brown, *Postmodernism*, 6–11, 23–31; Donnelly and Norton, *Doing History*, 3–7, 86–91; Evans, *In Defense*, 1–2 and Chapter Eight. Especially relevant to our treatment of Ferrell is Evans' conclusion: "Politically committed history only damages itself if it distorts, manipulates, or obscures historical facts in the interest of the cause it claims to represent" (p. 219). Discerning fact, of course, is part of the crux of the traditionalist versus postmodernist debate.

6. Donnelly and Norton, *Doing History*, 5; Evans, *In Defense*, 3–4.

7. Evans, *In Defense*, 30–37.

8. Wilson, "Introduction," 3–10.

9. Tim Tyson, "Can Honest History Allow for Hope? The Obligations of Scholarship Diverge from the Needs of Activists," *The Atlantic* (December 18, 2015).

10. Mark Donnelly, co-author of *Doing History*, emphasized that "conventional methods" are contested; see especially the co-authors' treatment of historical objectivity in chapters five and six. Donnelly email to the author, January 28, 2019.

11. Robert H. Ferrell (ed.), *Off the Record: The Private Papers of Harry S. Truman* (New York: Harper & Row, 1980), 7; Robert H. Ferrell (ed.), *The Autobiography of Harry S. Truman* (Columbia: University of Missouri Press, 1980).

12. Robert H. Ferrell (ed.), *Dear Bess: The Letters from Harry to Bess Truman, 1910–1959* (New York: W. W. Norton & Company, 1983), vii–ix.

13. The more expansive volume on Truman's life, *Harry S. Truman: A Life*, was published in 1994. Ferrell authored several more books focusing on Truman, for instance, his farming experience, choice as vice president, Pendergast connection, presidential leadership (among other presidents), and 'century celebration,' and he edited volumes on Truman and the Atomic bomb decision and the diary of Assistant Press Secretary Eben A. Ayer.

14. See Ferrell, *Ill-Advised*, xii.

15. Robert H. Ferrell, *Woodrow Wilson and World War I, 1917–1921* (New York: Harper & Row, 1985), 161; see Brenda Heaster, in Ferrell, *Ill-Advised*, xi.

16. Chapter One, in Ferrell, *Ill-Advised*, 168. Eugene P. Trani et al. published a 1977 volume on President Harding, including his health problems. Ferrell's former students, including Trani, wrote articles for a book to honor their Indiana history mentor; see *Presidents, Diplomats, and Other Mortals*, published in 2007.

17. Evans, *In Defense*, 17.

18. Good sources for both include Ferrell's edited volumes on Truman and Bess, and Ferrell's dad's (Ernest Sr.'s) account, *Stories I Want My Grandchildren to Know* (1980). Several copies still survive, for instance, at the Waterville Historical Society, Waterville, Ohio.

19. Ferrell wrote nine books on Truman and edited nearly half as many more, including the president's autobiography. For a listing of nearly all of Ferrell's books, see "Robert H. Ferrell." *Contemporary Authors Online*, Gale, 2018. Biography in Context.

20. *American Diplomacy: A History* (New York: Norton, 1959) and *George C. Marshall* (New York: Cooper Square, 1966).

21. See Chapter Three in Ferrell Sr., *Stories*, especially pp. 43–51.

22. See Ferrell's war letters, Box 74.

23. See, for instance, the "Battle of Who Run," in Ferrell, *Harry S. Truman and the Modern American Presidency*, 10–11.

24. See examples from Evans, *In Defense*, Chapter Eight, and from Donnelly and Norton, *Doing History*, 59 and 73.

25. For contrasting views to Ferrell's pro-Truman account, see Arnold A. Offner, *Another Such Victory: President Truman and the Cold War, 1945–1953* (Palo Alto, CA: Stanford University Press, 2002); or Alonzo L. Hamby, "A Biographer's Perspective II," in *Harry's Farewell: Interpreting and Teaching the Truman Presidency*, ed. Richard S. Kirkendall (Columbia: University of Missouri Press, 2004), 348–357, especially 351–354.

26. Ferrell, *Harry S. Truman*, 15.

27. Ferrell confessed to a well-read friend that Truman did not make whole the debt, likely paying off only $1,000 of the $8,000 total (after bank collapse), and further, that the future president did not fully compensate a local bank, given inflation, for a farm loan. Letter to Charles Blankenship, December 5, 2015 (in possession of recipient).

28. Ferrell continued to praise Truman well into the twenty-first century; see for instance, his comparisons of Truman to other presidents in *Presidential Leadership: From Woodrow Wilson to Harry S. Truman* (Columbia: University of Missouri Press, 2006).

29. Clearly several of the criteria of historical objectivity identified earlier cannot be identified in post-production text, but in as much as Ferrell, and historians generally, include their source processing and use to explain the topic and arguments, evidence can be identified.

30. For the full episode, see Ferrell, *Harry S. Truman: A Life*, 56–57.

31. A more complete list and discussion surrounding various criteria of historical objectivity can be found in Donnelly and Norton, *Doing History*, 59 and 73, and in Evans, *In Defense*, Chapter Eight.

32. Ferrell, *Harry S. Truman: A Life*, 124–132.

33. The analysis here focused on chapter 3, but for treatment of the full length of the Ferrell's explanation of Eisenhower's cover-up "crisis" through his years as president, see *Ill-Advised*, chapters 3–8.

34. Letter to Taft, October 14, 1949, Box 84.

35. Letter, Witsell to Ferrell, September 22, 1949, Box 84.
36. Letter to Taft, October 14, 1949.
37. Letter, Witsell to Taft, December 5, 1949, Box 84.
38. Letter to Taft, January 6, 1950, Box 84.
39. "My own case in itself is unimportant. . . . What is important, I believe, is that the Army . . . not waste time on the part of everyone concerned" (Letter to Taft, October 14, 1949). There is some uncertainty surrounding the chronology and construction of the narrative since the *New York Time's* newspaper clipping in Ferrell's files at LillyIU is undated, and the *NYT*-online archive listed the article's release date as February 19, 1949, well before the back and forth among Ferrell, Taft, and Witsell. Why it would be in Ferrell's file if it was not a result of his efforts makes no sense.
40. Letter to Taft, October 14, 1949; letter to Dad, August 2, 1951; letter to June, November 28, 1951—Ferrell "felt he needed more authority"; the "Designation of Insurance Beneficiary" form lists Ferrell in the "Air Target Research Branch, Division of Director of Intelligence," August 13, 1951 (all letters, Box 84); Ferrell had experienced the problems with Army bureaucracy during the war; see for example, letter to M/D, August 11, 1945, Box 74.
41. Letter to Taft, April 9, 1951, Box 84.
42. Perhaps worth nothing is what a close friend and fellow Yale student of Ferrell's, Dr. Robert Bryant, shared with the present author, that Ferrell supported FDR's policies, and demonstrated his Democratic stripes before the run-in with Taft. Interview, January 22, 2019.
43. Letter to Taft, May 1, 1951, Box 84.
44. Letter, Taft to Ferrell, May 11, 1951, Box 84.
45. Letter to Sir John [Pratt], November 3, 1952, Box, 84.
46. Letter to Mr. [William] Ruckelshaus, October 22, 1973, Box 49; letter to Dr. Brumberg, February 1, 1979, Box 35; letter to Gene, January 1, 1998, Box 58; letter to John Stewart, January 12, 1999, Box 58; letter to Mary Jane Gormley [JAH representative], June 1, 2001; letter to Jim, July 9, 2001, Box 95.
47. Letter to Chuck, September 1, 1951, Box 84; letter to Mrs. Castle, November 8, 1963, Box 77; Robert H. Ferrell, *American Diplomacy: A History*, 3rd ed. (New York: W. W. Norton, 1975), 516.
48. Letter to Ferrell from Rev. Theodore Hesburgh [Notre Dame President], December 30, 1966 (misfiled under March 1967), Box 20; letter to Bob, January 15, 1970, Box 10; letter to Indiana Senator Birch Bayh, March 26, 1974, Box 48; letter to Ferrell from Philip Crowl [U.S. Naval War College], December 11, 1973, (misfiled under May–July 1974), Box 48; Letter to Philip C. Brooks [Director Harry S. Truman Library], November 27, 1963, filed under Truman Library Conference, Box 41; letter to Bill, February 22, 1959, Box 72.
49. Letter to Ferrell from Arnie Offner, August 14, 2013, Box 207; letter to Clarence A. Berdahl, January 13, 1964, filed under Truman Library Conference, Box 41.
50. Letter to June and Flo, August 17, 1952, Box 44.
51. Letter to Ralph McDonald, May 10, 1952, Box 44.
52. Letter to John [DeNovo], August 17, 1952, misfiled under September 1952–February 1953, Box 44.

Dear Senator Taft 93

53. Letter to Dad, October 6, 1952, Box 44; letter to Flo and June, September 15, 1952, Box 44; letter to Murf, Marian, Karl and Q, December 22, 1952, Box 44; letter to Stephen, June 23, 1953, misfiled under September 1952–February 1953 (#7), Box 44; letter to John, circa September 1952–February 1953), Box 44; letter to Bo [Held], April 2, 1953, Box 44; letter to Rudin [Yale history professor], December 16, 1954, Box 72; letter to Paul L. Dressel [MSU Office of Research], February 27, 1964, Box 77; letter to Art [Ekinch], December 8, 1969, Box 7; letter to Lila, Carolyn, and Blackie, September 5, 1974, Box 48; letter to Bill and Gerry, June 10, 2005, misfiled under September–October 2011 (#2), Box 297; Ferrell Diary I [first box, 1949–1983], entry April 3, 1980, pp. 4–5), Box 216.
54. Letter to Gaddis [Smith], January 5, 1957, Box 1.
55. Ibid.
56. Letter to Stephen [Kertesz], June 23, 1953, Box 1.
57. Letter to Gaddis [Smith], January 5, 1957, Box 1.
58. Letter to Sumner Canary, October 17, 1966, Box 20; see also letter to Walter Sanderlin, April 24, 1978, Box 68—Ferrell's critique of BGSU's newly instituted "Coaster Culture" course.
59. Letter to Harold Pepinsky [IU Criminal Justice], June 11, 1991, Box 34—topics include IU Foundation dishonesty, summer school pay for "ghost" teaching, and misuse of Foundation cars for travel; letter to Jim, July 2, 1994, Box 25—Ferrell criticized the IU Foundation for supporting individuals who misused funds, paying excessive salaries, harassing alumni for funds, and using the Foundation plane to travel for convenience; letter to Dean Wolfe, November 23, 1993, Box 25; letter to Ken Duckett, January 30, 1999, letter to Don, January 19, 1999, Box 58; on President Ryan's dissertation, see File May 2001 (#2), Box 95; letter to [Barker [?], May 13, 1993, Box 34; on OAH problems, see letter to Thomas Manning, November 23, 1993, Box 25; on OAH President Arnita Jones (Executive Secretary)—letter to John, May 20, 2001, Box 95; letter to H.F. McMains, January 5, 1999; letter to Phil, January 4, 1999, Box 58; letter to Arnita Jones, October 6, 1993 (attached to letter to Ferrell from David [Danboy ?], April 6, 1994, Box 25; letter to Arthur Ekirch, October 1, 1993, Box 25; memo to Dean Shiner, November 1, 1973, Box 49; letter to Robert Menke, July 8, 1994, Box 25;
60. Letter to Thomas D. Clark, February 28, 1979; memo to William G. Panschar, March 21, 1979, Box 35; letter to James Madison [IU History Professor/Department Centennial Committee], July 27, 1994, Box 18; memo to C. Patricia Risesenman, July 1994, Box 25—Ferrell claimed that IU had created a summer school "diploma mill."
61. Letter to Ted, January 15, 1999, Box 58; letter to Charles Blankenship, April 7, 2003 (in possession of recipient).
62. Letter to [Gene] Davidson, October 30, 1952, Box 44.
63. Letter to Rossbachers, November 9, 1952, Box 44; letter to Dad, February 11, 1954, Box 46.
64. See letter to Manning M. Pattillo from Robert F. Byrnes (IU History Department Chair) and attachment, six pages describing the program, December 17, 1959, Box 73.
65. Maurice G. Baxter, Robert H. Ferrell, and John E. Wiltz, *The Teaching of American History in High Schools* (Bloomington: Indiana University Press, 1964), 8–10; letter to Victor Bogle, June 7, 1963, Box 77.

66. Baxter, Ferrell, and Wiltz, *The Teaching of American History*, 9.
67. Ibid., 26.
68. Letter to Joseph E. Weber [Professor of Chemistry Department, BGSU], June 6, 1963, Box 77.
69. Travel Requests, Lilly Program, Teaching American History, 1963, Box 77. See also Ferrell's high school site-visit reports for Georgetown, May 24, 1963; Goshen, April 23, 1963; and New Albany, May 23, 1963, Box 77).
70. See his chapters four and six, describing the typical Indiana high school American history classroom and administrators, parents, and school boards, in Baxter, Ferrell, and Wiltz, *The Teaching of American History* (page 11 notes that Ferrell has written these chapters). Also, in a telling chapter on high school history teachers, Ferrell wrote, "a typical [Indiana high school] teacher reads virtually nothing in his [*sic*] field from year to year. . . . About eighty percent of the teachers replied [in interviews conducted that they had read year to year] nothing." Ibid., 27 See Memo to Bernard Perry [IU Press Editor], February 19, 1964 Box 77.
71. Baxter, Ferrell, and Wiltz, *The Teaching of American History*, 117–119.
72. Letter to Morris Janowitz, March 3, 1967, Box 20.
73. Letter to Ferrell from Wanonah G. Brewer, October 6, 1957, Box 1.
74. Letter to James Koerner [author of *The Miseducation of American Teachers*], June 20, 1963, Box 18. See also Ferrell's words to a foreign student having to study "stupid . . . education courses in the U.S., that are full of an awful lot of hot air;" "the educationists are full of method, and not much knowledge" (letter to Margo, January 13, 1960, Box 73). See also Ferrell's comments to a publisher discounting the use of problems-based reading approaches to history when students so badly need "systematic, substantive reading" (letter to Arthur S. T. O'Keefe, May 30, 1960, Box 73).
75. James D. Koerner, *The Miseducation of Teachers* (Boston, MA: Houghton Mifflin Company, 1963).
76. Letter to David Thayer, November 16, 1959, Box 1.
77. Arthur Bestor, "Anti Intellectuals in the Schools," paper delivered at the AHA conference, December 28, 1952; see Ferrell mss., File February–September 1953, Box 44; David S. Brown, *Richard Hofstadter: An Intellectual Biography* (Chicago: University of Chicago Press, 2006), 134.
78. Memo to Henry, April 16, 1974, Box 48.
79. Thomas D. Clark, *My Century in History* (Lexington: University Press of Kentucky, 2006), 243.
80. Ferrell continued his efforts to upgrade history teacher competency well into the twenty-first century as participant in a teacher-researcher conference; see Kirkendall, *Harry's Farewell,* Preface and 336–347.
81. Bowling Green State University transcript for Robert H. Ferrell, Registrar's Office, Bowling Green, Ohio, 1947.
82. Brown, *Postmodernism*, 25–30; Donnelly and Norton, *Doing History*, 86–91; Evans, 199–219; Storey, *Writing History*, 59–74.
83. Tyson, "Can Honest History Allow for Hope," 3.
84. Barbara Winslow, "E. P. Thompson as Historian, Teacher and Political Activist," in *Against the Current*, January–February 1994 (accessed September 9, 2018 at https://solidarity-us.org/atc/48/p4731/).

85. Isaac McDaniel, "The Historian as Activists," *The Review of Politics* 57, no. 3 (Summer 1995), 541–544; Richard Aldous, *Schlesinger: The Imperial Historian* (New York: W. W. Norton, 2017), 149–165. Of course, Schlesinger Jr.'s work for the Kennedys, especially JFK, runs through much of the book. Henry Steele Commager worked as a propagandist during the Second World War, railed against McCarthyism, wrote and spoke on American exceptionalism for young and older audiences, and worked to create an American Studies program. See Neil Jumonville, *Henry Steele Commager: Midcentury Liberalism and the History of the Present* (Chapel Hill: University of North Carolina Press, 1999). Richard Hofstadter engaged in campus activism from undergraduate days in Buffalo through the heady 1960s while at Columbia University. See Brown, *Richard Hofstadter*.

86. A. F. (Floor) Haalboom, "Talking Activism and History—Part I," *Shells and Pebbles* [website blog] (accessed September 11, 2018 at http://www.shellsandpebbles.com/2015/10/14/talking-activitism-history-part-I/).

Part III

DISTINCTIONS

Chapter 5

Traditionalists, Debunkers, and Revisionism

We are all revisionists. But the cold war revisionists who attacked President Truman did not understand the time in which he was president nor the man himself.

—Robert H. Ferrell. In *Harry S. Truman and the Cold War Revisionists* (Columbia: University of Missouri Press, 2006), vii

Robert Ferrell's writings and professional struggles reveal that twentieth-century history, even that of the twenty-first, is not so far removed from its evolutionary roots. American historians continue to produce legend as history; create an historical consciousness; put history to good use for present-day purposes; debate the meanings of the primitive, progressive, or anachronistic; promote reading history for pleasure or as good literature; and shape the past with science as a model.[1] Similar to Robert Ferrell, John Lukacs, an historian of historiography, wrote "all history is revisionist" and shared a brief annotated version of the meanings of historical revisionism across time, from Thucydides to scholar priests' textual criticism to German-trained professional historians. Pro-German historians' revisionism was perhaps the first example with which the future Indiana historian eventually wrestled. Interpretations "came out of Germany after the First World War," whose aim was to correct the so-called "inaccurate and unilateral condemnation of Germany as having been primarily responsible for the outbreak of World War I," as written into the Treaty of Versailles.[2] Ferrell came of age at a time when the First World War–revisionists' ideas were making their way to history books and popular treatments. Then not so long after the Second World War, "the new school of revisionism" as he labeled it, trickled into re-interpretations of American involvement against Germany and Japan, and later, into pro-Soviet/anti-American accounts of Cold War causes.[3]

Ferrell's angst toward the new revisionists, and his approach to the past generally, began germinating from the admixture of three soils: northern Ohio upbringing (urban and rural), including world war understandings; East-coast graduate-level history training; and Hoosier-rooted, life-long career attachment. These cultivated in him an eclectic mix of what historian David S. Brown characterized in U.S.-Americanist historiography of the times as both an "interior" school of Midwestern progressivism and a school of East-coast liberalism. Early years' pro–Civil War union/anti-southerner influences would groom Ferrell to reject the "Vanderbilt" school.[4] Progenitors of the Middle West mentality included starpower storytellers Frederick Jackson Turner, Charles Beard, William Appleman Williams, and Christopher Lasch. As to the latter (Columbia) school, the Indiana historian fell under the spell of, or perhaps merely in-line with, Samuel Flagg Bemis at Yale, among others (e.g., Robert Maddox, Oscar Handlin, Arthur Schlesinger Jr.) favoring patriotic, pro-American, anti-Communist, international liberalism.[5] But Ferrell, as with his professional allies, was hardly uncomplicated, and conflicting influences showed their impact toward emerging scholarly challenges: changing perspectives on the purpose of history, interdisciplinarity, social science method and epistemology, historian identity, and so forth, whether tied to war-related-American leadership fault-finding, African American treatment, women and gender studies, or perspectives on America's role in the twentieth century generally, or more specifically, during the Cold War. An Ivy League alumnus and highly respected author, Ferrell found himself as part of the elite, yet seemingly conflicted, torn by birthplace-Jeffersonian-Republican sensibilities regarding the critical import of the yeoman-common man and democratic ideology.[6] His analysis of the origins of the Kellogg-Briand Pact in his widely celebrated first book, *Peace in Their Time*, was an omen of this bifurcated persona.[7] In a concluding sentence, perhaps exhibiting an "interior" progressive sentimentality along with adopted, smug East-coast liberalism, he wrote, "one should hope that by the 1950's American public opinion has become truly sophisticated and will give its unwavering support to a realistic American foreign policy."[8]

This chapter places in relief a glimpse of Ferrell-related historiography, his world of historians, his times and contributions. An active researcher, the Indiana scholar's identity seeps through the many critiques, both his and colleagues', that made their way into journals. The range of topical comments is instructive as is the variety of viewpoints. The first review explored here came in the early 1950s, with release of Ferrell's first book; the last one, into the twenty-first century. Stories of celebrated historians who came of age

Traditionalists, Debunkers, and Revisionism 101

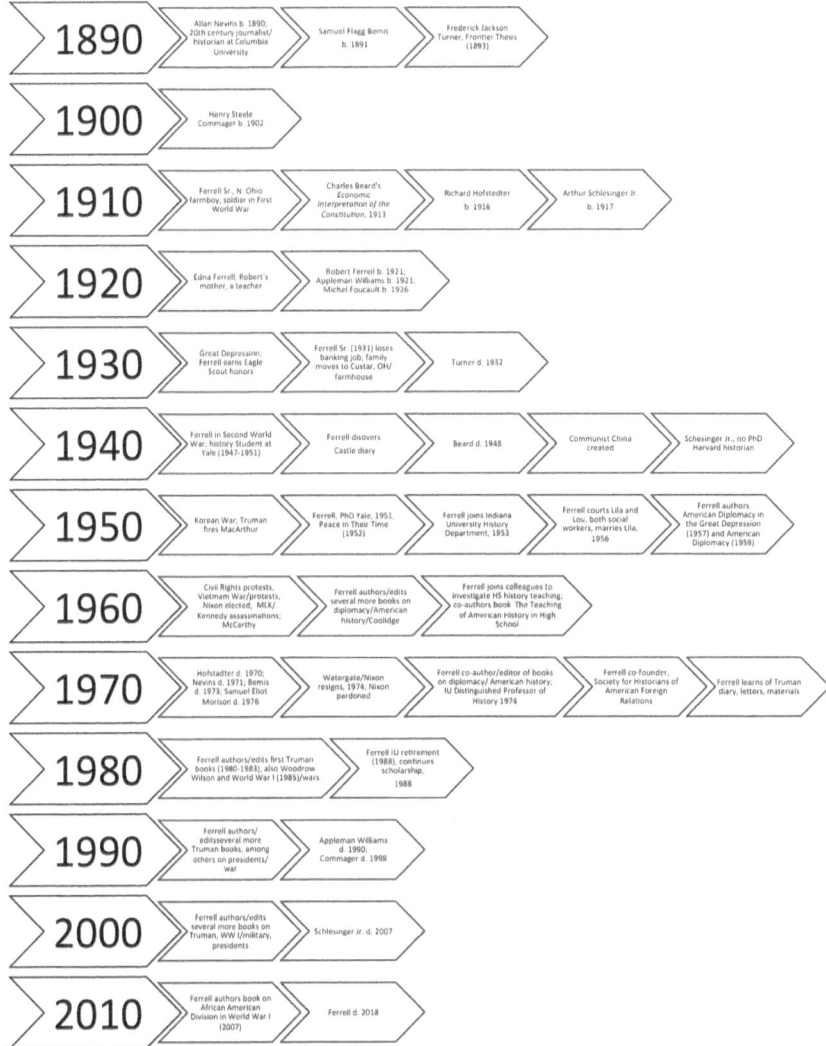

Figure 5.1   Ferrell-era historiography-related events.

during America's rise to world power provide an opportunity for comparison as well (see Figure 5.1). Identifying a manageable yet insightful subset of historians is aided partly by those mentioned in Ferrell's correspondence, book reviews and articles, and in biographies.[9] Ferrell lashed out at notable Midwesterners such as Beard and Appleman Williams, both products of so-called radical progressivism.[10] Beard, of course, more than likely spoke to Ferrell from the grave (d. 1948) or through his collegial pallbearers. The Hoosier historian encountered Appleman Williams at history conferences and in published critiques.[11] Ferrell would associate himself with other allies at times, Schlesinger Jr. or Commager.[12] Allan Nevins likely caught the attention of a young Bob Ferrell in lively journalistic accounts or in biographies long before the Ohioan graduated from Yale.[13] Nevins's works could be found in newspapers or magazines such as nationally syndicated editorials or articles written for the *New York Evening Post* or *World* or *New York Times Magazine* or in popular books on John Fremont or John D. Rockefeller. The latter publications may have been enticing to a young Ferrell, living in Cleveland's metropolis and having access to well-stocked libraries with parents encouraging him to use them.[14] An understanding of these late nineteenth-to-twentieth century storytellers, along with Richard Hofstadter, helps to inform us of Ferrell's professional and personal milieu and path to success.

One window into a historian's identity and perspective are the book reviews that make their way into peer-reviewed journals. Controversial topics likely draw more commentary or critique. At mid-twentieth century and beyond, the new school of revisionism and its antagonists provided an extensive outpouring of fireworks within the subfield of United States foreign relations.[15] Naturally, presidential biography intersects with international affairs and war. So, it is no surprise that Ferrell, a highly regarded scholar in these areas, found himself engaging colleagues regularly in print, nearly two book reviews each year through retirement in history journals alone. A search of the database JSTOR reveals the enormity of his interaction with so-called Cold War revisionists, among others.[16] The earliest review by historian Ferrell, surfacing in JSTOR, came in September 1953, his initial semester at Indiana, focusing on Wayne S. Cole's *America First: The Battle against Intervention, 1940–1941*.[17] His critique tells us something about how the Indiana scholar framed expectations of successful practitioners: dispassionate arguments, requisite evidence, thorough treatment of American isolationism and anti–Second World War attitudes toward participation. The commentary goes beyond the book's content and reveals something of the reviewer's bias, that the people of the time did not know of the strategic nor moral issues of the war as are known now or that the context for these anti-war attitudes was a throwback to pre–First World War idyllic times:

> a return to the unhurried and utterly safe years of the century before 1914, when Americans peacefully spread across and began to develop the vast resources of half a continent without the distraction of foreign wars. *America First*, perhaps, was an honorable if short-sighted attempt to preserve a way of life which had gone forever.[18]

One suspects that Ferrell overlooked (ignored?) the perspective of Native Americans, Gilded-age laborers, Jim Crow-era African Americans, or women suffragists.[19] More than fifty more reviews would follow until the retirement of IU's Distinguished Professor of History in 1988. Then nearly twenty more critiques would appear before Ferrell migrated to Ann Arbor from Bloomington, after wife Lila's tragic death, to be near daughter Carolyn and family, and to write more books. The omnipresence of Ferrell's ideas is demonstrated too by the multiplicity of journals that published his work, more than a dozen, including a multitude of pieces in each of those published by high status professional associations, for instance, the *American Historical Review*, *Mississippi Valley Historical Review*, *Journal of American History*, or *Journal of Southern History*.[20]

Reviews by Ferrell take the reader in many directions, and a deep look here at each individually is as unnecessary as it is undesirable, but looking at several as prototypes with supporting evidence from others parses the essence of the author's historical approach into at least five broad categories: his personal biases, advocacy for historical viewpoints, guideposts to proper scholarship, archival resourcefulness, and literary bent (see table in appendix). Reviews throughout his career zeroed in on revisionists and their arguments contesting traditionalist positions on the United States' worldviews and related activities, presidential actions, diplomacy, and world wars.[21] While Ferrell could be ardently oppositional to the Pearl Harbor and Cold War revisionists, he left the door open (a play on words, to be sure), for cogently argued and evidentially supported twists on interpretation. Beard, for instance, found plaudits from the Indiana historian for his economic theory (though "moncausal").[22] More important to Ferrell, Beard's writings exhibited "sharpness of language and acuteness of thought," which "took the reader irresistibly to the conclusion." The IU reviewer captured "the man as much as the book," turning to Beard's Indiana/Midwestern heritage that helped to explain the path to expression, "utter sincerity, droll wit, and homely approach to all problems." The best historians, in Ferrell's mind, knew those they studied intimately, their personalities, origins, eccentricities, and anecdotes. The wrong turn for Beard came as he pivoted to the 1930s, then 1940s, when in Ferrell's words, Beard's "wish was constantly father to the thought" (i.e., staying out of world war brought safety). The two men's persuasions, even ideologies, Beard's and Ferrell's, diverged as to the place of America in the world as it turned the page into the twentieth century, its claims to moral authority or cultural superiority, the former preaching "continentalism" (isolationism), the latter internationalism. Revealing something of Ferrell's bias, he noted, Beard "could not return the United States to the carefree era before the first World War." (Again, carefree for whom, one might ask.) An analysis of Ferrell's reviews provides one measure of the IU historian's attitudes toward practice.[23]

A trickle of Ferrell critiques underscore his willingness to engage less traditional perspectives on, or ways of doing, history as illustrated in reviews targeting the First World War social analysis, history telling through film, and women in the service of United States' foreign relations.[24] In *Opponents of*

War, 1917–1918, the authors, to Ferrell, had demonstrated in "subtle and convincing" ways how psychological conditions—"anti-labor and anti-Socialist feelings" or interethnic or racial discomfort—led to persecution of anti-war proponents. Ferrell also displayed sensitivity to Constitutional values (civil rights and liberties) and tolerance for cultural differences, something he may have encountered in the "Birds Nest" immigrant section of Lakewood. Though critical of a film documentary that tried to capture the experience of millions of American First World War participants, Ferrell suggested ways it could have succeeded by filling it with music "that makes the heart leap," with a script recounting memorable phrases, with a strong narrative voice that redounds in strength, not as one that speaks of "an old man's war." Of course, the story must tell of larger events and get the facts right, not render visuals that belie what really happened, hardly used bayonets or nonexistent quadriplegics.[25] One must also point to the IU historian's critique of women coming-of-age in service to American foreign policy. Ferrell begins the review with, "The author of this very interesting book writes with flair, and the subject is important," but the reviewer continues, "the women who have made large contributions to American foreign policy are few in number." The critique spends some time correcting assertions before adding a few remarks that belittle women who the book's author argued made a difference, Margaret Chase Smith and Bella Abzug. The criticisms likely are driven as much by Ferrell's Victorian attitudes toward women (though Ferrell does not completely dismiss women's potential), and perhaps by his sense of morality, as he noted that Abzug's foul language would have afforded his grandmother the "opportunity to wash [her] mouth out with soap."

Another sense for historian Ferrell comes by way of the feedback by colleagues on his books, and one of the first critiques came from W. N. Medicott's review of *Peace in Their Time: The Origins of the Kellogg-Briand Pact*, which played a refrain that would become repetitive among the reviews for many of his books: "Much of the inside story is already known."[26] This adds to the intrigue of why Ferrell found himself publishing so many books, and in addition, how this first book received those lofty awards. At least part of the answer may lie with Richard Leopold's overwhelmingly positive review of *Peace in Their Time*.[27] To Leopold, Ferrell gave "new depth and fuller meaning to what may seem a familiar subject"; "he writes with verve and distinction," excellent tone, without excessive second guessing or "special pleading," mindful of "humor, irony and sham" when detectable, is "eminently fair to all concerned." And furthermore, the reviewer noted, "The book is broadly conceived. Its story placed in a world setting." And finally, Leopold adds, the review of relevant archives is exhaustive. Attention to the review's phrases outlining the book's sections brings to mind celebrated nineteenth-century historians: The early chapters "set the stage" and "sketch the mood;" the next several chapters "skillfully trace the tortuous negotiations," and beyond this, the "pages describe, often amusingly, the formal signing in Paris."[28]

Truman biography engulfed the IU historian's attention with those "discoveries" at the president's library in Independence, beginning in the late 1970s, because it overlapped with other areas of interest, U.S. transition to world power, military conflicts of the American century (Truman served in WWI), presidential comparison and activities.[29] Perhaps nowhere is Ferrell's bias more boldfaced than his advocacy for the thirty-third chief executive.[30] Several cross-cutting reviews of Ferrell's early books on Truman provide a different lens than that of Ferrell's critiques. Scholars Robert Griffith, Donald McCoy, and William Pemberton may have been the most damning critics; Richard Lowitt, John Carroll, and Gerald Nash, or D. Karl Barry, the most complimentary.[31] Griffith's review is exceptional, in that it strays usefully into an essay on how to fix the scholarly impasse that Truman authors continue to indulge. In the reviewer's words, Ferrell's *Off the Record* and *The Autobiography* of Truman, "simply reaffirm the conventional portrait," while another non-Ferrell book repeats the revisionist's indictment (Truman as "architect of the Cold War and first Caesar of the new Imperial Presidency"). Ferrell's work offers a fresh look with just newly opened archives but is "disappointing." Part of this disappointment rests with inclusion of documents that have already been published, with the exception of the Potsdam conference materials and other documents excluded for no explicit reason. This led, in the reviewer's mind, to misrepresentation and downplaying of the "darker side to Truman's personality and character" (to mythologizing). Truman's life, personality, and times were hardly uncomplicated, to Griffith, and thus need an approach that "explain[s] the seemingly contradictory character of his presidency." The fix offered is a "closer examination of Truman's personality and character." So the critic provides it: Truman's extraordinary deference to parents and inferiority complex borne of personal deficiencies targeted by early peers and adult-year failures, the challenges of his era (e.g., rural to urban shift), the "personalistic" political norms, and so forth, set the stage for Griffith's psychosocial analysis that solves the heretofore stalemate in Truman historiography.[32] Ferrell was no fan of the historian as social scientist model, as this review promoted.

McCoy's and Pemberton's reviews overlap in their treatment of Ferrell's *Harry S. Truman and the Modern American Presidency*. To McCoy, Ferrell's history is "lively, forthright, but often unacceptable." The usual adjectives describe the biographer's depictions: "a sympathetic account," overlooks domestic concerns against foreign policies, "[o]verstatements abound," unsatisfactory explanations and conclusions that smack of a Truman apologist. McCoy complains that, "Ferrell has written essentially a case for Truman's greatness, citing his foreign policy, his institutionalization of the presidency, and his personal attributes, particularly his analytical abilities, decisiveness, and diligence." The reviewer adds that the "case is incomplete"; it avoids many criticisms of Truman; and finally, that the debate should move away from his greatness, and toward an assessment of Truman's impact and administration. William Pemberton's review of the same book echoes McCoy's disappointment; that is, problems of bias toward Truman, including overestimating his foreign policy achievement (i.e., Truman is responsible for effectively instituting containment while helping to dodge a third world war), and pointing to limited domestic accomplishments. Again, Pemberton adds the common criticism: "it adds little to the literature," the "synthesis fails to move scholarly research forward, and it neglects or treats superficially most of the major problems that Truman scholars have been dealing with for two decades." Unusual for criticisms of Ferrell, the reviewer notes, "It lacks the freshness and/or detailed analysis of other accounts."

Switching focus, what does one learn of Ferrell's identity as a historian from positive reviews? Richard Lowitt returns to common themes when focusing on Ferrell's Truman in the *Modern American Presidency* series: "terse, beautifully written, and cogently organized . . . the main points and ideas are crisply and succinctly stated," displays the author's "vast knowledge of the personal and private aspects" of Truman and diplomats and their documents (a deep familiarity with archival sources), "penetrating analysis of the vast changes in American foreign relations" with Truman at the helm. One learns again of the Indiana historian's advocacy for Truman, "fundamentally shifting the course of American foreign policy from neutrality and even isolation from world affairs to immediate and intimate involvement." Lowitt states that "Ferrell is no revisionist," by which he intends (remembering Ferrell's thinking, "all historians are revisionists") that he, Ferrell, is no "Cold War revisionist," and thus, avoids interpreting Truman's efforts as leading America toward modern-day imperialism or as one of the "perpetrators of the Cold War" with "insidious implications for domestic politics." "The Truman presidency, [the reviewer continues,] is cast in a *more heroic mold*" [italics added]. In contrast to Pemberton, Lowitt applauds the book's balanced treatment of domestic, biographical, and analytical portions, and adds the usefulness of the inclusion of "the most up-to-date bibliography of the Truman era."

Nash's review of Ferrell's Truman in the *Modern American Presidency* series duplicates much of Lowitt's slant on the author's writing, "succinct [yet] comprehensive accounts . . . simple and straightforward style," on his dismissive views toward Cold War revisionism and favorable treatment of Truman, crediting him "with qualities of greatness," and in this, the reviewer writes, "Ferrell presents his case in a forceful manner." Nash repeats that the Truman biographer has thoroughly excavated relevant-Truman sources, including those recently made available (e.g., Truman Papers, manuscript collections, interviews) and synthesized many existing studies. Agreeing with Lowitt, the reviewer applauds Ferrell for the bibliography, but notes the lack of footnotes. Carroll's *Off the Record* review compliments Ferrell on his rare ability to discover new primary sources, which "add vivid new details to Truman relationships," in the form of "personal diary, memoranda, and letters," with a few transcripts of telephone conversations and appointment calendar items. These are "invaluable to historians of the postwar era." Finally, merely to add color, but not much new to what the other reviewers have noted, D. Karl Barry addresses two of Ferrell's edited volumes, *The Autobiography of Harry S. Truman* and *Off the Record*, along with a third by another author on President Eisenhower. Comments by the reviewer dismiss the first book as shedding little new light, yet the second adds insights to Truman's personality; Ferrell's *archival find* presents "personal letters to family and close friends, an impressive number of diary entries on a wide range of subjects, and a wonderful sprinkling of unsent letters to newsmen, opponents, and a delightful one to his wife after a Christmas Day squabble." The Ferrell books are "not designed or edited" for scholars, perhaps to reach a broader audience. Barry explains that "the headnotes and running commentary are lively, partisan, and generally helpful to those who do not know the period or need to be reminded of their past commitments." Ferrell is called out for offering documents that present Truman "in a somewhat better light on some major issues than others that could have been used."

Whether overwhelmingly positive, negative, or mixed, the book evaluations speak to generally consistent attributes of Ferrell as historian; that is, his personal biases, historical perspectives, mixed application of conventionally accepted methods, merits of archival research, and attention to literary quality.[33] And it is the last two Ferrell characteristics that move the Midwest historian to a higher status as historian, for he tries not to be all things to all historians nor ignores essential conventional practices of most. Neither inventor of the wheel nor its replacement, he finds new applications for it or a new way of thinking about and describing its varieties, providing anecdotes that draw one in, even invoke wonder or amusement. In this, he clearly self-identified with the history-as-art literary tradition of nineteenth- and twentieth-century storytellers, to those labeled "greats" such as Francis Parkman or Samuel Eliot Morison, and/or a mixture of Allen Nevins and Richard Hofstadter. As with Morison physically retracing Columbus voyages, the IU historian believed to do history well is to know your subject well, if possible in person, place, and in relationships, but if not these, then at least in the archives, in interviews, in other sources, with those who experienced the world of the past one wishes to capture. Ferrell stands as a traditionalist more than not, but willingly dips his toes, at times, in the waters of new theories and in the insights of practitioners of cultural/social history.

Seen through the prism of his colleagues' paths, one may detect other characteristics of historian Ferrell, this through comparisons to personal circumstance, orientations toward events of the era, struggles within the profession, or issues that shaped ideas and ideologies. In *Beyond the Frontier: The Midwestern Voice in American Historical Writing*, David Brown described the uniquely situated Midwest orientation toward the past: "passionate about the possibilities of democracy . . . [and] unafraid of popular protest."[34] The region represented egalitarianism, optimism toward evolutionary change, WASP ties to the pioneers who made a Free-Soil Union impregnable, and the foundation of a university system rivaling those of eastern intellectuals; in sum, "a chosen people." Just as with Ferrell's ideological foundation, whether northern Ohio public culture and Methodism, father's patriotic war service and farm influence, or Eagle Scout achievement, the "interior" school, writ large, had its own starting point. Turner's historical manifesto blessed the frontier with democratic significance, even as it received an unenthusiastic initial welcome from his colleagues in Chicago. The end of the frontier signaled the need for new territories in order to keep democratic embers glowing. To more radical Midwesterners, however, it signified the lurch to imperialism and empire-building, not adherence to republican virtue. Other big names in pursuit of the past that followed Turner in the progressive tradition would rub more uneasily against Ferrell's views over the course of his career.

More important than Turner's thesis for Ferrell were the latter's struggles at the midpoint of the next century stemming from the early creation of a school of historians imbued with an understanding of the past through interdisciplinary theory. Turner and German-trained economist Richard Ely conjoined history, economics, and political science to create the leading "center for social science research" at the University of Wisconsin–Madison in 1892.[35] Previously, while at Johns Hopkins, Ely had organized the American Economic Association and wrote what became a classic study of the American labor movement. The country's changing environment, with increasing urbanization, immigration, and industrialization, brought about the push for problem-based studies. A nation-wide financial crisis in 1893 added to the urgency. This shift brought about the need in some minds for a different focus, a diverse methodology and set of sources, and a willingness to question past nationalistic and pro-capitalist notions as historical purpose. Turner likely introduced his doctoral students to a variety of sources overflowing in his office files: maps, population charts, statistics on voting and agricultural production, all to analyze the complexities of social and economic data to answer historical questions.[36] Even Beard, a Columbia University-trained PhD, noted Turner's impact on his influential *Economic Interpretation of the Constitution*, infusing the economic thesis with a political science classic (Federalist #10) and financial records.[37]

Ferrell and other history traditionalists were fighting upstream in a profession that was absorbing the topics, tools, outlooks, sources, and more, of social science disciplines, those for example of economics, anthropology, and sociology, requiring the most agile interdisciplinary swimmers. In 1971, historians David Landes and Charles Tilly led an effort to document some of the more dramatic changes and their oppositions across the twentieth century, battles which continue to the present.[38] As with Turner's office files, pastmasters had to navigate an eclectic mix of sources but that was only part of the increasingly fast-moving stream. As a "problem-oriented approach," social scientists assumed "uniformities of human behavior that transcend time and place . . . and the historian as social scientist chooses his [*sic*] problems with an eye toward discovering, verifying, or illuminating such uniformities. The aim is to . . . permit analogy and prediction." Traditional historians found (and continued to find) these aspects insulting to the integrity of the process of historical discovery, wedded to specific time and place, that society is far too complex for such simplification. Along with these differences came the notion of correct methods, and to the former that meant "methodological rigor" achieved by defining terms, stating hypotheses, clarifying assumptions, stipulating criteria of proof, all toward the development of a coherent theoretical model. The humanist historian, as Landes and Tilly labeled the traditionalist, is primarily concerned with the story weaving assumptions and interpretations into the narrative as discovered, "not to detract from its fluency and interest." A third divide, one drawing forth emotion like no other from oppositional historians, was reducing the historical imagination to numbers. Their leading argument was that "many aspects of human behavior are simply not reducible to numbers." Individuality, empathy, humanization do not lend themselves to quantification. Quantification led some to epistemological arrogance derived from absolutism that large data sets might suggest. Oppositionists resorted to name calling: Carl Bridenbaugh labeled the practice "Bitch-goddess;" Arthur Schlesinger Jr. countered that "all important questions are important precisely because they are not susceptible to quantitative answers." A final whirlpool of disagreement centered around whether tales of the past should prioritize more "clarity, precision, and analytic rigor" or literary ingredients such as "style, pace, and elegance," even ambiguity, to "stimulate thought."

Ferrell's objection to these social science perspectives courses through his writings but are especially dismissive in his review of a series of essays titled *Generalization in the Writing of History: A Report of the Committee on Historical Analysis of the Social Science Research Council*, coordinated by a University of Chicago historian, Louis Gottschalk, a Jewish immigrant.[39]

One only has to review an early and late remark of the critique by Ferrell to find where he stands on social science: "[H]istorians involved in this [report] . . . have turned out efforts which they might better have tucked in their desk drawers," and "the most common essay of all is written by Thomas C. Cockran, who wrote some odd information about social role." Ferrell often pointed to "generalizations" arrived at in his own works, but he employed the term synonymously with "a conclusion," not a theoretical stance or concept that portrayed a category tied to predictable behavior.[40] Ferrell, as with what Landes and Tilly suggest, is willing to cross over to the numbers side, to make a point, but these numbers are tied to unique events. For instance, he did not hesitate to reduce to quantification President Truman's decision to drop the atom bomb on Japan; that is, the number of Americans and civilians (among others) who might have been casualties if the president did not assent to the weapon's use.[41]

Beard presented Ferrell with a challenge that paralleled any concern the latter had for the former's possible Marxist perspective (or fear of economic determinism), resort to statistics, or interdisciplinary borrowing. In light of Ernest Ferrell Sr.'s patriotic fervor relaying stories of his dutiful service in the Great War to his future historian-son, Beard's "Midwestern turn" to borrow a phrase, came as cold water splashed across the face of Uncle Sam. Initially a pro-Wilson patriot as were most Americans, by the 1930s Beard began to question the president's war rhetoric and American motives. Imperialism not democracy or lasting peace seemed more likely the purpose. The evidence came from 1930s economics and Congressional committee hearings, Great Depression downturn and war-manufacturer profiteering.[42] Ferrell likely learned something of Beard's views in college textbooks at Bowling Green State University (1939–1942, 1945–1947). These interpretations changed minds and wrangled others. Another book written by the popular progressive, *President Roosevelt and the Coming of the War*, published in 1948 while Ferrell studied for his PhD again raised the hackles of any American patriotic soldier. Staff Sergeant Ferrell had joined America's efforts against the twin evils of Nazi fascism and Japanese militarism, and later, that of Soviet communism. In this case, Beard charged Roosevelt with fenagling American isolationists into war, deftly campaigning for neutrality while working behind the scenes to support the Allies and provoke Japan.[43] Ferrell's mentor, Bemis, would brush off the request of another student to write a dissertation on Beard, and the future Hoosier historian would join compatriots Schlesinger Jr. and Commager (among others) as they dismissed the radical's ideas, even as history proved many of them valid.

The culture of Madison, Wisconsin (home of the progressive school), in these years paralleled in many ways as that of Ferrell's early days near Cleveland.[44] Reforms borne of New England, German, and Scandinavian soils brought anti-slavery sentiment, strong support for public schools and workers' rights and a call for Christian charity. Academic reformers at the University of Wisconsin–Madison would attempt to address the perceived problems of genetic differences, of ethnic inferiority, and the overflow of immigration that contributed to them. Eugenics and immigration restrictions were touted as solutions. Eagle Scout Ferrell would not have found these attitudes so far from his Boy Scout training. As Brown noted, "the new social sciences presumed that discernible intellectual differences separated the races, thus justifying segregation, ethnic quotas, and the . . . colonialism in Puerto Rico, Guam, the Philippines and Hawaii."[45] Scout leaders following their organization's training manual inculcated in their troops the philosophy of G. Stanley Hall and his Child Study Movement, which promoted "recapitulation" activities that were thought to advance ("habituate") young, white males from inferior to advanced racial character traits.[46]

While Turner or Beard were coming of age as formidable figures in Americanist history circles, Allan Nevins, a journalist, found an audience for his work in nationally circulated publications such as the *New York Evening Post*, and related newspapers, the *New York World*, or *Herald*, or *Sun*, along with *New York Times Magazine* and industrialist biographies.[47] Those of his era, beginning at the height of progressivism, were caught up in the push and pull of producing a record of the past, a "new" school against an "old" that encompassed readable, morality-driven, compelling stories, filled with drama, larger-than-life personalities with agency, and preoccupations of the past relevant to the present. Nevins's approach, in some respects reflecting more the old school, underscored the nineteenth-to-twentieth-century transition of the field of history, from amateur practitioners ("nobs" as some labeled them) to university-trained and credentialed experts, from "reverential" or "romantic and literary" tales to "analytic and scientific investigations."[48] But Nevins spared no quarter rummaging through an eclectic set of archival materials to explore the past, from letters to speeches, court cases, legislative investigations, diaries, anecdotes, journals, newspapers, and oral histories."[49] *American Heritage*, a popular history magazine Nevins helped to publish in the 1950s was an exemplar of the bridge between professional and nonprofessional historians. It may have reflected as much the celebrated author's belief that history must serve to educate the public. The nuance of Ferrell fell somewhere between old and new school, hanging on to the merits of history as literature, paying tribute to the grace of Samuel Eliot Morrison's style, espousing history's democratic function, while pledging allegiance to elements of rigorous methodology, objectivity and truthful essences that were rooted in archive searches, first-hand (experiential) knowledge of what he studied, and the centrality of "national/international institutions and leaders."[50]

Nevins earned an MA in English, and as with other successful historians overlapping Ferrell's world (e.g., Arthur Schlesinger Jr., David McCullough), never found his way into a graduate history program. His training and ideological direction came partly with the tutelage of *New York Evening Post* editors William Cullen Bryant and E. L. Godkin, promoters of nineteenth-century liberalism. But Nevins's political philosophy found laissez faire and rugged-individual doctrine did not translate well to the needs of turn-of-the-century industrial or farming realities. He lauded scientific advancements and cooperative efforts, whether among labor and owners, as in the garment industry, or farmers among themselves, as more appropriate to the new era, leading to greater efficiency and productivity. Government had its role to play as well in regulating business in the public interest or providing loans to corporations to alleviate housing shortages. He also argued for the democratizing function of public universities and the press.[51] Ferrell's early brush with Nevins likely would have come in family discussions surrounding the journalist's treatment of prohibition and temperance, attitudes toward Roosevelt's handling of the Great Depression and related agricultural programs, and international relations among democratic countries facing rising dictatorships in the late 1930s. The last topic had immediate relevance to an adolescent nearing the age of military service. Nevins argued that the United States must embrace its role as a world power. Even more seductive for an avid teenage reader, young Bob may have gravitated toward Nevins's characterizations of explorers, businessman, and inventors.[52] Columbia University recognized the talents of this journalist cum historian and brought Nevins to New York in the late 1920s. Remembering Eagle Scout Ferrell's interests, one can surmise the adolescent would have found Nevins's biography of John Fremont's winning-the-West adventures laudable, surveying territories, describing natural elements such as vegetation and climate, and reporting on Native American threats. Another of his biographies, on John D. Rockefeller, a Cleveland native, would have caught the future Indiana historian's eye and guided the reader to appreciate the more noble aspects of Gilded Age titans. Nevins's biographies and editorials were punctuated by important political, economic, social, and consequently, moral issues of the day, and in contrast to Beard, he sang the praises of capitalism, business entrepreneurs, and trailblazers as in the cases of Abram Hewitt and Rockefeller. The two world wars had proved the necessity of the growth of big business to the nation's security.

William Appleman Williams continued the Wisconsin Progressive School tradition, posing threats to Ferrell's perspective in some ways while paralleling his ideological bent in others. Ferrell and Williams shared birth year (1921) and Midwest sensibilities (Ohio and Iowa, respectively) and experienced the challenges posed by unfolding events of their times: the Great Depression, the Second World War soldiering, Cold War cathartics,

McCarthyism, and Truman imposed security oaths. Yet they interpreted these events through separate lenses.[53] Williams expanded Beard's anti-imperialist thesis backward from nineteenth-century Gilded Age-industrialist to American Revolutionary elites, throwing more cold water on Ferrell's youthful nationalistic swagger. Turner's end-of-frontier concerns morphed into worries over minimal standard-of-living necessities as the yardstick that measured the potential for democracy's survival. Rather than military expansion and occupation (imposed across the American continent), the drive for free trade and global markets (cut-throat competition) to bolster domestic consumers' pocketbooks drove U.S. imperialism.

An interesting political twist to Williams's interpretation spoke to both the Left and the Right.[54] Williams promoted arguments of the New Left in his graduate-students' publication established in 1959, *Studies on the Left*; that is, issues such as income inequality; sterile suburban lifestyles; civil rights, anti-war, and campus activism; the women's movement; and imperial foreign policy/Cold War liberalism. As seen from the Left, examples of progressive reforms of the bygone era—"worker's compensation, railroad regulation, the Federal Reserve System—were initiated by a self-interested business class looking to manipulate markets, destroy competition, and undermine the labor movement."[55] The cooperative arrangements with state and local governments were merely a veneer. New Deal measures extended the logic, saving a corrupt, failing capitalistic system. Internationalism, with expanded markets, served as part of the larger corporate liberal thesis. Breadbasket conservatives, alternatively, argued that big government had squeezed local prerogative and that Americans needed to concentrate on domestic issues, not intervene in international concerns, the isolationist thread. From Ferrell's archival files, one can conclude he supported, at the least, IU students' free-speech rights and the civil rights of African Americans off campus in Bloomington.[56] Midwest populist and evangelical United Methodist Church egalitarianism surely underlay these positions. From diplomatic writings and Truman biography, one can gather his defense of the Truman Doctrine, Marshall Plan, and NATO, translated in the Indiana historian's mind to the necessity of U.S. global internationalism for security. Fighting the Nazi fascists and Stalin Communists had taught the world and the young Staff Sergeant from Lakewood, Ohio, something about ideological threats to freedom and democracy. There were right and wrong interpretations of the past and good and evil in the world in Ferrell's mind.[57]

Ferrell's perspective on the past fit more comfortably with Arthur Schlesinger Jr.'s or Richard Hofstadter's midcentury anti-intellectualism push back and rally around consensus liberalism though taking different paths getting there.[58] Schlesinger Jr.'s rise on his father's coattails, Harvard connections, and career attachment to Democratic Party politics, to Stevenson and President Kennedy, or to liberal ideology diverged from the more academic route of the others.[59] Growing up only a few hours apart, along Lake Erie, Ferrell and Hofstadter both were teenagers during the 1930s economic downturn, but their family's ethnicity and inculcation would structure the variance in initial perspectives. Hofstadter evinced a Jewish intellectualism characteristic of his family's ancestors (paternal-side Polish Jews), possessed a keen mind, and had the advantages of an open-minded and free school system in which he thrived. The future Columbia historian could not escape his immigrant identity which defined so many in the Queen City, while Ferrell was nestled comfortably in a WASPish western suburb of Cleveland, segregated from Eastern and Southern European workers recruited by industry in Lakewood's "Bird's Nest" on the other side of the tracks, only a few miles from his boyhood home.[60] While Beard's moncausal economic thesis was perceived as too simplistic to Ferrell, it was seductive to Hofstadter, but did not account for "larger ethnocultural tensions."[61] Ferrell had little use for the social sciences to enlighten the past, yet, Jews "ghettoized in the social sciences" in academia enticed Hofstadter to engage their theories.[62]

From early Buffalo college days through years as Columbia-PhD student then professor, Hofstadter, struck out on a series of zig-zag moves: communist embrace, then alienation; self-identification as an intellectual against mindless working-class masses, Marxism, or indeed against any ideological straightjacket; a student seeing past "old liberalism" to a "new liberalism," attributed to surging demographic diversity, to shared sting of Great Depression, New Deal remedies, and world war-and-beyond struggles. Hofstadter described the old liberalism as the marriage of a complex set of ideas, a myth of a dominant class that identified with WASP values, "scientific" undergirding of natural selection, individualism, property rights and laissez faire economics. Historical renderings of a string of notable figures (e.g., presidents from Jefferson to Jackson, Lincoln, Theodore Roosevelt, Hoover, among others) gave testimony to the myth. But to those labeled "consensus historians," the old liberalism had run its course in the American century.[63] Hofstadter's *Social Darwinism in American Thought* had provided the pretext to what would be the most celebrated historiographical revisionism of mid-century, according to biographer Brown; that is, *The American Political Tradition*, a pivot to "consensus liberalism." This new historiographic framework laid aside salient conflicts that structured the outdated progressive era perspective (labor versus capital and interclass and interracial warfare), amidst an era of communist threat and postcolonial appeals to nationhood. A rising affluent society, the consensus school had it, continued to believe in its democratic, egalitarian ethic.

In the 1950s, Ferrell likely would be categorized, if such were possible, as a "neoconservative," while Hofstadter possessed what Brown considered (using Neil Jumonville's criteria) a "neoconservative sensibility": willingness to critique direct democracy and mass culture; an appreciation of "complexity and ambiguity;" an embrace of meritocracy over egalitarianism; and respect for academic freedom, a diversity of ideas, and a multiethnic, immigrant-enriched society.[64] In the post-war era, anti-Communist surge and rise of McCarthy slurs, the social science disciplines, with focus on "personality types," authoritarianism (tethered with values such as efficiency, order, stability), mythic nationalist glory, the irrational over the economic, appeared to offer what archival documents could not, another twist away from the Ferrell perspective. Ferrell's typed love letters to Lila and Lou or missives to academicians highlighted his distaste for Freudian explanations and sociological frameworks. But Hofstadter, as with Columbia colleagues, pursued social-psychological dimensions to understand better the behaviors of mass followers of fascist leaders or McCarthyism. As importantly, Hofstadter's insight into the sources of America's divisiveness (rural-urban clash, move toward secularism, growing reliance on government resources and direction, Populist [rural]-Progressive [middle-class urbanite] schism, anti-Semitic-East Coast financier connection, and race- and ethnic-status-identity politics) fed into the meaning imputed by these social scientists.[65]

The 1960s strife of civil rights protests, Vietnam War rebellions, assassinations, and campus crusades would clarify priorities of men such as Hofstadter or Ferrell. Both understood the changing dynamic of college institutions infused with democratic purpose, a mix of mainstream and radical students facing off, the charge to engage debate while campuses faced threats to order and nonviolent free speech. Neither historian was willing to embrace chaos in classrooms or administrative hallways, yet both prioritized free speech with the caveat that it was not to be disruptive to learners.[66] Schlesinger Jr. barred contemporary politics from entering his classroom.[67] Certainly decades before, Hofstadter had played a role in militant campus uprisings himself as president of the University of Buffalo's National Student League, and later in civil rights marches in the South. Ferrell, while a student at Bowling Green State University, found more comfort performing at concerts, then went off to soldier against fascism, and returned a serious student, an ardent anti-communist and strong advocate of Constitutional freedoms. Hofstadter's book *The Progressive Historians* (1968) linked his circuitous evolution from a 1930s militant, to consensus, to newfound appreciation for conflict, and appeal to a historical framework that spoke to the times.

The biographical traces of Turner, Beard, Nevins, Appleman Williams, Hofstadter, or Schlesinger Jr. highlight Ferrell's world, the larger evolution of history as a profession, the conflicts among colleagues, and the challenges of his era. Comparisons to the IU historian across five dimensions boldface the characteristics of one who succeeded as scholar like few others: personal bias, advocacy for historical viewpoints, guideposts to scholarship, archival resourcefulness, and literary style. The temptation, of course, is to make more of these comparisons than they are—quick and too easy generalizations as contrasts. Beard and Appleman Williams, the first a socialist, the second, a Marxist, would differ markedly from Ferrell's personal biases and advocacy for historical viewpoints. These two Wisconsin School scholars, as Brown labeled them, along with Columbia School Hofstadter, would cast about for primary sources, purposes of history, and interdisciplinary approaches, the dreaded social science interlopers to Ferrell, and would find analytic frames or quantification, for instance, as useful to doing history as the narrative approach was to Ferrell. Nevertheless, the Jewish intellectual scholar Hofstadter promoted a liberal internationalist outlook that fit well with other liberal Democrats, Schlesinger Jr. and Ferrell. Schlesinger Jr. found too much excitement in Democratic Party circles to evince the role of conventionally defined objective historian in line with what the IU historian would approve—an imaginative crafting of the past within the boundaries of the trail of evidence. It is the similarities, Ferrell to Nevins, the journalist cum historian, where one finds perhaps the most overlap, across one could argue all five dimensions, and it is from these similarities that one traces the lineage of the Indiana historian, back to the "greats," Francis Parkman or Samuel Morison, unique to be sure in their own ways, but reflective of so much of the bright-light history that was Ferrell.

The comparisons to a small set of professional colleagues is only part of the tale, but if combined with Ferrell's own biography and critical book reviews, the picture of Buckeye-turned-Hoosier storyteller and related historiography finds more fullness. Stemming from those early years, as Eagle Scout, son of the First World War patriot, soldier in the Second World War, and avid reader of grand narratives and biography, the IU pastmaster touted the blessings of United States' involvement in twentieth-century world affairs, and painted the personalities and scenes of heroes and villains. Anglo roots, evangelical pieties, and rural family traditions proved influential in his attitudes toward the "lesser" mortals (non-WASP males), perhaps to be protected or civilized as reinforced by Boy Scout training manuals. Personal attributes that the Truman biographer shared with his Independence, Missouri-born favorite subject transformed Ferrell to apologist, even promoter, extolling the greatness of the thirty-third president, against the tide of historians. Americans, growing nostalgic after the politics of the 1960s and 1970s, smiled on Ferrell's mythological Truman (but even more on David McCullough's). Nineteenth-century, German-based Ranke training with "Wave-the-Flag" Bemis as mentor, world events—fighting against deceitful Nazis, then Communists in the age of nuclear weapons—and the stimulus of what many thought were wrong-headed radical progressive colleagues, pushed Ferrell to push back in substance and methodological diatribes.

It is fair to claim that Ferrell did not restructure historical thinking through a frontier thesis nor reinterpret the founding fathers' motives. Even professional allies appear to agree he did not bring any significant new interpretations, new schools of revisionism Ferrell might say, to topics explored. He did not share in the fortune of a young Schlesinger Jr. following in the footsteps of the father nor as an insider to Camelot politics of the age that would inflate his notoriety. Ferrell's upbringing and path through Yale would keep him far from the antidemocratic, overly critical stances toward American capitalists and American foreign policy that Beard or Appleman Williams would trailblaze. Yet the scholarship of Ferrell abounds, and the reason flows from following the literary tradition and primary source detail of other great storytellers.

NOTES

1. John Lukacs, *The Future of History* (New Haven, CT: Yale University Press, 2011), 1–5; Brown, *Beyond the Frontier*.
2. Lukacs, *The Future of History*, 143–147.
3. Ferrell, "Pearl Harbor and the Revisionists," 215; Robert H. Ferrell, "Truman Foreign Policy: A Traditionalist View," in *The Truman Period as a Research Field: A Reappraisal, 1972*, ed. Richard S. Kirkendall (Columbia: University of Missouri Press, 1974), 14–15.
4. Brown, *Beyond the Frontier*, xiii–xviii; see also Brown's discussion of racial controversy that swirled around the evolution of the Mississippi Valley Historical Association (pp. 88–100), one that found Ferrell more than likely on the anti-segregationist side, as he helped to bring its journal to Indiana University's Bloomington campus; see interoffice memo, Ferrell to IU History Department Faculty, June 1, 1962 (among other letters), files May and June, 1962, Box 18.
5. See Mark T. Gilderhus, "Founding Father: Samuel Flagg Bemis and the Study of U.S.-Latin American Relations," *Diplomatic History* 21, no. 1 (January 1997), 1–13. (Accessed May 11, 2019 at academic.oup.com.) Gilderhus labeled "Wave the Flagg" Bemis' historical approach as nationalistic, characterizing U.S. motives as legitimate: the maintenance of independence with Republican government focus, need for expansion due to Manifest Destiny, and defense of the continental Republic from security threats. His critics saw his treatment as blind to capitalist shortfalls, racist mistreatment of indigenous peoples, and problematically interventionist (e.g., Cuba, Philippines and South America,). See also Allen, "Samuel Flagg Bemis," esp. 202–205; or Boia (ed.), *Great Historians of the Modern Age*, esp. 723–724. Ferrell knew Handlin in the latter's role as editor of a biography series; see Robert H. Ferrell, *Indiana Magazine of History* 53, no. 4 (1957), 467–469, including his first Truman biography, in that series.
6. In two letters, Ferrell bragged on the democratic spirit of the nation's breadbasket region compared to the East: In the first letter, he critiqued the students at

East Coast schools for their "snobbishness" and "anti-democratic tendency," "not present in the Middle West"; in the second, he noted, "I miss Indiana quite a lot . . . I cannot go for the English snobbery, of which there is a good deal here [Yale]; this is not home, which is Ohio-Indiana." See letters to Frank [former MSC colleague], December 1, 1955, Box 43, and to [Harold] Grimm [I.U. History Department Chair], October 8, 1955, File 1, Box 43.

7. Ferrell both applauded and criticized the "popular movement for peace in the United States" leading to the adoption of the pact. He characterized the peace movement as such: they were filled with "goodness," with the most noble of intentions, yet exhibited naivete ("immature idealism") and ignorance. See Ferrell, *Peace in Their Time*, 264–265.

8. Ibid., 265.

9. David Brown identified "professional" historians Turner, Beard, C. Vann Woodward, Hofstadter, and Schlesinger Jr., as ones making the most lasting impressions on their culture, with Hofstadter ranked "the greatest" of these; see Brown, *Richard Hofstadter*, xiii–xiv.

10. See, for instance, Ferrell's critique of Beard in the *Indiana Magazine of History* 50, no. 2 (June 1954), 175–176, or of Appleman Williams' "open door" theory of U.S. foreign policy and history practice, in Ferrell, *Harry S. Truman and the Cold War Revisionists*, 3–13. Brown, *Beyond the Frontier*, 18.

11. Ferrell, "Truman Foreign Policy," 14–15; Ferrell critiqued Appleman Williams' "theory of the Open Door," that of long-standing U.S. expansionist commercial policy and its application to the origins of the Cold War, outlining and rebutting major arguments of the revisionists (e.g., Truman's shift from FDR's U.S.-Soviet policy, U.S. intervention in the USSR's Eastern European security zone, and atomic diplomacy). He concluded that despite the efforts over the years, the revisionists "have not proved a single one of their points;" see esp. pp. 23–45.

12. Robert H. Ferrell, *Indiana Magazine of History* 50, no. 2 (June 1954), 174–176; Robert H. Ferrell, *The Georgia Historical Quarterly* 71, no. 3 (Fall 1987), 553–554.

13. Ferrell appears to have gravitated toward Samuel Eliot Morison as well, categorizing Nevins, Morison, Commager, and Schlesinger Jr. as "great scholars" like those of the century past, George Bancroft or Francis Parkman, who "knew their subjects, and could write readable prose." Ferrell, *Indiana Magazine of History* 50, no. 2 (June 1954), 174. Worthy of note too is the influence on Ferrell of Morison, this through Bemis, a student of Morison, then mentor to Ferrell; see Pfitzer, *Samuel Eliot Morison's Historical World*, 229–231.

14. Letters from Ferrell to his mother during his war service reveal an active interest in book sharing; see Box 74. Historian David Edward Herold reported that "The number of biographies [of the popular variety] published annually in the United States increased during the 1920s and 30s," including Allan Nevins' Grover Cleveland. See his *A Species of Literary Lion: Essays on Morison, Freeman, Devoto, and Becker, and the Writing of History* (PhD Diss., University of Minnesota, 1973), 6.

15. Ferrell and colleagues participated in the debates surrounding Cold War revisionism well into the twenty-first century; see, for instance, Richard S. Kirkendall

(ed.) *Harry's Farewell: Interpreting and Teaching the Truman Presidency* (Columbia: University of Missouri Press, 2004), or Norman E. Saul, *The Historian* 71, no. 1 (2009), 107–108. Arnold Offner argued Cold War views that would have received a scrunched up face with crinkled nose—a stern look—from Ferrell, his mentor at IU; see Offner's *Another Such Victory*, esp. xi–xii (on Truman's parochial, nationalistic, black and white/rigid world views, and wholly inadequate leadership), or concrete examples, on atom bomb diplomacy, misperceptions of world politics or Middle East maneuvering, 108–109, 115, 123–124.

16. The present author searched JSTOR at the University of Texas-Austin using the following delimiters: Robert H. Ferrell (author), articles and reviews (peer-reviewed), history, and relevant time frames. Nearly all seventy-nine works by Ferrell that arose in the search were book reviews (1953–2002), and of course, there were plenty of reviews, in addition to these, by others focused on Ferrell's books. A search in other databases without less stringent delimiters (e.g., Academic Search Complete) revealed a trickle of other writings (and topics) but generally not of sufficient variance to outweigh the thrust and characterization of Ferrell deduced from the JSTOR collection; see, for instance, Ferrell on Merle Miller's questionable methods/characterization of Truman, in "Plain Faking?," *American Heritage* 46, no. 3 (May/June 1995); the Atom Bomb-Truman controversy, in *National Forum* 75, no. 4 (Fall 1995); on Truman and "First Cold Warrior," *American Communist History* 9, no. 3 (December 2010); on biography as anecdote to boring history, in "From the Stacks," *OAH Magazine of History* 20, no. 1 (January 2006); on the unfortunate tendency to produce overly lengthy biographies, in "The Large Book Versus the Small," *Indiana Magazine of History* 100 (December 2004), or the case against "antiheroes," in "The Villains of the 'Red Scares' of 1950s" (interestingly enough, coauthored with Peter Szatmary, a non-historian, awarded English and MFA degrees), *Phi Kappa Phi Forum* 90, no. 3 (September 2010).

17. Robert H. Ferrell, *Indiana Magazine of History* 49, no. 3 (1953), 326–328.

18. Ibid., 328.

19. Perhaps chided enough over the ensuing decades by New Left or social and cultural history colleagues or other late twentieth-century historians, Ferrell came around to view pre-1914 America as not so enchanting; see Robert H. Ferrell, "America Made E–Z," *National Review* (September 28, 1998), 60–61.

20. It is worthy to note that Ferrell concentrated most of his scholarly efforts on producing books but did write numerous articles for publications such as the *Journal of Modern History*, *The Historian*, the *Journal of American History*, and the *Indiana Magazine of History*, along with several for a wider audience.

21. A more detailed treatment of the unprofessional practices of the Beardian (and Wisconsin school/progressive) strand of revisionism came in a Ferrell article that delved more deeply into historian misconduct (and "vitriolic and angry" mis-directedness, p. 217). Violations of conventional history standards asserted include, for example, misrepresenting evidence (e.g., beliefs about Japanese intentions), uncritical use of evidence (e.g., partisan participants, inaccurate/unreliable/unauthenticated source citations, reading post-event understanding into past interpretations, oversimplification of events, and confounding/inexplicable application of sociological

theory (pp. 217–224). Ferrell goes on to elaborate a military-rooted explanation as to the cause for the surprise attack; see Ferrell, "Pearl Harbor and the Revisionists," 215–233.

22. Robert H. Ferrell, *Indiana Magazine of History* 50, no. 2 (June 1954), 175–176. For twenty-first-century writings, see Ferrell, *Harry S. Truman and Cold War Revisionists*.

23. In a particularly scathing book review, Ferrell went after the incompetence of the thesis advisor and the publisher as much as the author. The condemnation began with "It is difficult to know where to start in showing how this book could have been better. Its organization is badly at fault: too much detail, too little generalization . . . a conclusion that recapitulates the entire book. There was little understanding that the book's subject has been treated by many writers, and that the author hence should cut his detailed narrative and concentrate on a clear thesis. And that thesis, too, would have to be novel." The remainder highlights the reviewer's understanding of the topic, methods, archival sources, and the publishing world: "The documentation is at fault, for the author should have used the captured German archival material. His publisher announces that the study is 'definitive'—written without either the British or French archives! The printing of the book is poorly done, with a type face that in its boldness almost jumps off the page. There are plenty of misprints, and a fair-sized number of misspellings and grammatical lapses. The book jacket has a copied photograph from *Life Magazine* when a short trip to the top of the National Archives building would have put the author in the midst of an enormous collection of uncopyrighted photographs of the time." See *The Historian* 24, no. 1 (November 1961), 117–118.

24. Robert H. Ferrell, *Indiana Magazine of History* 53, no. 4 (1957), 467–469; Robert H. Ferrell, *The Journal of American History* 77, no. 3 (December 1990), 1110–1111; or Robert H. Ferrell, *Reviews in American History* 25, no. 3 (1997), 499–503.

25. Ferrell would take the opportunity to criticize David McCullough, the Pulitzer Prize-winning author whose Truman biography overshadowed that of the Indiana historian's; see letter to Barton J. Bernstein [History Department, Stanford University], January 25, 1999, Box 58; letter to James Grant, May 25, 2001, Box 95; letter to Charles Blankenship, August 14, 2001 (in possession of recipient).

26. *The English Historical Review* 68, no. 269 (1953), 663–664; other examples: Ferrell "hardly offers a fresh understanding," in Donald F. Drummond, *The Mississippi Valley Historical Review* 45, no. 1 (1958), 165–167; Ferrell adds nothing new, in Arthur S. Link, *Indiana Magazine of History* 54, no. 2 (1958), 193–194; Ferrell "generally goes along with current opinions among historians, in John D. Hicks, *Indiana Magazine of History* 55, no. 4 (1959), 412–413; Ferrell "covers the main issues . . . without great originality," in Arthur Schlesinger Jr., *The American Historical Review* 72, no 2 (1967), 740–741; on three of Ferrell's Truman books, he adds nothing to what is known, in Barry D. Karl, *The American Historical Review* 87, no. 2 (1982), 560–561; or Ferrell "simply reaffirm[s] the conventional portrait created by Truman and his friends and family," in Robert Griffin, *Reviews in American History* 9, no. 3 (1981), 296; "Ferrell provides no major reinterpretations of the Truman presidency," in William K. Klingaman, *The Public Historian* 7, no. 2 (1985), 82–84;

adds little to received wisdom from Truman's point of view," William E. Pemberton, *The Journal of American History* 70, no. 4 (1984), 921–922. Worthy to note also is an effort by Ferrell, perhaps, to bring a large-scale interpretive twist to United States history if it would have joined the League of Nations (a counterfactual), that is met with plenty of reasonable refutations; see William Stueck, *Pacific Historical Review* 55, no. 3 (1986), 490–491. Appleman Williams review of Ferrell the same year as Medicott's early critique may have been one of the initial head-long encounters of the 'new revisionist school'; see William Appleman Williams, *The American Historical Review* 58, no. 2 (1953), 329–331. Medicott and Appleman Williams both noted that Ferrell's work lacked the insights that John E. Stoner's earlier study on S. O. Levinson and the Pact of Paris (1942) offered. In Appleman Williams's words, "Stoner is more accurate [than Ferrell] when he points out that the question of American-Soviet relations overshadowed the issue of outlawry for both Senator Borah and Raymond Robins. Though these men supported Levinson's campaign, neither viewed it as other than a substitute for rapprochement between Washington and Moscow. This is but one of several considerations which suggest, perhaps, that the neat characterization of Borah as merely negative and isolationist is both inaccurate and misleading," 330.

27. Richard W. Leopold, *The Mississippi Valley Historical Review* 39, no. 3 (1952), 577–578.

28. Leopold, *The Mississippi Valley Historical Review*, 578; Ferrell's literary bent and talent is noted especially in his books detailing the overlapping drama of presidents, diplomacy, and war, for instance in his *Woodrow Wilson and World War I, 1917–1921*; see reviews by Gary B. Ostrower, *The Pennsylvania Magazine of History and Biography* 110, no. 2 (April 1986), 300–301, or John M. Carroll, *The Historian* 50, no. 2 (February 1988), 311.

29. Ferrell (ed.), *Off the Record*, 7. Ferrell's Truman books include edited volumes (*Off the Record*, 1980; *The Autobiography*, 1980; *Dear Bess*, 1983 [a best seller]; *Truman in the White House*, 1991; *Harry S. Truman and the Bomb*, 1996), and authored books (*Harry S. Truman and the Modern American Presidency*, 1983; *Truman: A Centenary Remembrance*, 1984; *Harry S. Truman: Life on the Farm*, 1991; *Harry S. Truman: A Life*, 1994; *Choosing Truman*, 1994; *Truman and Pendergast*, 1999; *Harry S. Truman (American Press Reference Series)*, 2003; *Harry S. Truman and Cold War Revisionists*, 2006; *Presidential Leadership*, 2006).

30. See, perhaps as "bookends," his *Harry S. Truman and the Modern American Presidency*, esp. p. 191, and *Presidential Leadership*, esp. pp. 134–135.

31. Robert Griffith, *Reviews in American History* 9, no. 3 (September 1981), 295–306; Donald R. McCoy, *The American Historical Review* 88, no. 5 (1983), 1344–1345; William Pemberton, *The Journal of American History* 70, no. 4 (March 1984), 921–922; Richard Lowitt, *Indiana Magazine of History* 79, no. 4 (1983), 358–359; John M. Carroll, *The Register of the Kentucky Historical Society* 80, no. 3 (Summer 1982), 356–358. Gerald D. Nash, *Illinois Historical Journal* 77, no. 4 (1984), 309–310; *The American Historical Review* 87, no. 2 (April 1982), 560–561; Karl Barry, *The American Historical Review*.

32. As summary, Griffith wrote: "It was this central tension between the local and the national, the traditional and the modern, the provincial and the metropolitan—and

not just the conflict of liberal and conservative, Democrat and Republican, northerner and southerner, or president and congress—which defined the Truman presidency. It was a tension which Truman himself never fully mastered. On the one hand his personal insecurities were reinforced by the received culture of modern America, which counseled deference to the values of education, status and hierarchical authority. On the other hand his personal resentments were sustained by the commonsensical and anti- modernist values of an older and very different America." See *Review in American History* 9, no. 3 (September 1981), 305.

33. In 1985, nearing official retirement, Ferrell's *Woodrow Wilson and World War I, 1917–1921*, was published; other books followed, which prompted more reviews. Meaty examples of book reviews cited here continue to be illustrative (with few exceptions) under the five descriptions that define his historian identity characterized by colleagues in earlier reviews. More adjectives might be added to 'his personal bias' or 'advocacy for historical viewpoints' such as ethnocentric, traditionalist (e.g., focus on politics, diplomacy, and military), internationalist. See, for instance, on Ferrell's Woodrow Wilson book: William Stueck, *Pacific Historical Review* 55, no. 3 (August 1986), 490–491; Ostrower, *The Pennsylvania Magazine of History and Biography* 110, no. 2 (April 1986), 300–301; John M. Carroll, *The Historian* 50, no. 2 (February 1988), 311; John M. Mulder, *The Register of the Kentucky Historical Society* 84, no. 3 (Summer 1986), 332–333; see also reviews on other Ferrell presidential books (e.g., *The Strange Deaths of President Harding* [1996] or *The Dying President* [1998]), respectively; David W. Levy, *Illinois Historical Journal* 90, no. 3 (Autumn 1997), 222–223; and Judy Barrett Litoff, *The Register of the Kentucky Historical Society* 96, no. 2 (Spring 1998), 209–211.

34. Brown, *Beyond the Frontier*, xvii. Recounting the Midwestern school of progressivism in this chapter draws extensively on Brown's work.

35. Numerous examples of interdisciplinary history are detailed in the discussion of American historians who theorized "a stage model" of the revolutionary process in 1938, underscoring "bottom up" as well as top-down stories, or investigated British economy modeling (1949), or studied *Ante Bellum* South slavery economics (1958), among others; see Landes and Tilly (eds.), *History as Social Science*, 7–19.

36. Brown, *Beyond the Frontier*, 54.

37. Ibid., 56.

38. Landes and Tilly (eds.), *History as Social Science*, 7–19; Ferrell's former students cum twentieth-to-twenty-first-century professors have written on these struggles, in *Presidents, Diplomats, and Other Mortals*, esp. Wilson, "Introduction" or p. 168; Ferrell characterized himself in "the tradition of the great historian Leopold von Ranke" with "the task of trying to capture the past as it really was," but with the caveat that that is not entirely possible. See Ferrell, *Harry S. Truman and the Cold World Revisionists*, 35.

39. *Indiana Magazine of History* 59, no. 4 (December 1963). See also Ferrell's disparaging remarks toward sociologist George Lundberg for applying social science to international affairs, especially his plunging into "a morass of sociological definitions," attached to concepts such as "security," negative emotional conditioning, or "principles of human ecology and sociology." Ferrell shared that Lundberg's strategy

permitted rigged arguments "under the guise of science," all for naught; see Ferrell's "Pearl Harbor and the Revisionists," 222–223. Perhaps it is worth noting here Ferrell's inconsistency, using social science in his book reviews and praising Schlesinger Jr.'s "cycles of American history," a recurring pattern of American politics; see for example, Robert H. Ferrell, *Indiana Magazine of History* 53, no. 4 (1957); and on Stalin's "personality disorder," Robert H. Ferrell, *American Historical Review* 72, no. 2 (1967), and on Schlesinger Jr., Ferrell, *The Georgia Historical Quarterly* (Fall 1987), 553.

40. See, for instance, Robert H. Ferrell, *The American Historical Review* 69, no. 4 (July 1964), 1084; also Ferrell willing to make generalizations (i.e., draw conclusions)—domestic concerns pushed global concerns aside, or capitalists lost virtue while fascists/communists went their way, or morality lost out to nationalism, in Fred L. Rippy, *The Journal of Modern History* 30, no. 2 (June 1958), 165.

41. Ferrell, *Harry S. Truman and the Cold War Revisionists*, 40–43; see also Robert H. Ferrell, "Looking Back: The Truman Books," *Indiana Magazine of History* 92, no. 2 (June 1996), 168–169; Ferrell, "Truman Foreign Policy," 29–31. For the broad scope of arguments surrounding numbers and Truman's bomb decision, see Richard B. Frank, "President Harry S. Truman's Farewell Address and the Atomic Bomb: The High Price of Secrecy" (105–142), in Kirkendall (ed.), *Harry's Farewell*, esp. pp. 129–134.

42. Brown, *Beyond the Frontier*, 59–61.

43. Robert H. Ferrell, *Indiana Magazine of History* 50, no. 2 (June 1954), 176; Brown, *Beyond the Frontier*, 56.

44. Ibid., 21–24.

45. Ibid., 23.

46. Benjamin Rene Jordan, *Modern Manhood and the Boy Scouts of America: Citizenship, Race, and the Environment, 1910–1930* (PhD Diss., University of California San Diego, 2009), 71.

47. Gerald L. Fetner, *Immersed in Great Affairs: Allan Nevins and the Heroic Age of American* History (Albany: State University of New York Press, 2004), 115, 122, 128. Fetner's work underlies the majority of the Nevins' biography discussed in this section.

48. Fetner has written of Nevins' skepticism toward the university-trained focus on "monographs . . . conveying a thesis supported by facts rather than telling a story;" and more, "training seeking to develop a more objective approach . . . [a] trust only to government and administrative materials." Fetner, *Immersed in Great Affairs*, 45–46, 49.

49. Ibid., 79, 121, 162.

50. On the emergence of universities as "the primary gatekeepers" of the twentieth-century history profession, see Brown, *Richard Hofstadter*, 5–6. A student of Ferrell's wrote, "the 'Ferrell Approach' begins with the passionate conviction that the study of history offers . . . an understanding of how and why the society and world in which we live came to be . . . and [that conviction] leads to . . . writing history . . . for a broad general readership. And, of course, *that* conviction . . . leads to . . . the primacy of the historical narrative as the methodology by which these aims are best

realized" (Wilson, "Introduction," 3); Samuel Eliot Morison's efforts are described as an exemplar, as a play on the title of his book suggests, historian as a literary artist; see Wilson, "Introduction," 4–5; see also descriptions of Francis Parkman's and Morison's writings to educate or to stimulate and please, or from first-hand experiences and deep archive searches as precursors to doing history well, in Herold, *A Species of Literary Lion*, 5, 15–16, 24–28, 36–38.

51. Fetner, *Immersed in Great Affairs*, 26–29.

52. According to A. Lovell Elliot, Ferrell's childhood friend, unlike his active brother Ernie (June) Ferrell Jr., young Bob would retreat to read and play the piano during Elliot's visits. Telephone interview with the author, September 2018. Richard Sandomir wrote, once Ferrell returned from serving in the war, "he began to read the work of historians like Arthur M. Schlesinger Sr., Allan Nevins and Ida Tarbell." See "Robert H. Ferrell, 97, Truman Authority Inspired by Diaries, Dies," *New York Times*, August 22, 2018. Fetner stated that, "[d]uring the 1920s, bookshelves began to be filled by an arsenal of biographies, some scholarly, some popular, some debunking." And "the academic community responded favorably to this development [by] creating courses in biography and in a few cases even departments," see his *Immersed in Great Affairs*, 67.

53. Appleman Williams received a Purple Heart for service in the Second World War, but unlike Ferrell, found the experience "intellectually and emotionally" repulsive; a self-described Marxist, he "stressed social alienation" and "endless wars" as products of destabilizing markets and "capitalist individualism." Imperialism and its attendant problems replaced and reinterpreted the logic of the frontier. See Brown, *Beyond the Frontier*, 137.

54. Ibid., 111, 122–123, 141.

55. Ibid., 122.

56. Ferrell wrote to support an editorial writer who had denounced the poor treatment of "colored university students" at a local roller rink. See letter to Fred H. Gregory, July 26, 1962, Box 18.

57. Letter to Stephen Kertesz, June 23, 1953, Box 44; letter to Ferrell from Kertesz, July 3, 1953, Box 44.

58. Discussion of Richard Hofstadter relies extensively on Brown, *Richard Hofstadter*.

59. See Aldous, *Schesinger*.

60. Ferrell's orientation likely had more in common with Brown University historian Carl Bridenbaugh who delivered the presidential address to the American Historical Association in 1962, emphasizing the unfortunate shift in the history profession, refashioning the craft toward "dehumanizing methods," of "social scientific history written by scholars coming from ethnic backgrounds," and away from the profession's "uplifting," "Yankee, literary roots." See Brown, *Richard Hofstadter*, 134.

61. Ibid., 17.

62. Ibid., 73. See also Brown's discussion of the impact of Theodor Adorno/authoritarian personality, Max Weber/status politics, Karl Mannheim/social positioning and perception, Robert Merton/latent function, and Kevin MacDonald/individual psyche; ibid., 90–93.

63. Ibid., chapter 3; Brown noted, "The Wasp worldview, described by Hofstadter as isolationist, individualistic, nationalistic, and capitalistic, broke before a sharp cultural realignment shaped by demographic change, depression, and war. As practiced by Hofstadter, consensus history was the product of multiple traditions." Ibid., 54. Consensus history or consensus historians, as discussed by Jumonville, has more fissures than some have attributed to it; see Jumonville, *Henry Steele Commager*, esp. 206–209. See also Pfitzer, *Samuel Eliot Morison's Historical World*, 229: In line with "a conspirational theory, "rooted in the distrust of the Soviets, "consensus historians" pressed to "reaffirm the unanimity of democratic values and to pursue a vigorous anticommunist crusade against those who would challenge the hegemony of those values in their histories. The anticommunist crusade took many forms within the profession."

64. Ibid., 88. Ferrell supported several dimensions of what Brown highlights in Neil Jumonville's 1950s-era "neoconservativism" (or liberalism): strongly anti-Communist, generally unsympathetic to American critique, suspicious (more than fearful) of democratic masses and direct democracy, sensitive to societal complexity (though not so much for its ambiguity), and a nod to meritocracy, even as defined in Harry Truman's rise to prominence. For example, see Ferrell's cautious attitude against the democratic uprising in Gamal Abdel Nasser's Egypt; letter to Bill, February 22, 1959, File 1, Box 72.

65. The discussion of this is in Brown's description of Richard Hofstadter's *Age of Reform*, in *Richard Hofstadter*, Chapter Five.

66. See, for instance, Ferrell's advertisement submission ("An Open Letter to the University Community") to the *Indiana Daily Student* [newspaper] that argued IU has a responsibility to uphold free speech in a democratic society, this in connection to the behavior exhibited against a student protest regarding Cuba-U.S. relations, circa Fall 1962, Box 18; Brown, *Richard Hofstadter*, 180–181, 184–186.

67. Aldous, *Schlesinger*, 126.

Chapter 6

Then and Now

> *Well-written history is still being produced (and will be produced) by professional historians. More well-written history is, and will be, produced by 'amateur,' that is, nonprofessional historians.*
>
> —John Lukacs, *The Future of History* (New Haven, CT: Yale University Press, 2011), 90

I wrote this book for several purposes. First, I wanted to understand how a successful historian, Robert Ferrell, approached the past, and consequently, to evaluate his work against that of emerging conceptions of the field. Another thrust was to explore how Ferrell's experience, scholarship, and professional approach fit in with the evolution of professional practice among more celebrated pastmasters during his lifetime. On a more personal level, I was interested in learning something about Ferrell's life, exploring archival sources of his own making, interviewing those who knew him, so I could understand better who he was, and in turn, how that might inform his craft and topical orientation. I had benefited, as had so many others, from his mentoring, but in all those office visits and personal conversations, he always turned the focus to my life, and perhaps not surprisingly, kept his muted. It was a seductive puzzle to solve, taking a look behind the admired-mentor's public persona, to uncover what made him who he was.[1] I also came to the investigation to learn more about what historians describe as their task, as a collective group, from historians of history, so that my understanding of Ferrell could be situated among other historians, a sort of historiography of historians of the Ferrell era. As I came to know my former IU history professor and his work better, I realized how his path could inform and be informed by that of history programs and their graduates. With Lukacs's words in mind, perhaps this history of Ferrell will find some value for future historians in-training or nonhistorians who are interested in the world of successful history making and personal intrigue.

In an IU Oral History project interview, conducted decades ago, Ferrell himself guided this investigation. He recommended that students of history explore the archives.[2] So, I dove into his archived papers at the Lilly Library in Bloomington at Indiana University, with an eye toward telling something of his story, discovering strands as they arose from the documents, seeking historical puzzles to answer. Several topics were easily noticeable, and admittedly the peculiar aspects caught my attention, his letters from the war, the mixed bag of academic achievements, and those matrimonial courting missives. Just as Ferrell had coached, stories sprouted with perceivable beginnings, middles, and endings from his archived papers. Of course, as Gordon Leff has noted, Ferrell's "history [was] made intelligible by periodizing it into epochs and grouping its events into categories . . . social wholes."[3] In 1940s American society, the Second World War experience is just such a "whole." The future Indiana scholar gaining admission to an Ivy League graduate program near mid-century as an aspiring academic is another. The matrimonial courting ritual for American unwed adults is also a recognizable "social whole."

Did I find among Ferrell's ideas any new frontier thesis, new ways of structuring how historians might think about topics or eras? There was no Arthur Schlesinger Jr. cycles-of-history, no Richard Hofstadter consensus narrative, no William Appleman Williams centuries-long-imperialist-America quest equivalences. Even accounting for his decades of focus, Ferrell made little headway among colleagues arguing for President Truman's greatness, though he made a strong case for Truman as the architect of post–Second World War containment. What one finds in the professor's papers (and writings generally), however, are wonderful stories, written with flair, with fascinating new details that have informed what was already known, material that a current IU historian described as "inherently interesting," and that a former IU student, successful biographer, and life-long confidant found delightfully "surprising."[4] Ferrell's twenty-first century thesis that General MacArthur built his career on a lie, described in the book, *The Question of MacArthur's Reputation*, no doubt has raised eyebrows.[5] Beyond the aphorism, the devil is in the details (and one might add archives), Ferrell knew, of course, that that is where the most attractive (descriptive) story can be found, or the best understanding, or where one finds the most enjoyment. A former journalist, now historian, at the IU professor's alma mater noted that the detailed storylines I shared of the Buckeye-turned Hoosier's life "reads much like a good novel."[6]

It is worth noting that contemporary efforts by historians to redefine "historical scholarship at its best" easily could have applied to celebrated features of Ferrell's efforts, aside from quantity of books published or intriguing tales of personal life.⁷ For example, the American Historical Association's (AHA) Ad Hoc Committee on Redefining Scholarly Work noted, "A fuller conception of scholarship might properly include bringing together old and new knowledge in a fresh narrative or perhaps in another form of presentation designed to reach a public audience." A constant archival archeologist, Ferrell mixed old with new on a regular basis. He also served the United States Department of State in editing foreign affairs volumes for public and scholarly consumption.⁸ His work on behalf of the American diplomatic and foreign policy community found him offering advice to policy makers as well, another mark of new thinking on what should count ("to bring historical scholarship to bear directly on policy issues"), according to the historical association's expanded recognition of accomplishment. The AHA committee added that scholarship should also be broadened to include creating "effective educational materials, whether for the college level or for K–12." As already discussed at length, Ferrell and colleagues teamed up to deliver curriculum across Indiana high schools (creating book lists too to aid school librarians). Even beyond his official years at Indiana University, the distinguished octogenarian-historian participated with others to refine interpretations and teaching of the Truman presidency into the new millennium.⁹

Beyond the efforts of professional organizations, historians have identified qualifications that make for outstanding practitioners, even "superhistorians," across time. While it is as inappropriate as anachronistic to discuss the qualities of bright lights such as Herodotus, Thucydides, Augustine, Voltaire, and so forth, as touchstones for Ferrell's era and contemporaries, a search for his name in book discussions of highly regarded United States-Americanist historians of the twentieth century, resulted in two mentions: the first time, as the IU scholar elaborated the accomplishments of historian C. Van Woodward, and the second, as understudy to highly celebrated mentor, Samuel Flagg Bemis.¹⁰ Bemis earned the title "founder of the study of [American] diplomatic history" (the best symbol of the "twentieth-century American school of multiarchival international history"), published dozens of books and significant articles, and won Pulitzer Prizes for history (Pinckney's Treaty), and decades later for biography (the two-volume *John Quincy Adams*), and authored a widely adopted textbook on American diplomacy.¹¹ He also served as AHA president. It is through Bemis, no doubt, that Ferrell became a convert to the sanctity of archives and gained access to Washington's diplomatic community. As with Bemis, Woodward's books also earned prizes, Pulitzer and Bancroft. He reinterpreted Southern history partly as apologist, comparing it to other "American Plantations" and northern disingenuousness, and served as president of three top historical associations, AHA, OAH, and Southern Historical Association. W. E. B. Du Bois, a "superhistorian," according to John Barker, took Ferrell's understanding of Ranke training and

Woodward's ideas on racism a different direction.[12] Frustrated by an immovable majority white culture toward his dispassionate and lucid arguments, data, and truths about the long history of inhumane and inequitable treatment of his race, Du Bois became an advocate, even propagandist, putting aside conventional standards of historical and social science objectivity. Thus, according to Barker, he qualifies as a superhistorian based on his influence on others through persuasion and organization (e.g., Niagara Movement/ NAACP, *The Crisis* editor) and the provision of an alternative interpretation to Eurocentric-shaped American history that ignored "the most brutal American experience." Moreover, while boosting the self-image of African Americans, he simultaneously projected that "the roots of whites and blacks could not be separated"; that is, they shared a common appeal to American ideals.[13] Du Bois's orientation became the prototype for other marginalized groups, American and otherwise.

Historians blaze trails in such unique ways it is difficult to measure Ferrell against notable colleagues, Bemis, Woodward, or Du Bois. Others crafting the past have achieved wide-spread recognition based on an explicit set of criteria. In the late 1990s, a group of twenty-five historians (as described by Robert Allen Rutland) chose twelve "leading historians of American history" active since the end of the Second World War on the basis of "the quality (not volume)" of their work, their impact in their subareas, "undergraduate and graduate teaching" effect, public-oriented accomplishments, and worthy personality traits.[14] Nearly all had also "broken new ground." Students of American history likely would recognize a majority of the names: Bernard Bailyn, John Hope Franklin, Gerda Lerner, Howard Roberts Lamar, David Potter, Edmund Morgan, among others discussed earlier. Ferrell did not make the list nor would he be found among those historians who "barely fell short," ten more, including Oscar Handlin who shared the IU-Truman-biographer's Cold War revisionist complaints and edited Ferrell's 1983 Truman book for The Library of American Biography. Another effort to identify worthy United States-Americanists, admittedly with the qualifiers that they be Americans who wrote on United States history and have been active within the past hundred years, settled on thirteen, again with no Ferrell.[15] (To be fair, the IU historian had only 16 years of experience at the time of selection.) Not surprisingly, there was some overlap with those identified by Rutland's group, for example, Hofstadter, Potter, Schlesinger Jr., and Woodward. It is true that in regard to those not making the cut, the jurors underscored the difficulties of being comprehensive, but here again, others considered second benchers did not include the Hoosier pastmaster. The criteria in this case included: "weight of authorship" (substance of high quality and impact); "influence," either as inspiration to other researchers or with interpretations; and "representativeness"—shaping historiographical development.[16]

It is perhaps no surprise, with the book-review critics of Ferrell in mind, to understand why he was not recognized on these lists. No doubt one prominent factor was an often repeated theme, that he "hardly offers a fresh understanding," or "generally goes along with current opinions of historians," or "covers the main issues . . . without great originality." A related issue is the duplication found in his publications (e.g., the arguments for Truman's greatness or his organizational talent or savvy vice-presidential jockeying or counterarguments against Cold War revisionism and related subthemes). One can see an extreme case in regard to several of these repetitions among various Ferrell books that run decades apart.[17] Yet, there are reasons, with criteria of his colleagues in mind, that he might be considered more worthy aside from publications. He was a cofounder of the Society for Historians of American Foreign Relations. He applied lessons from scholarship to problems for public purposes in widely diverse settings (e.g., foreign affairs and public schools). He influenced the research agenda and publication success for dozens of new historians, both at Indiana University and elsewhere. Based on IU Alumni feedback, his influence flowed well beyond history scholarship too, improving the communication skills of countless undergraduate (and graduate) students completing his courses, with plenty of marked up papers to prove his devotion. Ferrell also did not hesitate to fight for just causes regardless of unpopularity or powerful opponents. Importantly, the Hoosier scholar had formidable talent for archival research and literary skill, and this had much to do with the publication of so many books. A wonderful example is that Truman Library archival find (PFS Box 333) while investigating Truman's Great War experience, which led to the discovery of diary entries, personal letters, memoranda, and so forth. This and more helped Truman's most prolific biographer produce fourteen books, including the best seller, *Dear Bess*.

Ferrell's scholarship and personal life, or better said, the traces of these left behind, including post-retirement-oral-interview reflections, are useful material in regard to contemporary disciplinary subfields. Assaying twenty-first-century "new approaches" to history, one can identify the difficulty of recovering what happened in Ferrell's experiences and/or in evaluating his scholarship.[18] The extant interviews with him recount episodes that underscore contemporary struggles with "memory as history," for example, that of his Second World War service and mainstream accounts or how he gained acceptance to Yale. New paths in gender history contrast with Ferrell's scholarship on presidential wives, their lives, aside from focus on husbands. The IU professor's personal life also lends itself to analysis of mid-twentieth century and after perspectives on women in private, public, even professional historian roles. Another example, his diplomatic textbook narratives provide gist for current-day contrasts to postcolonial scholars.

Memory studies informs Ferrell's personal and professional story.[19] In two oral interviews, the IU historian shared that his memory of turning to the study of history as a career was marked simply by cycling out to the Egyptian pyramids during his service in the Second World War. Another of these oral recollections tied his acceptance to the History graduate program at Yale to the singular fact that its faculty was looking for someone west of the Hudson, and he just happened to be the one.[20] Yet analyzing documents closer to those decision points, both of his making and otherwise, and consulting secondary literature, suggests a more extensive set of considerations as to what may have happened in both cases. His latter-day utterances do not capture the complexity nor very likely the realities at the time of those significant life events (see chapter 1).

Historian Geoffrey Cubitt outlines three assumptions that help to define memory studies, all of which have some bearing on these Ferrell remembrances: how one makes use of the past, how the past evokes an identity, and how one selectively remembers.[21] Ferrell's entrance to Yale is puzzling in part because there are conflicting possible storylines, some of which are less worthy of celebration. By the time of the interviews (long after a successful career at IU), he is at a point, as a well-respected historian, that does not require proving his status. This was not always the case, as we noticed when he argued for appointment to the Army Reserves four decades before. Thus, his memory of getting into Yale may signify an opportunity to portray himself as perhaps not quite deserving, either from an attempt to paint a modest identity or as a way to gloss over the actual factors, perhaps causing some uneasiness in the telling, that put him there (e.g., early poor marks in history, a Music Education focus, alumni advantage, male and WASP attributes [Yale as male-only], the Second World War soldiering and GI bill, patriotic zeal and overlapping rural experience with Samuel Flagg Bemis, his eventual mentor). His path to a history career as "told" in extant archival documents cannot be reduced to pyramid-cycling trips, especially as one examines his letters from the war. What he is more sure of during the 1940s (pre-career) is that he did not want to continue with Music Education: It did not fit with Ferrell's emerging identity, with what he knew of those who pursued that career choice and with the problematic situational factors that one found teaching music in public schools. Pursuing a graduate degree, Ferrell wrote his parents would lead to better opportunities and job security, and history was only one of several disciplines he considered.[22] The disjuncture between Ferrell's memories and how chroniclers might share his history based on archival and secondary sources helps one to understand how history can be distinguished from memory.[23]

Ferrell's private and professional world intersected with another emerging area of history, women and gender studies.[24] For the greatest part of his time in Bloomington, the Indiana historian was mystified that either topic could be a legitimate target of chroniclers of the past, whether the subjects were defined as a type of social history or an analytic perspective "that focuses on the ways that relationships between women and men have been constructed through language . . . [and] social practices."[25] Chapters 1, 2, and 5 in the present volume characterize how Ferrell responded to history-profession "rebels" that introduced socially constructed realities, social and cultural histories, and postmodernism against his traditionalist approach, including elite, top-down, and male-centered. The fact that gender history came intermixed with narratives of marginalized groups and Marxist baggage (ideological, philosophical/teleological, social science interdisciplinary) also left him cold. He may have grown up in the vortex of Midwest progressivism, but his ideology overlapped as much with what David S. Brown labeled the Columbia School of liberalism—anti-Communist, pro-capitalist, pro-American democratic patriotism and international liberalism, with a cautious eye toward the intelligence or ability of the democratic masses.[26]

Chapter 2 incorporated a good bit of Ferrell's attitudes toward women, role expectations for a wife (and others), and complications that the social sciences were creating for his Rankean notion of history and interactions with professional women as romantic partners. Though likely, heavily influenced by his father Ernest Sr.'s patriarchal attitudes toward family (along with the norms of the 1930s through the 1970s, at least), parallel Boy Scout inculcation, and Second World War experiences, and dominant ideology among his colleagues, Ferrell could not ignore other exemplars of womanhood in his early years, those that could not be categorized as inferior or reflective of the Victorian era (housewife and mother, with dominant husband and father).[27] Historian Joanna Alberti has identified the conflicting expectations for women among women and men in gender studies.[28] The females in Ferrell's maternal ancestor's lineage attended college, taught school, and achieved professional status as medical doctors. A close aunt, Ocie (Rentsch) Brown, earned a master's degree in history. Thus, the Indiana historian knew something of the professional service and achievement of the opposite sex (if not the less static gendered characterizations that came later—masculinity to femininity)—long before historian Laura Lee Downs marks the history subfield's emergence in the late 1960s growing from the second-wave of feminist militancy.[29]

For the most part, Ferrell fit in with United States-Americanists, in primarily male-dominated professional organizations and departments of history that dismissed women's history (or "herstory") and women as historians, until the feminist movement overcame societal resistance in other spheres.[30] The minute subset of family examples surrounding him hardly overcame the conscious reality women faced, for example, limitations on social and professional roles. It is worthy to note that Ferrell's aunt, mother, cousin, wife, and daughter all chose careers in teaching or social work, a not uncommon path for females working outside the home. The challenge to Ferrell of social worker professionalization during courtship provided some degree of discomfort to the historian-as-suitor, both personally and within his career (i.e., social science/interdisciplinary confusion; potential mates and their training in just what he found wanting in [or conflating] his discipline). Later he would face women coming to IU's history department and exploring gender as a focus, an abhorrent thought to what he considered legitimate history.[31]

What may be of greater import here to new millennium women and gender historians generally is the potential to revisit archival material relevant to Ferrell's scholarship, for example, Harry Truman's relationship with wife Bess (or daughter) in all those letters.[32] According to the IU biographer's interpretation of the president's missives, "The birth of daughter Margaret in 1924 was, next to marriage to Bess, the most important event in Harry Truman's life."[33] In this context, one might investigate why Truman was so fearful that "Margie" (or Marg or Marger) "would lose her small-town simplicity and openness," and more importantly, what meaning that had for him (and men) and his daughter (and women) at the time? Would this have been a fear of a father toward a new-born son? Of course, Truman was a relative unknown at the time, and not too accomplished, when Margaret arrived, and as Truman climbed in political status, Ferrell noted that the letters to Bess "increased to flood proportions," and therein lies another interesting dynamic, a husband and wife relationship that had to negotiate (and renegotiate) the career fortunes of a spouse over time.[34] Bess ("the Boss" as Harry would describe her) would remain in Independence through much of President Truman's time in the White House. The corpus of some 1,200 letters likely would be of great interest to gender historians who are drawn to the evolution of women coming of age from early to the latter half of the twentieth century.[35]

Traditionalist scholars in the latter half of the twentieth century found themselves pushed to engage the interdisciplinary nature of history regarding gender with other emerging subfields. Historian Rochona Majumdar summarized "the conceptional foundations of postcolonial history," with several crossing into discussions of race and gender.[36] Ferrell had established himself as a leader in the field of American diplomacy and foreign relations in the midst of the decolonizing movements of the 1960s and would not have found much of the terrain unfamiliar, as his top selling textbook suggested, exploring imperialism, nationalism, empires, nation-states and post-war superimposed boundaries.[37] These ideas were all part of colonial-empire builders imposed divisions on peoples not quite fitting together, the result often connected with wars and markets. Before engaging too forceful a critique, however, it is useful to remember that a young Bob Ferrell grew up tutored in the widely accepted notions of hierarchal race classifications (advanced versus savage civilizations or cultures, or Eurocentric-cum-U.S.-American worldviews).[38] Nevertheless, a telling example from the Hoosier diplomatic historian's analysis of "the heritage" of the Vietnam conflict provides something of the culturally dominant flavor of his times: "The government of France, nearly a century ago, entered the Far East at a time when imperialism was not a dirty word. The French nation . . . thought that some *gloire* might be available outside France and even outside Europe."[39] Not a dirty word for whom?, the postcolonial researcher might query. What, in fact, would the Vietnamese have thought? The answer to many became all too clear by the late 1960s, yet Ferrell was unwilling to join with AHA colleagues in condemning American involvement in the Vietnam War.[40] The newer breed of postcolonialism scholarship set in contrast to this includes redefining (or overturning) earlier accepted versions of reality, even cherished abstractions that focus on nation-states to the exclusion of broader global characterizations. Ferrell would likely have had little regard for the "pluralities of historical interpretations."[41] But recognizing this and analyzing his accounts of colonization (e.g., the Philippines, Korea, Vietnam) place in relief interpretations of postcolonialism and the new imperial history.[42] Aside from scholarship, if we reflect on his thoughts while in India during the Second World War, for instance, as recounted in the local newspaper (see chapter 1), one can use his description of veils worn by women (and of other cultural artifacts) within the context of postcolonialism debates, as described by Majumdar (e.g., nationalist discourse and gender or gender and the clash of civilizations).[43] This case of looking back is not, of course, an effort to correct Ferrell, but to place his accounts in their context, to see the historian and his interpretations as time, place, and culture specific.

Regardless of current debates in the discipline and their intersection with Ferrell's work, or his status among other high achievers in the profession, the Hoosier storyteller added a richness to historical narrative that endeared him to colleagues, students, and history-loving readers generally, those who enjoy stories for all their unpredictable twists and turns, personalities, and anecdotes. A review of several examples from his decades-long widely adopted textbook rounds out what is now understood about the Ferrell approach. In one anecdote, Ferrell noted that amidst the post–Second World War imbroglio over Middle East oil and have-and-have-not national antagonisms, "It was so easy to poke fun at Middle Easterners, especially Egyptians." When the American Ambassador in Cairo queried "his senior military attache to tell him the size and strength of the army of one of the smaller countries, the answer was that 'they have about five thousand men under arms, about half of them are usually absent without leave, and the other half are looking for them. When they find them they change places.'"[44] Ferrell found another bit of humor, decidedly pro-Western, arising out of the 1948–1949 Berlin airlift crisis: "American commandant, Brigadier General Frank L. Howley . . . recounted the Russian difficulty in constructing a war memorial at Pankow during the blockade. The Soviets had contracted to a West German builder for a large statue of Lenin, and the German thoughtfully sent over all the material except Lenin's head, which he kept as security until he should receive payment." The German builder demanded payment in the more valued West marks; the Russians wanted to pay in East marks. The Russian general pressed for the head, as the unveiling was to take place the following week: "we must have the head!" Too bad, came Howley's reply. "The Russians paid in West marks."[45]

Then, flipping back in time, Ferrell described the troubled country just to the South, this during the Mexican Revolution, and all those transition leaders coming after President Porfirio Diaz, first Francisco Madero, next Victoriano Huerta, then Venustiano Carranza, each with peculiarities ably described. But Madero's is sufficient to make the point of the author's skills.[46] Madero was a "dreamer," and finding "himself doodling on a pad of paper . . . psychic forces began to move the pencil which inscribed in firm letters, 'Love God above all things and thy neighbor as thyself.'" After some experimentation with "spirit writing," "he got in touch with the great minds of the past who helped . . . [him begin] to write excellent essays." From this came the belief "that he was the chosen instrument to regenerate Mexico." The lunacy continued, as Ferrell told it. Upon meeting with the American ambassador to Mexico, Madero "placed a third chair in the circle and announced to the ambassador that a friend was sitting there. The friend was invisible, Madero explained, but there nonetheless." These insights, and hundreds perhaps thousands more, underscore the most cherished gift of historian Ferrell, wonderful stories with intriguing personalities tied to significant events, written with uncanny wit, humor, irony, and impact.

NOTES

1. Several former students wrote obituaries of Ferrell. See, for example, James Grant, "Robert H. Ferrell, a Historian of Breadth and Clarity," *New York Times* (August 17, 2018); Emmett Tyrrell Jr., "Death of a Historian, Robert H. Ferrell," *The Washington Times* (August 21, 2018).

2. Interview with Robert H. Ferrell, conducted by Glenn, transcript p. 42, November 3, 1994, IUOralHistory.

3. Gordon Leff, *History and Social Theory* (Tuscaloosa: University of Alabama, 1969), 4.

4. Email, Professor Eric Sandweiss to author, October 10, 2018; email, Louis Galambos to author, March 31, 2019. Email, Jim Grant to author, August 16, 2018.

BGSU historian Michael Brooks noted that Ferrell's world is "a fascinating read"; email to author, December 17, 2018; with an interesting twist, the Director of the Herbert Hoover Presidential Library wrote to Ferrell, "Thank you so much for your wonderful letter! I swear, you write the best damn letters—always full of good information." See letter to Ferrell from Timothy Walsh, January 26, 2001, File December 2001–February 2002, Box 97.

5. Robert H. Ferrell, *The Question of MacArthur's Reputation: Cote de Chatillon* (Columbia: University of Missouri Press, 2008), Chapter Five.

6. Michael Brooks to author, March 29, 2019.

7. Thomas Bender, Philip M. Katz, Colin Palmer, and the AHA Committee on Graduate Education, *The Education of Historians for the Twenty-first Century* (Urbana: University of Illinois Press, 2004), 23–24.

8. Letter to Clarence A. Berdahl (and attached "Report of Advisory Committee on Foreign Relations, 1963"), January 13, 1964, File Truman Library Conference, Box 41; see also in same folder, "Notification of Personnel Action" Excepted Appointment [of Ferrell] as Historian (Consultant-WOC), Bureau of Public Affairs, Historical Office, Office of Director, effective date November 1, 1963, for three years; and again, same folder, letter to Ferrell from Robert Manning (Assistant Secretary, DOS), October 11, 1963.

9. Ferrell participated at a gathering with dozens of teachers from several states, "in the hot midsummer of 2003," with "researchers, teachers, and staff members" at the Truman Library "to explore how to interpret and teach the Truman presidency." And further, the organizers clarified that "What was new about the conference in 2003 was its focus on the high school history classroom." See Kirkendall (ed.), *Harry's Farewell*, xiii–xv, and Ferrell's chapter, "Harry S. Truman: A Biographer's Perspective I." Kirkendall's edited book was another result of the conference.

10. Robert H. Ferrell, "C. Vann Woodward," in *Clio's Favorites: Leading Historians of the United States, 1945–2000*, ed. Robert Allen Rutland (Columbia: University of Missouri Press, 2000); Allen, "Samuel Flagg Bemis," 194; Gilderhus, "Founding Father" or see https://www.pulitzer.org/winners/samuel-flagg-bemis. Aside from historian biographies, other books reviewed included Lucian Boia (ed.) *Great Historians of the Modern Age: An International Dictionary*, esp. the section, "United States," 715–781; Barker, *The Superhistorians*; Daniel Snowman, *Historians* (New York: Palgrave Macmillan, 2007).

11. H. Hale Bellot, *American History and American Historians: A Review of Recent Contributions to the Interpretation of the History of the United State* (London: University of London Press, 1952), 287; see also Boia (ed.), *Great Historians*, 723.

12. Barker, *Superhistorians*, esp. 239–267.

13. Ibid., 256.

14. Ferrell, "C. Vann Woodward," in Rutland, *Clio's Favorites*, 2.

15. Allen, "Samuel Flagg Bemis," in Cunliffe and Winks (eds.), *Pastmasters*. There is some confusion here as the editors noted later that five listed are British and were chosen to highlight a foreign perspective on the United States; see pp. 9, 14.

16. Ibid., xi–xii.

17. From his *Harry S. Truman and the Modern American Presidency* (1983) to *Presidential Leadership* (2006) among several other biographical treatments in between these years.

18. See for instance the subfields postcolonial, gender, and memory studies, in Marek Tamm and Peter Burke (eds), *Debating New Approaches to History* (London: Bloomsbury Academic, 2019).

19. Geoffrey Cubitt, "History of Memory," in *Debating New Approaches to History*, ed. Marek Tamm and Peter Burke (London: Bloomsbury Academic, 2019), 128–129.

20. Interview with Robert H. Ferrell, conducted by Sheehan, February 13, 1998, transcript, p. 3; and by Glenn, November 3, 1994. IUOralHistory.

21. Cubitt, "History of Memory," 128–129.

22. Letter to M/D, January 8, 1945, Box 74; letter to M/D, August 15, 1943, Box 74.

23. Ibid., 130.

24. Laura Lee Downs, "Gender History," in *Debating New Approaches to History*, ed. Marek Tamm and Peter Burke (London: Bloomsbury Academic, 2019), 101–125.

25. Downs, "Gender History," 102.

26. Letter to Bill, February 2, 1959, Box 72.

27. By 1992, Ferrell, along with coauthor Lawrence E. Wikander, had edited *Grace Coolidge: An Autobiography* (Worland, WY: High Plains Publishing Company, 1992), and it is worthy to note that Mrs. Coolidge wrote of her own Victorian-era expectations for marriage partners: "If [marriage] is to be a going concern it must have a head . . . [and] in general this is the husband." See pp. 33–35, 65. Coolidge had earned a college degree and taught at a school for the deaf.

28. Johanna Alberti, *Gender and the Historian* (London: Pearson Education, 2002), esp. Chapter One.

29. Downs, "Gender History," 100, 102.

30. Alberti noted that "men dominated writing of history and defined what historians should and could do" from 1969 to 1999; see her *Gender and the Historian*, 1.

31. Ferrell wrote, "I have been trying to forget the name of the present "chair" of the [history] department at Indiana University. . . . She is the sponsor of the project on the intersection of gender, sexuality, and popular culture in the history of the United States in the twentieth century." The chair, he continued, "arrived on campus perhaps ten years ago with a salary three times mine." See his letter to Jim, June 9, 2011; decades earlier, Ferrell registered concern that a historian, Joan Wilson, an applicant for an IU History Department position, might be hired; see his diary entry April 13, 1981, pp. 1–2, Box 216.

32. Robert H. Ferrell (ed.), *Dear Bess: The Letters from Harry S. Truman, 1910–1959* (New York: W. W. Norton, 1983). Ferrell also tackled indirectly and unknowingly issues raised later by Laura Lee Downs: "intersectionality, individual subjectivity and its material and bodily contexts, agency, and the role of emotions in shaping both" (Downs, "Gender History," 109) though without couching them in these terms (e.g., presidents Warren Harding (Nan Britton) and Dwight Eisenhower (Kay Summersby); see Ferrell, *Ill-Advised*, 59–60. As mentioned earlier, Ferrell also

co-edited the stories of First Lady Grace Coolidge, in Wikander and Ferrell (eds.), *Grace Coolidge*.

33. According to Ferrell, "the . . . letters from Harry to Bess span the years 1910 to 1959 and number well over twelve hundred," this at the Truman Library. See *Dear Bess*, 306.

34. Ibid., 307.

35. Ibid., vii.

36. Rochona Majumdar, "Postcolonial History," in *Debating New Approaches to History*, ed. Marek Tamm and Peter Burke (London: Bloomsbury Academic, 2019), 49–74.

37. See for instance Ferrell's discussions on the Philippines, the Middle East, India, Korea or Vietnam, in Ferrell, *American Diplomacy*, chapters 15, 18, 28–29, 31. With Majumdar's ideas as background, one wonders what the postcolonial debaters would have thought of Ferrell's interpretation that the acquisition of the Philippines heralded the age of American imperialism. Ibid., 434.

38. Ferrell shared "a confusion of the historians many years ago that has lingered to the present-day. . . . The historians now think, according to a historian at Santa Barbara by name of Hasegawa, that the war in the Pacific of 1941–45 was a clash of two cultures, both humanly justified. Etc. I will not add cubits to my stature by this book, for the whole dispute over revision is full of animosity even now. But, well, I let 'em have it." See letter to Charles Blankenship, April 5, 2006 (in possession of the recipient).

39. Ibid., 797.

40. Letter to Bob, January 15, 1970, Box 10.

41. Majumdar, "Postcolonial History," 56. Further, Majumdar notes that, "postcolonial historians focus on the ways in which colonial categories were operationalized on the ground by the natives, often described by the colonizers as uncivilized or backward." Ibid., 57.

42. One might consider Ferrell's usefulness, partly, as an aspect of an evolving historiography, lacking the narratives of imperialist-country returnees or networks of people and issues (e.g., failed states/environmental crises) that transcend nation-states and their borders. Majumdar, "Postcolonial History," 58, 61–63.

43. Ibid., 59.

44. Ferrell, *American Diplomacy*, 739.

45. Ibid., 641.

46. Ibid., 417.

Appendix

Ferrell Book Reviews as Guide to Crafting the Past

Categories	Cross-referenced examples in published reviews
A. Ferrell's personal bias	1, 2, 9, 12, 14, 16, 18
B. Ferrell's advocacy for historical viewpoints	1, 2, 4, 5, 6, 8, 9, 10, 12, 14, 18,19
C. Ferrell's measures of worthy scholarship (e.g., methods, source criticism and application, personal and intellectual integrity)	1, 2, 3, 4, 5, 6, 7, 8, 9, 10, 11, 12*, 13, 14, 16, 17, 18
D. Importance of archival engagement	1, 10, 14, 16, 17, 19
E. History as literary art	2, 3, 4, 6, 7, 11, 12, 14, 16, 17, 19

Note. Cross references (A, B, C, D, E and 1, 2, 3, 4, 5, 6) are used in the Table citations and examples that follow.

1. *The Wisconsin Magazine* 41, no. 1 (Autumn 1957), 63–64.—A. "The reader will come away from the book wishing that it were possible to live again in those heady days of America's rise to world power prior to the Great War of 1914–1918"; "It was a wonderful time to be alive . . . in those sunlit days of high politics . . . of great powers and *backward nations*"; B./C. "Beale's book *proves* that the picture of Roosevelt [TR] in Pringle's now twenty-five-year-old biography was wrong . . . [but] that he was a man of many talents; in diplomacy Roosevelt showed every attribute of the ideal negotiator"; C./D. "impeccable piece of research . . . the *author went through every available scrap of material on his subject*"; "Historians will have to change a number of interpretations as a result of it";

2. *Indiana Magazine of History* 53, no. 4 (1957), 467–469.—A./B. "Why not show that the sorry tampering with civil rights in 1917–1918 was part of a long history of unconstitutional acts during wartime or supposed periods of national danger?" C. "The volume fails to attain any kind of broad perspective"; "descriptive and not analytical . . . refuses to generalize and takes refuge in a recital of facts"; "should not professorial writers attempt to get away from the narrow, narrative approach, and tell their readers what their subjects mean for the broad course of history?"; E. "passive-voice verbs reflect the book's colorless writing";
3. *Indiana Magazine of History* 53, no. 1 (March 1957), 100–101.—C. "The scrupulous fairness of Perkins' biography, its *willingness to see both sides* of its subject is surely one of the most successful aspects of the book"; C./D. "the new book . . . may prove disappointing to some readers . . . when it comes to giving a feel for [the] subject," knowing the subject, the "mass of detail, of both a personal and public nature." "Especially does one wish *for descriptions of Hughes the man*";
4. *The Mississippi Valley Historical Review* 47, no. 2 (September 1960), 352–353.—B./C. Roosevelt's ideas on world order, the topic, of little historical value; E. "well written, in clear and careful if humorless prose"; problem of the book is "its organization, topical rather than chronological";
5. *The Historian* 23, no. 3 (May 1961), pp. 388–389.—B. "The Second World War receives too much attention here to the slighting of other phases of America's foreign relations in the twentieth century. The First World War was probably more crucial for the fate of America and the world"; "the genuine effort of American diplomats to meet postwar problems is dismissed as so much foolery—which those efforts were not"; C. "It is easy *to judge from hindsight* and Davids may have given in to that temptation"; "the opening of the book is designed more to attract what student reviewers like to describe as "reader interest" rather than to *state a serious historical proposition*";
6. *The Mississippi Valley Historical Review* 50, no. 1 (June 1963), 149–150.—A./B. Ferrell counters the thesis using both personal recollection and knowledge of public sentiment and Roosevelt politics on the eve of December 7, 1941; C. the difficulty of supporting a too broad generalization (i.e., the contention that "the 'important roots' of American isolationism were the needs, desires, and values of American agricultural society, and that when for many reasons agriculture lost importance in the national economy, isolationism gave way to internationalism"; E. lacks a detailed grasp of the human side, in this case the attributes of Senator Gerald P. Nye, isolationist, and his context;

7. *The American Historical Review* 69, no. 4 (July 1964), 1083–1084.—C. judicious with generalization; grasps large volume of secondary works; broadens perspective with infusion of new topics to what is known; E. "The prose sparkles.";
8. *The American Historical Review* 70, no. 3 (April 1965), 827–828.—B. overlooks significant contextual considerations; C. Source material (interviews) cannot be verified; thesis is not supported; the work may "confuse the historical record"; author displays "malice" toward the subject studied; sophomoric logic; overwhelmingly pro-Israel;
9. *The American Historical Review* 71, no. 2 (January 1966), 729–730.—A. "It [Second World War] became a fight against the most amoral government since the statistically clouded times of Genghis Khan"; C. insignificant thesis, "a scholarly disaster";
10. *The American Historical Review* 71, no. 3 (April 1966), 1092.—B./C. "a cleaver analysis of President Wilson's moral leadership of the world, which the author rightly says was too high in sentiment"; C. "Organization is topical and chronological, so that the inquiring student can grasp the general chronology and the broad, controversial topics"; "If the book holds no great surprises, it has no special pleading or weird interpretation." Extraordinarily balanced; D. The author "has gone to the manuscript sources and thereby brings novelty to this timeworn narrative. He has close knowledge of the published materials, books and articles, and he has not ignored the work of others";
11. *Indiana Magazine of History* 62, no. 2 (1966), 163–164.—C. confused/improper use of footnotes to credit sources; E. "no undergraduate will go through this sort of prose with any feeling of interest not to mention enjoyment. . . . None of the figures in this book comes to life. . . . One recalls the lament of Theodore Roosevelt . . . that he was going to tell the historians that history was literature and, he added, they were not going to believe it. After fifty-four years has that message still failed to get through?";
12. *The American Historical Review* 72, no. 2 (January 1967), 534.—A./B./C. "If flawed, its failure [is not] . . . to take positions beyond the available evidence. . . . For the most important single factor in the deterioration of American-Soviet relations may well have been the Russian dictator, a peculiar individual, whom one distinguished American expert on Soviet affairs has described as possessing a "personality disorder"; C./E. "clear, straightforward prose, [which] analyzed the origins of the so-called cold war";
13. *The American Historical Review* 73, no. 2 (December 1967), 625.—C. ignores recent research, extreme bias/unbalanced treatment, lacks

thoughtfulness/simplistic narrative ("black and white"), notes/bibliographic shortcomings;
14. *The Journal of Modern History* 40, no. 1 (March 1968), 150–151.—C./D./E. Edited volume of letters, "virtually a diary of the author's attendance at the [post-WWI Paris] peace conference"; "They *contain few if any diplomatic revelations, and yet are eminently worth reading for atmosphere of that now bygone time*"; A./B. "It was a heady occasion when nearly fifty years ago the young professors . . . *helped President Wilson remake the world*";
15. *The Pacific Northwest Quarterly* 59, no. 4 (October 1968), 228–229.—C. pro-internationalist/anti-conservative bias, "factual lapses, uncritical use of source material; mere chronicle"; C./D. inattention to relevant sources; prematurely published, ignoring just released documents; E. "This book is ably written and marches along to its conclusion. It lacks humor";
16. *The American Historical Review* 74, no. 3 (February 1969), 1112.—A./E. "*In a deservedly praised essay Samuel Eliot Morison once advised* students of history to avoid writing 'dull, solid, valuable monographs' . . . the present monograph surely should not suffer . . . the Morisonian stigma for it is sprightly, solid, and valuable"; A./C./D. "This *excellent analysis* of the interwar periodicals of peace *deserves close attention by students of American history, and also by individuals concerned with present campus causes*";
17. *The Journal of Modern History* 41, no. 1 (March 1969), 122–123.—C./D./E. "Alton Frye has written *an admirable monograph, well organized, well written, ably researched*. It is difficult to flaw this book in any way"; D. "The present book *has gotten deeply into the massive unpublished documentation* to show Hitler's view of and actions toward the western hemisphere";
18. *The American Historical Review* 75, no. 2 (December 1969), 612–613.—A./B./C. "*Ingeniously organized into chapters dealing with Roosevelt the isolationist, the interventionist, the realist, and the pragmatist* . . . the various sides of the man, and *come down firmly on what, at least to me, seems the right one*: Roosevelt the decent human being who, sometimes with undue attention to political opponents, *sought to lead the country against the evil international forces of his time*"; "[the author] contends that Roosevelt had little concern for Poland . . . Truman, decided to breathe life into the Polish agreement, the cold war ensued. This point seems questionable, for the Western Allies were without power in Eastern Europe, as Roosevelt so well understood during the Yalta sessions. *The cold war arose out of Russian intransigence rather than out of misunderstand*ing"; C./D. "What makes Roosevelt's correspondence unique, however, is the magnitude of the issues, the

results of which sometimes border on catastrophe"; "The series begins auspiciously because most of us have been led to believe that the first Roosevelt administration was uninteresting in terms of foreign affairs. The present *documents prove* it fascinating";

19. *The American Historical Review* 75, no. 4 (April 1970), 1205.—B. "President's [FDR's] disorganization and off-handed, almost careless, approach to large issues" yet he is politically shrewd, consulting closely with important institutional players; D. "not much pertinent manuscript material that the author failed to see"; E. "lively, colorful, shrewdly intelligent account," perhaps too much detail for readers.

Bibliography

"150 Additional Awards." *The American Magazine* 128 (September 1939): 70.

Abramovitz, Mimi. *Regulating the Lives of Women: Social Welfare Policy from Colonial Times to the Present.* Boston: South End Press, 1996.

Alberti, Johanna. *Gender and the Historian.* London: Pearson Education, 2002.

Aldous, Richard. Schlesinger: *The Imperial Historian.* New York: W. W. Norton, 2017.

Allen, H. C. "Samuel Flagg Bemis." In *Pastmasters: Some Essays on American Historians*, edited by Marcus Cunliffe and Robin Winks. New York: Harper & Row, 1969.

Barker, John. *The Superhistorians: Makers of Our Past.* New York: Charles Scribner's Sons, 1982.

Baxter, Maurice G., Robert H. Ferrell, and John E. Wiltz. *The Teaching of American History in High Schools.* Bloomington: Indiana University Press, 1964.

Becker, Thea Gallo. *Images of America: Lakewood.* Charleston, SC: Arcadia, 2003.

Bellot, H. Hale. *American History and American Historians: A Review of Recent Contributions to the Interpretation of the History of the United States.* London: University of London Press, 1952.

Bender, Thomas, Philip M. Katz, Colin Palmer, and the AHA Committee on Graduate Education. *The Education of Historians for the Twenty-First Century.* Urbana: University of Illinois, 2004.

Bestor, Arthur. "Anti-Intellectuals in the Schools." Paper delivered at the AHA Conference (December 2, 1952).

Boia, Lucian, ed. *Great Historians of the Modern Age: An International Dictionary.* New York: Greenwood Press, 1991.

Brown, Callum G. *Postmodernism for Historians.* New York: Routledge, 2005.

Brown, David S. *Beyond the Frontier: The Midwestern Voice in American Historical Writing.* Chicago: University of Chicago, 2009.

———. *Richard Hofstadter: An Intellectual Biography.* Chicago: University of Chicago, 2006.

Butler, Margaret Manor. *The Lakewood Story*. New York: Stratford House, 1949.
Cassuto, Leonard. *The Graduate School Mess: What Caused It and How We Can Fix It*. Cambridge, MA: Harvard University Press, 2015.
Cayton, Andrew R. L. *Ohio: The History of a People*. Columbus: The Ohio State University, 2002.
Clark, Thomas R. *My Century in History*. Lexington: University Press of Kentucky, 2006.
Cubitt, Geoffrey. "History of Memory." In *Debating New Approaches to History*, edited by Marek Tamm and Peter Burke. London: Bloomsbury Academic, 2019.
Cunliffe, Marcus, and Robin Winks, eds. *Pastmasters: Some Essays on American Historians*. New York: Harper & Row, 1969.
Dewald, Jonathan. "Rethinking the 1 Percent: The Failure of the Nobility in Old Regime France." *The American Historical Review* 124 (June 2019): 910–932.
DiNitto, Diana M. *Social Work: Issues and Opportunities in a Challenging Profession*. Needham, MA: Allyn & Bacon, 1997.
Dominelli, Lena. *Sociology for Social Work*. London: Macmillan Press, 1997.
Donnelly, Mark, and Claire Norton. *Doing History*. New York: Routledge, 2011.
Dore, Martha Morrison. "Clinical Practice." In *The Columbia School of Social Work: A Centennial Celebration*, edited by Ronald A. Feldman and Sheila B. Kamerman. New York: Columbia University Press, 2001.
Downs, Laura Lee. "Gender History." In *Debating New Approaches to History*, edited by Marek Tamm and Peter Burke. London: Bloomsbury Academic, 2019.
Duffy, Elizabeth, and Idana Goldberg. *Crafting a Class: College Admissions and Financial Aid, 1955–1994*. Princeton, NJ: Princeton University Press, 1998.
Evans, Richard J. *In Defense of History*. New York: W. W. Norton, 1999.
"Favorite Profs." *Indiana University Alumni Magazine* (Fall 2013): 11.
Ferrell, Ernest Sr. *Stories I Want My Grandchildren to Know*. Columbus, OH: Author, 1980.
Ferrell, Robert H. "America Made E–Z." *National Review* (September 28, 1998): 60–61.
———. *American Diplomacy: A History*. 3rd edition. New York: W. W. Norton, 1975.
———. *America's Deadliest Battle, Meuse Argonne, 1918*. Lawrence: University Press of Kansas, 2007.
———, ed. *The Autobiography of Harry S. Truman*. Columbia: University of Missouri Press, 1980.
———. "C. Vann Woodward." In *Pastmasters: Some Essays on American Historians*, edited by Marcus Cunliffe and Robin Winks. New York: Harper & Row, 1969.
———, ed. *Dear Bess: The Letters from Harry S. Truman, 1910–1959*. New York: W. W. Norton, 1983.
———. "First Cold Warrior." *American Communist History* 9 (December 2010).
———. "From the Stacks." *OAH Magazine of History* 20 (January 2006).
———. *George C. Marshall*. New York: Cooper Square, 1966.
———. "Harry S. Truman: A Biographer's Perspective I." In *Harry's Farewell: Interpreting and Teaching the Truman Presidency*, edited by Richard S. Kirkendall. Columbia: University of Missouri Press, 2004.

―――. *Harry S. Truman: A Life*. Columbia: University of Missouri Press, 1994.
―――. *Harry S. Truman and Cold War Revisionists*. Columbia: University of Missouri Press, 2006.
―――. *Harry S. Truman and the Modern American Presidency*. Boston: Little, Brown and Company, 1983.
―――. *Ill-Advised: Presidential Health and Public Trust*. Columbia: University of Missouri Press, 1992.
―――. "The Large Book Versus Small." *Indiana Magazine of History* 100 (December 2004).
―――. "Looking Back: The Truman Books." *Indiana Magazine of History* 92, no. 2 (June 1996).
―――, ed. *Off the Record: The Private Papers of Harry S. Truman*. New York: Harper & Row, 1980.
―――. *Peace in Their Time: The Origins of the Kellogg-Briand Pact*. New Haven, CT: Yale University Press, 1952.
―――. "Pearl Harbor and the Revisionists." *The Historian* 17 (Spring 1955): 215–233.
―――. "Plain Faking?" *American Heritage* 46 (May/June 1995).
―――. *Presidential Leadership: From Woodrow Wilson to Harry S. Truman*. Columbia: University of Missouri Press, 2006.
―――. *The Question of MacArthur's Reputation: Cote de Catillon*. Columbia: University of Missouri Press, 2008.
―――. "Truman Foreign Policy: A Traditionalist View." In *The Truman Period as a Research Field: A Reappraisal, 1972*, edited by Richard S. Kirkendall. Columbia: University of Missouri Press, 1974.
―――. *Unjustly Dishonored: An African American Division in World War I*. Columbia: University of Missouri Press, 2011.
―――. *Woodrow Wilson and World War I, 1917–1921*. New York: Harper & Row, 1985.
―――, and Lawrence E. Wilkander, eds. *Grace Coolidge: An Autobiography*. Worland, WY: High Plains Publishing, 1992.
―――, and Peter Szatmary. "The Villains of the 'Red Scares' of the 1950s." *Phi Kappa Phi Forum* 90 (September 2010).
Fetner, Gerald L. *Immersed in Great Affairs: Allan Nevins and the Heroic Age of American History*. Albany: State University of New York Press, 2004.
Gilderhus, Mark T. "Founding Father: Samuel Flagg Bemis and the Study of U.S.-Latin American Relations." *Diplomatic History* 21 (January 1997): 1–13.
Grant, H. Rodger. *Ohio on the Move: Transportation in the Buckeye State*. Athens: Ohio University Press, 2000.
Haalboom, A. F. (Floor). "Talking Activism and History—Part I." *Shells and Pebbles* [website blog] (accessed September 11, 2018).
Hamby, Alonzo L. "A Biographer's Perspective II." In *Harry's Farewell: Interpreting and Teaching the Truman Presidency*, edited by Richard S. Kirkendall. Columbia: University of Missouri Press, 2004.
Helfgot, Joseph H. *Professional Reforming: Mobilization for Youth and the Failure of Social Science*. Lexington, MA: Lexington Books/D. C. Heath and Company, 1981.

Herold, David Edward. *A Species of Literary Lions: Essays on Morison, Freeman, Devoto, and Becker, and the Writing of History* (PhD Diss., University of Minnesota, 1973).

Howell, Martha, and Walter Prevenier. *From Reliable Sources: An Introduction to Historical Methods*. Ithaca, NY: Cornell University Press, 2001.

Hughes, H. Stuart. *History as Art and as Science*. New York: Harper & Row, 1964.

Jackson, Robert L. *The Clubhouse Model: Empowering Applications of Theory to Generalist Practice*. Belmont, CA: Wadsworth/Thomas Learning, 2001.

Jordan, Benjamin Rene. *Modern Manhood and the Boy Scouts of America: Citizenship, Race, and the Environment, 1910–1930*. Chapel Hill: University of North Carolina Press, 2016.

Jumonville, Neil. *Henry Steele Commager: Midcentury Liberalism and the History of the Present*. Chapel Hill: University of North Carolina Press, 1999.

Kahn, Alfred. "Themes for a History: The First Hundred Years." In *The Columbia School of Social Work: A Centennial Celebration*, edited by Ronald A. Feldman and Sheila B. Kamerman. New York: Columbia University Press, 2001.

Kaplan, Lawrence. "Robert H. Ferrell: An Appreciation." In *Presidents, Diplomats, and Other Mortals: Essays Honoring Robert H. Ferrell*, edited by J. Garry Clifford and Theodore A. Wilson. Columbia: University of Missouri Press, 2007.

Kirkendall, Richard S., ed. *Harry's Farewell: Interpreting and Teaching the Truman Presidency*. Columbia: University of Missouri Press, 2004.

Kirkendall, Richard S., ed. *The Truman Period as a Research Field: A Reappraisal, 1972*. Columbia: University of Missouri Press, 1974.

Knepper, George W. "Ohio Politics: A Historical Perspective." In *Ohio Politics*, edited by Alexander P. Lamis. Kent, OH: Kent State University Press, 1994.

Koerner, James D. *The Miseducation of Teachers*. Boston: Houghton Mifflin Company, 1963.

Landes, David, and Charles Tilly, eds. *History as a Social Science*. Englewood Cliffs, NJ: Prentice Hall, 1971.

Leff, Gordon. *History and Social Theory*. Tuscaloosa: University of Alabama, 1969.

Leighninger, Leslie. *Creating a New Profession: Beginnings of Social Work Education in the United States*. Alexandria, VA: Council on Social Work Education, 2000.

Lindstrom, E. George. *Story of Lakewood, Ohio*. Lakewood, OH: Author, 1936.

Lukacs, John. *The Future of History*. New Haven, CT: Yale University Press, 2011.

Majumdar, Rochona. "Postcolonial History." In *Debating New Approaches to History*, edited by Marek Tamm and Peter Burke. London: Bloomsbury Academic, 2019.

McDaniel, Isaac. "The Historian as Activist." *The Review of Politics* 57 (Summer 1995): 541–544.

Messer-Kruse, Timothy. *Banksters, Bosses, and Smart Money: A Social History of the Great Toledo Bank Crash of 1931*. Columbus: The Ohio State University Press, 2004.

Miller, Carol Poh, and Robert Wheeler. *Cleveland: A Concise History, 1796–1990*, Bloomington: Indiana University Press, 1990.

Offner, Arnold A. *Another Such Victory: President Truman and the Cold War, 1945–1953*. Palo Alto, CA: Stanford University Press, 2002.

Pfitzer, Gregory M. *Samuel Eliot Morison's Historical World: In Quest of a New Parkman*. Boston: Northeastern University Press, 1991.

"Ralph Waldo Emerson." In *The Norton Anthology of American Literature: Volume I*, edited by Nina Baym, Ronald Gottesman, Laurence B. Holland, et al. New York: W. W. Norton & Company, 1989.

Ricards, Michael P. *The College Board and American Higher Education*. Madison, WI: Fairleigh Dickinson University Press, 2010.

Schmidt, Peter. "A History of Legacy Preferences and Privilege." In *Affirmative Action for the Rich: Legacy Preferences in College Admissions*, edited by Richard D. Kahlenberg. New York: The Century Foundation Press, 2010.

Snowman, Daniel. *Historians*. New York: Palgrave Macmillan, 2007.

Storey, William Kelleher. *Writing History: A Guide for Students*. New York: Oxford University Press, 1996.

Usher, Brian. "The Lauche Era, 1945–1957." In *Ohio Politics*, edited by Alexander P. Lamis. Kent, OH: Kent State University Press, 1994.

Tyson, Tim. "Can Honest History Allow for Hope? The Obligations of Scholarship Diverge from the Needs of Activists." *The Atlantic* (December 18, 2015).

Wheeler, Kenneth. "How Colleges Shaped Public Culture of Usefulness." In *The Center of a Great Empire: The Ohio Country in the Early Republic*, edited by Andrew R. L. Cayton and Stuart D. Hobbs. Athens: Ohio University Press, 2005.

Wigger, John. "Ohio Gospel: Methodism in Early Ohio." In *The Center of a Great Empire: The Ohio Country in the Early Republic*, edited by Andrew R. L. Cayton and Stuart D. Hobbs. Athens: Ohio University Press, 2005.

Wilson, Theodore A. "Introduction: Individuals, Narratives, and Diplomatic History." In *Presidents, Diplomats, and Other Mortals: Essays Honoring Robert H. Ferrell*, edited by J. Garry Clifford and Theodore A. Wilson. Columbia: University of Missouri Press, 2007.

Winslow, Barbara. "E. P. Thompson as Historian, Teacher and Political Activist." *Against the Current* (January–February 1994) (accessed September 9, 2018).

Index

9th Air Force Service Command (AFSC) Headquarters, 12, 13, 16

Abramovitz, Mimi, 43n81
Abzug, Bella, 104
AFSC. *See* 9th Air Force Service Command
AHA. *See* American Historical Association
Air Detachment Group, 13
Air Force Intelligence, 24
Alberti, Joanna, 133
Alexandria, 16
alternative teacher education, 88
America First: The Battle against Intervention, 1940–1941 (Cole), 102
American Banking Institute, 60
American Century, 34
American Economic Association, 108
American Heritage, 111
American Historical Association (AHA), xi, 3, 11, 26, 35, 83, 88, 94n77, 124n60, 135; Ad Hoc Committee on Redefining Scholarly Work, 129; Committee on Graduate Education, 137n7. *See also Education of Historians for the Twenty-First Century*
American Historical Review, 103, 120–21n26, 143–45

American Magazine Youth Forum, 9
American Political Science Association, 35
American Political Tradition (Brown), 114
American Revolution, 36
"The American Scholar" (Emerson), 53
American Social Science Association, 31
American University, 15, 23
Americanization, 58
Anglo-American relations, 17
anti-capitalism, 3, 4
Army Air Force, U.S., xvii, 13
artifacts, as surrogates of past, 5
Aylward, James, 79

B of LE. *See* Brotherhood of Locomotive Engineers National Bank
Badger, Joseph, 51
Baedeker guidebooks, 18
Bailyn, Bernard, 130
Ballot, H. Hale, and evolution of history as discipline, 34
Bancroft, George, 35, 118n13
Barker, John, 129
Barry, D. Karl, 105, 107
Barthlomew, Betsey, 51
Battle of the Bulge, 18
"Battle of Who Run," 91n23

153

Baxter, Maurice, 26, 93n65, 94nn66, 70, 71
Bayh, Birch, 92n48
Beard, Charles, 35–36, 100, 101, 103, 108, 110–17, 118n10
Becker, Iowan Carl, 35
Bee Gee News, 8
Bemis, Samuel Flagg, xiii, 10, 11, 12, 23, 38n9, 40n34, 84, 100, 110, 116, 118n13, 129, 130, 132
Bengasi, 16
Benns, F. Lee, 11, 12
Bestor, Arthur, 88
Beyond the Frontier: The Midwestern Voice in American Historical Writing (Brown), 108
BGSU. *See* Bowling Green State University
Bible Stories for Young Children, 64
Bird's Nest (in Lakewood, Ohio), 58, 114
Blaine, Rick, 12
Bloomington, Indiana, 29, 30, 31, 41n40, 44n88, 86, 103, 113, 128, 133
Boulevard St. Germaine, 18
Bowling Green State University (BGSU), xiii, 6, 8, 9, 24, 26, 54, 89, 110, 115
Boy Scouts of America (BSA), and training, 55–57, 60, 65, 68n28, 133
Brand, Myles, 86
Brehm, Walter E., 84
Brewer, Wanonah G., 87
Bridenbaugh, Carl, 109, 124n60
Britton, Nan, 138n33
Brooks, Philip C., 92n48
Brotherhood of Locomotive Engineers National Bank (B of LE), 60
Brown, Callum G., 19nn7, 9, 20nn18, 19, 43nn67, 68, 72, 44nn86, 90, 93, 90nn4, 5, 94n82; on contrast between postmodernists and traditionalists, 4
Brown, David S., xv, 100, 108, 111, 114, 116, 117n4, 118n9, 125nn63–65, 133

Brown, Walter Folger, 63
Bryant, Robert, xv, 24, 29, 30, 92n42
Bryant, William Cullen, 112
BSA. *See* Boy Scouts of America
Byrnes, James, 86

Cairo, Egypt, 12–15, 23, 135
Camp Deolali, 13
Canary, Sumner, 7, 20n26, 86, 93n58
Carranza, Venustiano, 136
Carroll, John, 105, 107
Carter, Lorenzo, 51
Castle, William, 12, 84
Cayton, Andrew, 50, 64, 66n4, 69nn35, 37, 41, 43, 70n68
Child Study Movement, 55, 111
Christ Church cathedral, 17
Church of Nazarene, 29
Cireniaca, 16, 17
civil rights, 89, 104, 113, 142; African American, 77, 113; protests, 3, 115
Clark, Thomas D., 93n60, 94n79
Cleaveland, Moses, 50
Cleveland Plain Dealer, 59
Cleveland Press, 59
Cockran, Thomas C., 110
Cold War, 4, 5, 100, 105, 119n15, 143, 144; causes, 100; liberalism, 113; origin, 3; revisionism, 106, 118, 131
Coldwater, Michigan, 28
Cole, Wayne S., 102
Columbia School of liberalism, 133
Columbia University School. *See* New York School of Social Work
Columbia University, 42n58
Commager, Henry Steele, 95n85, 102, 110
Commercial Bank, 63
Connecticut Land Company, 50
contingency, 12, 33
Coolidge, Calvin, 33
Coolidge, Grace, 138n28, 139n33
Council on Foreign Relations, 7
Cubitt, Geoffrey, and memory as history, 132

Custar, Ohio, xii, 53, 57, 59–61, 63–64, 66, 67n16
Cycles of American History (Schlesinger Jr.), 123n39

Daniels, Jonathan, 79
Davidson, Eugene, 23, 70n57
Debating New Approaches to History (Tamm and Burke), 138nn19, 20, 25, 139n37
Department of State, U.S., 84, 129
Department of the Army's Adjutant General's Office, 82, 83
Derby Evening Sentinel, 39n19
Dewey, Thomas, 59
Diaz, Porfirio, 136
Dore, Martha Morrison, 44n92
Dorsett, Lyle, 79
Downs, Laura Lee, 133
Du Bois, W. E. B., 36, 129–30
Duckett, Ken, 43n74, 90n2, 93n59

Economic Interpretation of the Constitution (Beard), 108–9
Education of Historians for the Twenty-first Century (Bender et al.), 137n7
Educational Wastelands: The Retreat from Learning in our Public Schools (Bestor), 88
Eisenhower, David Dwight, xii, 74, 80, 81, 107, 138n33
Eisenhower, Mamie, 81
Eli Lilly Foundation (Lilly Endowment, Inc.), 71
elite college admissions (1940s), as function of multiple factors, 10–11
Elliott, Franklin Reuben, 51
Ely, Richard, and interdisciplinary theory, 108
Emerson, Ralph Waldo, 53
empirical method, 72
England, 17
English-Speaking Union, 17
evangelical Protestant faith, 29

farming practices, 35
Federal Reserve Board, 63
Federal Reserve System, 113
Ferrell, Carolyn (Carolyn Ferrell Burgess), 14, 15, 25, 40n38, 50, 54, 67n16, 74, 93n53, 103
Ferrell, Ernest, Sr.: as banker, 60, 61; as bank examiner at RFC, 60; bank failure and, 64; and critic of Standard Trust Bank mismanagement, 60; as First World War soldier, 54, 58; as graduate of Wooster College, 52, 64; as President of Waterville Bank, 61; training at American Banking Institute, 60, 64
Ferrell, Orlando, 57, 58
Ferrell, Robert H.: and twenty-first-century history emerging subdisciplines, 127, 132, 134; as activist, 71, 73, 83–85, 89; and activities as Staff Sergeant, xvii, 7, 8, 10, 17–18, 65, 75, 110, 113; and admission to Yale, 5–11; as admixture of old and new history approaches, 129; as advocate of history education improvement, 71, 87–89; as *American Magazine* contest winner, 9–10; appointment to Indiana University faculty, 23–24, 29; and approach (to history), 5, 72, 73; aunt Ocie (Rentsch) and uncle Mark Brown, xii, 37, 40n39, 41n50, 133; and battles with twentieth-century revisionists, 3–5, 99, 100, 102, 103, 105, 106; Bemis influences on, xiii, 10–12, 23, 84, 100, 110, 116, 129, 130, 132; and "Bob Ferrell Describes India as Weird and Mysterious," 13, 21n65; book reviewer critiques of, 102–4, 116, 131; book reviews as clues to historical approach and bias of, 101–3; Boy Scout inculcation of, 16, 52, 55, 56, 57, 60, 65, 111, 116, 133; Bronze Star Certificate awarded to, 10; Cleveland, Ohio, birthplace of,

xii, 29, 49, 102, 110; as co-founder of SHAFR, 84; versus Harry Truman, 73–80, 89, 91n28, 105, 106; as contrast to notable historians, 130; and criteria for historian comparisons, 108, 115–16; as critic of Army Reserve recruiting policy, 83, 132; on critique of Lila and Lou professional roles, 29–30; and Depression-era flight-to-farm living, 17, 52–53, 61, 64; as director of Lilly Endowment-funded American History Teaching Program, 86–87; as Eagle Scout, xi, 9, 55, 56, 65, 108, 111, 112, 116; and early years, xii, 24, 37, 49, 51, 54, 65, 66; as editor of U.S. Department of State Foreign Affairs series, 84; Ernest, Jr. (June), brother of, xii, 9, 16, 66n21, 22n74, 28, 53, 124n52; Ernest and Edna (Rentsch) Ferrell, parents of, xii, 51, 52, 54, 58, 64; family Republicanism and, 53; GRE scores of, 8–11; historical objectivity and, xviii, 73, 78, 79, 81, 89; as Indiana University Distinguished Professor of History, xi, 102; and influential Yale alumni family members, 9; as lecturer at Michigan State College, xiii, 24, 64, 85; as liberal Democrat, 61, 70n57; on Lila and Lou comparisons, 28, 36; and love life as postmodernist allegory, 26, 38; on MacArthur dismissal and Constitution, 71, 72, 83, 84, 128; as Methodist, xii, 11, 51, 58, 65, 66; Morison, as new social history influence on, 107, 116, 118n13, 124n50; New England influences on, 50; overseas comparisons to American Midwest of, 13; parallel struggles within profession and love life of, 26; parental values of, 55, 57, 65; parent aspiration as models for, 54, 55, 65, 102; as presidential biographer, xvii, 33, 50, 74, 77–78, 102; and professional network, 23–24; pro-Truman bias of, xviii, 25, 54, 65, 73, 76, 78, 80, 89, 103, 105–7, 116; and public school music, 7; as publishing consultant, xi; and relationship with Captain Bradford, 16; religious influences on, 16, 49, 57, 75; research recommendations of, 6; as research specialist in Air Force Intelligence, xiii, 24, 83; romantic beginnings of (Loueva and Lila), 23–38; Sanderlin as mentor to, 7, 8; Second World War as occupational influence on, xiii, xvii, 5, 12, 18, 65, 75, 99, 116, 131–33, 135; on social science and history, 25, 31–34, 100, 109, 110, 114, 115, 116, 133, 134; on social work as Christian duty, 27; successful attributes of, 33, 107, 127, 128; and teaching of American history in high schools, 86–87, 88, 129; as traditionalist/empiricist, xvii, 4, 5, 25, 37, 103; on Truman greatness, 75, 106, 116, 128, 131; as undergraduate student at BGSU, 6–9, 89; urban and rural identity of, xii, 51, 100; views on emancipated women of, xi, 10, 30, 65, 104, 131, 133–34; war travels of, 12–18; Yale PhD, 5, 11, 82, 83, 110

Ferrell Robert H., works of: "America Made E-Z." (article), 119n19; *American Diplomacy in the Great Depression: Hoover-Stimson Foreign Policy, 1929–1933*, 23, 84, 139nn38, 45; *American Diplomacy: A History*, xi, 84, 91n20, 92n47; *America's Deadliest Battle, Meuse Argonne, 1918*, 68n21; *The Autobiography of Harry S. Truman*, 90n11, 107; "C. Vann Woodward" (essay), 137nn10, 14; *Dear Bess: The Letters from Harry S. Truman, 1910–1959*, 90n12, 121n29, 131, 138n33, 139nn34, 36; "First Cold Warrior" (article),

119n16; "From the Stacks" (article), 119n16; *George C. Marshall*, 91n20; *Grace Coolidge: An Autobiography*, 138n28; "Harry S. Truman: A Biographer's Perspective I" (essay), 137n9; *Harry S. Truman: A Life*, 73, 78, 90n13, 91nn30, 32, 121n29; *Harry S. Truman and Cold War Revisionists*, 19n1, 120n22, 121n29; *Harry S. Truman and the Modern American Presidency*, 73, 89n1, 91n23, 105, 121nn29, 30, 106, 138n18; *Ill-Advised: Presidential Health and Public Trust*, 73, 74, 89n1; "The Large Book Versus Small" (article), 119n16; "Looking Back: The Truman Books" (article), 123n41; *Off the Record: The Private Papers of Harry S. Truman*, 73, 75, 90n11, 105, 107, 121n29; *Peace in Their Time: The Origins of the Kellogg-Briand Pact*, xi, 11, 84, 89n1, 100, 104, 118n7; "Pearl Harbor and the Revisionists" (article), 19nn5, 6, 19, 44n89, 117n3, 120n21, 123n39; "Plain Faking?" (article), 119n16; *Presidential Leadership: From Woodrow Wilson to Harry S. Truman*, 91n28, 121nn29, 30, 138n18; *The Question of MacArthur's Reputation: Cote de Catillon*, 128, 137n5; "Truman Foreign Policy: A Traditionalist View" (article), 117n3, 118n11, 123n41; *Unjustly Dishonored: An African American Division in World War I*, xi, xiiin1, 37, 38n1, 45n94, 89n1; "The Villains of the 'Red Scares' of the 1950s" (article), 119n16; *Woodrow Wilson and World War I, 1917–1921*, 90n15, 121n28, 122n33

First World War, xi, 3, 37, 45n94, 54, 57–58, 64, 71, 75, 78, 81, 99, 103, 104, 110, 116, 131, 142n5

Flexner, Abraham, 33
foreign relations, U.S., 12, 18, 35, 84, 102, 103, 106, 134, 142
Foucault, Michel, 44n90
Fountainbleau, 18
Franck, Cesar, 18
Frank, Richard B., 123n41
Franklin, John Hope, 89, 130
French Revolution, interpretations as example of postmodernism, 4
Freud's psychoanalytic theory, 31, 33

Gallagher, Mark, 7
Gallagher, Robert, 8
Garrett, Annette, 31
Generalization in the Writing of History: A Report of the Committee on Historical Analysis of the Social Science Research Council (Gottschalk), 109
Germany, 18
GI Bill, 11
Godkin, E. L., 112
Gottschalk, Louis Reichenthal, 36, 109
Graduate Record Exam (GRE), 8–11
Great Depression, 8, 11, 28, 58, 61, 63–64, 66, 85, 110, 112, 114
Great War. *See* First World War
Griffith, Robert, and psycho-socio historical analysis, 105
Guardian Bank in Cleveland, 52, 60, 63
Gutman, Herbert, 36

Hall, G. Stanley, 55, 111. *See also* Child Study Movement
Hamby, Alonzo L., 91n25
Handlin, Oscar, 5, 20n15, 100, 117n5, 130
Harding Junior High, 49
Harding, Warren, 74
Harry S. Truman Presidential Library and Museum. *See* Truman Library
Helfgot, Joseph H., 34, 42n58, 43n76, 44n83

Hesburgh, Theodore, 92n48
Hewitt, Abram, 112
Hickman Springs High, 10
The Historian, 3, 19n5, 119nn15, 20, 120n23, 121n28, 122n33, 142
historians: consensus, 114, 125n63; humanist, 109; professionalism of, 34; social and cultural, xvii, 33, 119n19; as social scientist, 109; super, 129, 130
historical approaches, postmodernism in contrast to empiricism, 5
historical objectivity, 79, 91nn29, 31; conventional professional, xviii, 78; Ferrell writing on Truman and, 81; and method, 73, 74; philosophical stance toward, 78; standards of, 73, 78
historical truth, approach to, 4; lack of certainty of, 5
history profession, and evolution, 115
history teaching improvement campaign, 71
history-as-art. *See* historians, humanist
Hofstadter, Richard, 95n85, 102, 107, 113–16, 118n9, 125n63, 128, 130
Horace Mann Junior High, 49–50
Howley, Frank L., 136
Huerta, Victoriano, 136

imperialism, U.S., 4, 106, 108, 110, 113, 124n53, 134, 135, 139n38
Indiana Daily Student, 125n66
Indiana Magazine of History, 117n5, 118nn10, 12, 13, 119nn16–18, 20, 120nn22, 24, 26, 121n31, 122n39, 123nn39, 41, 43, 142–43
Indiana University (IU), xi, xiiin2, xv, xvi, xvii, 3, 5, 6, 12, 19n1, 23, 35, 37, 49, 66, 84, 129, 131
Indiana University Alumni Association, xii
Indiana University Foundation, 93n59
Indiana University History Department, 11, 85–87, 117n4, 138n32

Indiana University Oral History Project, 128
Indiana University School of Education, 87, 88
inductive reasoning, 5, 32
Ireland, 17
IU. *See* Indiana University (IU)
Ivy League, xi, xiii, xviii, 7, 9, 10, 11, 65, 69n38, 100, 128

Jameson, J. Franklin, 36
Janowitz, Morris, 88
Jarrett, Beverly, 23, 38n2
Jefferson and Washington University, 7
Jerusalem, 15, 16
Johns Hopkins University, and social science school, 42n59
Johnson, Lyndon, 81
Jones, Arnita, 93n59
Jordan, Benjamin, 55, 57, 68n25, 123n46
Journal of American History, 103, 119n20
Journal of Southern History, 103

Kahn, Alfred F., 42n59
Kansas City Times, 79
Kaplan, Lawrence, 11
Kelley, Datus, 51
Kellogg, Frank, 84
Kennedy, John F., 84, 89, 114
Kertesz, Stephen, 5, 19nn13, 14, 43n73, 93n56, 124n57
Kirtland, Jared, 51
Knepper, George, 59, 69nn42, 47
Knight, W. W., 63
Koerner, James, 87, 88, 94n74

Lake Shore Electric Line (interurban street cars), 51
Lakewood Public Library, 50
Lakewood United Methodist Church (LUMC), xvi, 51, 64, 67n12
Lakewood, Ohio (suburb of Cleveland), 29, 49, 51, 53, 57–58, 61, 64, 66, 67n16

Lamar, Howard Roberts, 130
Landes, David, 109, 110
Lasch, Christopher, 100
Lausche, Frank J., 59
Lebaree, Leonard, 21n56
Leedham, Charles L., 81
Leff, Gordon, 128
Leighninger, Leslie, 44n91
Leopold, Richard, 104
Leptus Magna, 16
Lerner, Gerda, 89, 130
Levine, David O., 11
Libya, 16
Lilly Library (Bloomington, Indiana), xiiin2, xvi, 5, 19n1, 68n30, 128
Lilly Program in American History (at Indiana University), 88
London, 17
Lowitt, Richard, as exemplar of positive Ferrell book reviewer, 105–7
Lukacs, John, 99, 127
LUMC. *See* Lakewood United Methodist Church
Luxemburg, 18
Luxor, 15–16

MacArthur, Douglas, 72, 83, 84, 128
Maddox, Robert, 5, 19n1, 20n15, 100
Madero, Francisco, 136
Majumdar, Rochona, and post-colonial history, 134
Malin, James, 35
The Man from Independence (Daniels), 79
Marshall Plan, 77, 113
Marshall, George, 75
Marxism, 4, 33, 110, 114, 133
Mattingly, Thomas W., 80, 81
McCoy, Donald, 105–6
McCullough, David, xii, 112, 116, 120n25
McDonald, Ralph, 6, 20n25, 92n51
Medicott, W. N., 104
Meggitt, Auntie (Verna) and Uncle Ivan, 52, 61

Mehlinger, Howard, 88
Messer-Kruse, Timothy, 61
"Me Too" movement, 26
Mexican Revolution, 136
Michigan Department of Social Welfare, 29, 31
Michigan State College (MSC), xiii, 11, 24, 37, 64, 85
Middle East culture, 13–16
Midwest conservatism, xiii
Midwest historians as innovators: Becker, Carl, 35; Du Bois, W. E. B., 36, 129, 130; Gottschalk, Louis Reichenthal, 36, 109; Gutman, Herbert, 36; Jameson, J. Franklin, 36; Malin, James, 35; Robinson, James Harvey, 35; Susman, Warren, 36; Turner, Frederick Jackson, 36, 100, 108–9, 111, 113, 115, 118n9
Midwest progressives. *See* University of Wisconsin–Madison
Miller, Richard, 79
Milton Township Rural School, 53
Mississippi Valley Historical Association. *See* Organization of American Historians (OAH)
Mississippi Valley Historical Review, 103
Mobilization for Youth Federal Program, 34
Morgan, Edmund, 130
Morison, Samuel Eliot, 37, 107, 111, 116, 118n13, 124n50
Mosley, Philip E., 7
MSC. *See* Michigan State College

Namier, Lewis, 41n54
Nash, Gerald, 105, 106
National Student League, 115
NATO. *See* North Atlantic Treaty Organization
Naval War College, 23
Nevins, Allan, 102, 107, 111, 112, 115, 116, 118nn13, 14, 123n48, 124n52
New Deal, 77, 113, 114

160   Index

New England, 50
New Haven Officers Board, 82
New Haven, Connecticut, xiii, 9, 11, 40n30
New Left, xvii, 56, 113, 119n19
new liberalism, 114
New York Evening Post, 102, 111, 112
New York School of Social Work, 41n56, 44n92
Nicholson, James, 51
Nixon, Richard M., xii, 3
nonjudgmental psychology, 27
Nordmann, Bernard, 39n16, 39n20, 40n37
North Africa, 16
North Atlantic Treaty Organization (NATO), 77, 113
Notre Dame, 5, 17, 18

OAH. *See* Organization of American Historians
objectivity, illusion of, xviii. *See also* historical objectivity
officer candidate school (OCS), 12
Offner, Arnold A., 91n25, 92n49, 119n15
Ohio Bank, 63
Ohio Methodists, 58
Ohio politics, 59
Old Stone Presbyterian Church, 52
Opponents of War, 1917–1918, 103–4
Organization of American Historians (OAH), 44n88, 71, 117n4, 129

Palestine, 15, 16
Park, Guy B., 79
Parkman, Francis, 107, 116, 118n13, 124n51
Patterson Field, Ohio, 12
Pemberton, William, 105, 106
Pendergast, Tom, and Truman, 77–81
The Pendergast Machine (Dorsett), 79
Pentagon, xiii

Pepinsky, Harold E., 93n59
Perry, Bernard, 23, 38n2
Pflueger, Loueva (Lou), 23–24, 26–33, 36–37, 38nn6, 9, 39nn12, 30, 40n30, 41n51, 42n61, 43n78, 115
postmodernism, xvii, xviii, 4, 6, 12, 36, 44n90, 133. *See also* historical approaches
postmodernists, xii, xvii, 3, 4, 11, 37, 44nn90, 93, 74, 75; allegory, 26; critique, 4, 73; debate, 90n5; philosophy, 5, 36; repartee, 24
Potter, David, 130
Powell, Colin, xii
Pratt, Waldo, 38n9, 39n15, 40n32
presentism, 26
problem-oriented approach, 109
The Progressive Historians (Hofstadter), 115
"Program in American History at Indiana University," 86
psychoanalytic terminology, as foundation for social work, 32
racial and ethnic minorities, 25
radical progressivism, 101

Reconstruction Finance Corporation (RFC), 61, 63, 64
Red Cross Clubs, 17, 18
Rentsch, Burt, 9, 11
Rentsch, Christine (Chris), 24, 29, 30
Republicanism, 58
The Restoration of Learning (Bestor), 88
The Review of Politics, 3, 19n3, 95n85
revisionists: twentieth-century, ideologically driven school of, 3; Cold War, 4, 99, 102, 103, 106, 130, 118n15; as interpreter of, 4, 106; overlap with postmodernists, 4
RFC. *See* Reconstruction Finance Corporation
Richmond, Mary, 44n91
Robinson, James Harvey, 35
Rockefeller, John D., 112

Roosevelt, Franklin Delano, xii, 3, 35, 49, 59, 62, 69n49, 73, 74, 110, 112, 142, 144
Roosevelt, Franklin, 3, 15, 35
Ruckelshaus, William, 92n46
Rutland, Robert Allen, 130
Ryan, John, 86, 93n59

Sabratha, 16, 17
Sakhara, 13
Sanderlin, Walter, 7, 8, 93n58
Saturday Evening Post, 61
Schlesinger, Arthur Jr., 3, 89, 100, 102, 109, 110, 112, 113, 115–17, 118nn9, 13, 120n26, 123n39, 124n52, 128, 130
School of Social Work, 42n58
scientific history methods, 35
Scott, Hilda, 10
Second World War, xiii, xvii, 5, 12, 18, 34, 42n58, 65, 75, 95n85, 99, 112, 116, 124n53, 128, 130–33, 135, 142, 143
Security-Home Bank, 63
SHAFR. *See* Society for Historians of American Foreign Relations
Shoshone (Indian tribe), 68n30
Siller, Kit and Bob, 23, 27, 28, 39n30, 40n30
Smith College (Springfield, Massachusetts), 24, 27, 29, 32
Smith, Gaddis, 38n3, 93nn54, 57
Smith, Margaret Chase, 104
Snyder, Howard McC., 80
social construction of reality, 36
Social Darwinism in American Thought (Hofstadter), 114
social science: approach to history and versus traditionalist, 31; disciplines, 25, 109, 115; theories, 28, 35, 68n30. *See also* psycho-social theories
Social Service Review, 31
social work, 25, 27, 29–34, 36, 41n55, 42nn61, 63, 43nn78, 80, 44n91, 134; versus history as profession,
32, 33; mission, 31, 33; new studies in, 42n59; programs as training, 31, 42n59, 43nn78, 80; psychoanalytic terminology as foundation for, 32
Society for Historians of American Foreign Relations (SHAFR), 84, 131
sociologists, as postmodernists, 5
South Asian culture (India), 13, 135
Southern Historical Association, 129
Sprout, Earl, 28
Sprout, Lila, 23–33, 36, 37, 38, 38n11, 39n12, 39n30, 40–41n40, 41n50, 42n61, 65, 103, 115
Standard Trust Bank, 60
State of Michigan Department of Social Welfare, 29, 31
State of Ohio Banking Department, 63
Staten Island, 12
St. Clair, Arthur, 58
St. Clotilde church, 18
Stevenson, Adlai, 61, 84, 89, 113
Stock Market crash, 51
Stonehenge, 17
Stories I Want My Grandchildren to Know (Ferrell Sr.), 20n40, 40n36, 66n2, 91n18
Studies on the Left (Williams), 113
Study Commission on Teacher Training and Licensing, 87–88
Summersby, Kay, 138n33
Susman, Warren, 36

Taft Elementary School, 49
Taft, Robert A., 71, 72, 82–84
Thayer, David, 87–88
Thompson, E. P., 94n84
Thompson, Henry, 63
Tiffin, Edward, 58
Tilly, Charles, 109, 110
Toledo, and financial industry collapse, 61–64
totalitarianism, 7
Trani, Eugene P., 90n16
Tripoli, 16, 17
Tripolitania, 16, 17

Truman Doctrine, 77, 113
Truman Library, 73, 131, 137n9
Truman, Bess Wallace, 73
Truman, Harry S., xvii, xviii, 3, 11, 33, 49, 59–81, 83, 89, 90n13, 91nn18, 19, 27, 28, 105–7, 113, 116, 119n16, 120n26, 122n32, 128, 129, 134, 144n18
Truman, Margaret, xii, 134
Truman: Rise to Power (Miller), 79
Tuileries gardens, 17
Turner, Frederick Jackson, 36, 100, 108–9, 111, 115

U.S. Constitution, 35
U.S. Treasury Department, 35
unethical historical practices, 4
United Brethren Church (Custar, Ohio), and commitment to equality and temperance, 57
United Kingdom, 16, 18
United Methodist Church, 113
United States Department of State, 129
University of Buffalo, 115
University of Missouri Press, 23, 99
University of Wisconsin–Madison, 108, 111
USS West Point, 12

V-E Day, 17, 18
Versailles, 18
Vietnam War, 84, 115, 135
Vietnam, 3, 135, 139n38
von Ranke, Leopold, xvii, 43n67, 122n38

Wales, 17
Warner, Amos, 42n59. *See also* social work, new studies in
WASP. *See* White-Anglo-Saxon-Protestant
Waterville Bank, 61
Waterville High School, 53, 67n16
Waterville, Ohio, 17
Wells, Herman B., 86
Western Michigan Teacher College, 86
Western Reserve, 50
White-Anglo-Saxon-Protestant (WASP), xii, 11, 12, 74, 75, 108, 114, 132
Wigger, John, and Methodism in Ohio, 57, 69n35
Williams, William Appleman, 100–102, 112, 113, 115–17, 121n26, 124n53, 128
Wilson, Woodrow, 33, 74, 75, 78, 143
Wisconsin Progressive School, 112
Witsell, Edward F., 82–84
women and gender studies, 100, 132
women as professionals, 25, 29, 30, 38, 65, 133
Woodward, C. Van, 118n9, 129–30
Wooster College (Ohio), 52, 64
World Civilization Exam, 6
World War I. *See* First World War
World War II. *See* Second World War

Yale University, xi, xiii, xvii, 5–12, 21n54, 23, 24, 35, 38n3, 41n50, 54, 71, 82, 83, 84, 100, 102, 117, 131, 132

About the Author

Douglas A. Dixon earned his PhD at the University of Georgia. A native of Evansville, Indiana, he served in the U.S. Foreign Service and on the faculties of several universities. Before receiving his doctorate, he taught U.S. history, economics, world geography, and literature in public schools. His articles have appeared in popular and academic publications, most recently focused on Peace Corps beginnings and myths, political conservatives in mid-twentieth-century America, and Latinx immigrants in the Midwest. Dixon resides in Austin, Texas.

www.ingramcontent.com/pod-product-compliance
Lightning Source LLC
Chambersburg PA
CBHW032149010526
44111CB00035B/1424